Reminiscing Donegal

Reminiscing Donegal:

Short Stories from Donegal

E.F.Ward

Published by Edward Ward

2019

First Printing: 2019

ISBN 978-0-9554177-4-0

Dedication

This book is dedicated all those who helped and inspired me to bring this book to fruition:

Ryan Ward whose inspiration and help was the catalyst in compiling this book.

Bryan Byrne who sat with me for days discussing the book and encouraging me to continue, by recounting the ancient Donegal practice of 'garniel', that is visiting neighbours, acquaintances and friends on a regular basis.

Patrick Boner who encouraged and pushed me on when I was lacking interest to continue.

To the many Taibhsis who invaded my dreams, especially on Oiche Shamhana, to remind me that they had lived, and to ask me when will I join them?

My wife Margret and my children who tolerated me while I chased ghosts of the past.

E F Ward

Contents

Foreword

Dear Reader,

A gaunt man drags a spade behind him through the fields and along the boreens, driven by grief, and brings strange and unwanted tidings to his neighbours.

A lonely figure keeps its distance on the Strand: everyone knows what it is and come to accept it, until one man helps it find peace and a lasting rest.

A fisherman discovers a surprisingly close connection between central London and the remote glens of Donegal, and is lured to his fate in one of them.

A tale of Fortunes made abroad, and of fortunes almost lost near home, when the last few miles of a long journey become the most dangerous.

These vignettes illustrate only a few of the stories recounted in this work. Our Author has collected and interpreted them from tales told to him around the flickering glow of the turf fire before the days of electricity, when a piercing cry at night could not be investigated with the bravery instilled by a bright electric torch. Uncertainty hovered behind the moving shadows, and who knows what travelled through the dark countryside outside, as quiet as the clouds racing across a moonlit Donegal sky?

Prepare to be amused, scared, and amazed. Dive in and swim in the sea called "Reminiscing Donegal"

John Masters

Nullifidian

Ar Chúl Éaga, 2019

Preface

The book is an insight into the storytelling that was prevalent in the homes of Donegal where I was born, before the advent of television.

The Seanchais (storytellers) were the method of entertainment, and the stories would be repeated word for word, to the delight and trepidation of the listener.

I have endeavoured to record some of these myths and legends that are part of a receding way of life. In these rural areas of Donegal, pre-Christian beliefs were, and are, hidden beneath a veil of Christianity. Beneath this surface of conformity there lies our beliefs of the past, masked by rejection and denial.

The Shanachai who told and retold these yarns, sometimes year later, could retell them as accurately as or better than most of our digital recorders. There was no scratching or loss of content on disc or tape. Their recorder was the human memory, and these stories were repeated from generation to generation. These alluring stories flowed softly from the lips of the Shanachais, like water running down a hill.

The stories they told were as sweet as honey, and had the effect of stirring the imagination of everyone who had the privilege to listen to them. The art of the Shanachai would have the listeners spellbound, between wonder and trepidation. As a child, you would be afraid to look at or out of a window, fearing some ghost or dark shadow would see you. And later that night in bed, your eyes would be firmly closed and the blankets were pulled over your head. You were afraid to look, in case something would see you, or you would see something. This was our entertainment, perhaps better than the television or films of nowadays.

This book is my vain attempt to record some of the stories that were and are part of our past heritage or history. While they are folklore, folklore becomes history when it is written or recorded.

I ask you, is our old Irish folklore not as important, or even more important, than other people's folklore? Are we so immature or ashamed of our history that we the people cannot appreciate what we have? I for one would like to yell it from the mountain tops, and say that our folklore is superior because it is that of our own people.

I know of many families who boast that the Banshee come to their people. Was this a badge of honour, or perhaps a link to their past belief in pre-Christianity? In my youth I heard various accounts of the Banshee crying before a death. The person that was about to die could hear the Banshee cry twice, but on the third time they would not hear her, for they would be dead. And the question is, how many times have you hear the Banshee cry?

In my youth, there were stories of the Devil dragging his chains in a certain place.

Some of the Shanachais would have the young people fascinated as they described Mermaids; of a beautiful young girl as she danced in the moonlight without her clothing, and how the moonlight flittered across her body. The young, whose testosterone was beginning to awaken were fascinated.

Names of people have changed to protect the innocent, but also to hide the guilty.

EF Ward

Aye, Life is Strange

In the hidden veiled glen of Draugurbeg lived an old woman, Cailleachdubh. She was a very old woman who could be described as eccentric or of an unbalanced mind. She came to the area many years ago during a severe winter. No one knew from where she came, nor did she say.

That year the snow fell continuously from November until March, and Cailleachdubh was given shelter in many of the houses in the area. She was eventually welcomed to stay with an old woman Nida Buí, who lived alone and was in failing health. Cailleachdubh cured her with the herbs that she dug out of the snow. Nida Buí was so pleased with her that she offered her the house to stay in as long as she wished. Cailleachdubh remained in the house and the two woman were content with this symbiotic arrangement. Nida Buí owned the house and was pleased that Cailleachdubh would look after her in her old age. When Nida Buí died, Cailleachdubh remained in the house and the neighbours were pleased to have someone they could call whenever they were unwell. In time she became part and parcel of the community. And the neighbours thatched her house and made it comfortable for her.

At that time, whenever there was a wake in the neighbourhood, the prevailing custom was to provide drink to those who attended. It was often said that it was a poor wake and showed a lack of respect to the person that died, if there was a not a drop of the creatur that was not spilt at their wake. Some of the people at the wakes would sing songs helped with a decent drop of poitín. There would be plates full of cigarettes and plenty of cut tobacco to fill the pipe, and boxes of snuff. Cailleachdubh was always welcome at any wake as she was a chaointe (crying). She would cry a lamentation that was fascinating, equivocal and haunting. (The custom of a caointe had its roots in the pre-Christian religion, and the Catholic Church tried to ban it.) Maria Bánan an old woman often said, "You can cry and laugh at the jubilation in sorrows. I hope to God that I will live long enough that Cailleachdubh will sit at my coffin as caointe."

Often Cailleachdubh would be requested to come to wakes as caointe that were a distance from her house. It was known that she would attend wakes on some of the islands as the welcome caointe. At times she could be absent from her house for a few days at a wake and the party and afters. Whatever house she entered she was always given whatever food they were eating and a bed for the night or nights.

Now Cailleachdubh's wee house was partly hidden by the numerous varieties of trees. There were old Irish apple trees, oak, ash, holly bushes and yew trees. At one time a person said that she should cut down the blackthorn, and the yew trees as they could poison animals. Her reply was, "Everything has its use if you know its secrets. Some people say that the blackthorn is a symbol of beauty and poetry. In my garden there is a cure for most ailments. The blackthorn can give strength and comfort but it also can inflict the wounds of rejection, like a spurned lover. Even the yew tree has its use, if you know how to use it. But the blackthorn is the most wonderful plant for cures and health. You can eat the leaves in the summer. Do you know, it is the plant of the underworld? And the time for harvesting the blackthorn is when November ends and December begins. This is the best time to harvest a blackthorn stick to protect you from ghosts or evil spirits. It is unlucky to cut the blackthorn outside of this time. The worst time to cut a blackthorn stick is in the spring of the year, particular in the month of May. The Cásbáis of death lives beneath the blackthorn tree, and it could bring evil luck to anyone who damages it. If you respect the blackthorn it will bring you luck and health. The sloe berries can be used to make a health drink which is both mystical and medicinal."

Cailleachdubh at times could be harping on about the medicine that is lying at one's feet. She, like most old people perhaps could be bordering on the edge of psychosis. But there is a very fine line between wisdom and insanity. She was an herbalist who would make a poultice for strains or swellings and bottles of medicine for people or animals. A lot of the people had more faith in her than in a doctor. Most doctors would dismiss anyone if they mentioned Cailleachdubh, saying, "She is a fraud for the disillusioned and a panacea for the gullible."

Doctor McCoskey was the only doctor in the area who would recommend her. His usual retort was "Did you not visit Cailleachdubh?" If the person had ringworm or skin allergic his reply was, "I can give you a handfuls of pills if you want, but perhaps you should give Cailleachdubh a try. If you are not happy with her come back to me in a few days' time."

Most of the neighbours respected Cailleachdubh and would come to her whenever they or their animals were sick. The neighbours would give her a load of turf for her fire, and she was welcomed to come to their fields and take turnips, cabbage or potatoes. John Rua, a neighbour of hers who fished, always took her some fish, as did other fishermen. Cailleachdubh seldom used the word thanks. Whenever she received anything her only retort was, "May health and plenty always stand by your side."

Nance Hamish was a woman who always behaved like she was important and looked down on others. Her family in the past had more than others; but now she was living on the past glories of yesteryear. One day she was in the local shop of Danny Bán's when Cailleachdubh came in. Nance Hamish did not acknowledge Cailleachdubh but said, "Perhaps I will come back when the stink clears. Then maybe I might get something for a wedding."

Cailleachdubh quickly snapped, "Oh! The world must be coming to an end if Nance Hamish is going to get a man. Is he blind or insane! For you are like the blackthorn bush with all the thorns, sticking out of you. The flowers on the blackthorn bush are beautiful; but your petals are withered and gone a long time ago. And all that remains are the venomous thorns."

Nance Hamish beat a hasty retreat out of the door muttering in a low voice, "Some people have no breeding or manners!"

After she was gone Danny Bán said, "You put that one in her box! I didn't know if it was you or me she was growling at. The moment she comes in here until she leaves there is nothing but complaining about something or somebody. I don't think that even God would please that one."

"Ah" uttered Cailleachdubh, "Maybe she has a little money, but it is as much good to her as the big stones that are around my house. I can't spend the stones and she will never spend her money, both will remain long after we are gone."

"Aye" said Danny Bán, "Nance Hamish mightn't know it but she is her own worst enemy. I don't think she has a friend this side of hell. Not like you who is welcomed into every house in this parish, or the next ten."

"Aye" cried Cailleachdubh, "Danny Bán, you could charm the birds from the sky to sit on the palm of your hand with your sweet palaver. But I will say something for you; you never insulted anybody. You know how to please with your honeyed words; but you will catch more flies with a spoon of honey than a jar of vinegar. However, you were always a decent man with a big broad smile on your face."

Danny Bán was glad that he did not upset Cailleachdubh, not alone for her custom, but to keep life without any discords. He was aware that there was always someone in the locality who could upset the district. To run a business, you had to have skin on you like leather, that is not be easily offended; and it is prudent at times to be deaf.

Life in the area continued as usual, with little incidents that happen in every district, and Cailleachdubh was called for whenever there was any malady. Cailleachdubh became the midwife and herbalist for any sickness of the people or their animals.

If a vet was called and said the animal should be destroyed as there was no hope of the animal surviving, people as a last resort would ask Cailleachdubh if she could help.

Cailleachdubh would reply sharply, "What did the vet say?" "The vet said there is no hope for the animal, it should be put down as it will never get better again."

Cailleachdubh usual quick riposte was, "Maybe he should be put down himself."

One-day John Mór noticed that his good milking cow was unwell, and he decided to give her a good feed of fresh cabbage. However, when he went to see the cow again it did not eat anything. She only drank a small drop of water from the bucket. John Mór was worried and following the customary discussions with the neighbours he decided to call the vet. The vet came that day and perhaps for a few days, giving the cow a multiple of injections. But the cow was not getting any better. Eventually the vet said. "Perhaps it would be better to put the cow down, as I can do no more."

John Mór was reluctant to have his good cow killed and he said he would ask Cailleachdubh if she could do something."

The vet laughed saying "Cailleachdubh is only a witch and fraud and she couldn't cure herring with all the salt in Ireland. Don't you know that your own priest Fr Jimmy has warned people to stay away from her? If he hears you have anything to do with her he will never hear your confessions."

"Well" drawled John Mór, "If I go to Cailleachdubh and she can't help the cow get better, what have I to lose? As for Fr Jimmy, I never go to him for confessions to anyway. And, am I not confessing to God, not to some puffed up vainglorious snarling fictitious replica."

The vet was quite for a while and then said, "John Mór I never thought that you were a pagan. It surprises me the way you spoke about Fr Jimmy; after all he is your priest. It is not nice to speak badly about anybody."

John Mór replied slowly, "Who said I claimed Fr Jimmy as mine? I did not. And if you do as you say and not speak badly about anyone, why are you calling Cailleachdubh a witch? You know it annoys me when people say, don't do as I do, but do as I say. I try not to let arrogance slip out of my mouth, and I hope that others would do the same."

The vet was lost for words as John Mór was usually very reserved in speech and his outburst of words may be explained by his worry about his cow.

Then the vet then replied, "Aye John Mór I suppose that you are right to try everything, vets don't know it all. As you say you have nothing to lose. Wasn't it Karl Marx that said, 'You have nothing to lose but your chains?' Aye good luck to you and would you tell me if the cow gets better."

"Aye" uttered John Mór, "I am sorry that I let my tongue fly. I know at times; I have a quick temper when anything upsets me. And I say things that I shouldn't. I apologise most profusely for my ignorant outburst."

"Ah" said the vet, "Forget it, we all say something's we shouldn't say. I sometimes say something that I should not. I should not have been so abrupt in telling you to put your cow down. But good luck to you."

John Mór went to visit Cailleachdubh and told her about his cow, and how the vet said the cow would never get better. "I suppose it is useless for me annoying you but I thought that I would give it one last try."

Cailleachdubh snapped, "John Mór, where is the cow now, and why did you wait so long before you came to me. I will have to see the cow first before I will know what is wrong with her. And tell me where or what was the cow eating?"

John Mór replied unhurriedly, "You know, it was in the field below the house. You know, beside the wee stream that runs into the lough. And that night I gave her a feed of cabbage, but she did not eat all."

Cailleachdubh paused before replying, "Aye beside the stream; let me think. Was there any froth around her mouth next morning, and how was the cow in the morning: was it standing or lying down?"

John Mór replied, "Cailleachdubh, there was a little froth around her mouth but not much, and the cow seems to be lying down most of the time. My heart is broken trying to get her to stand up. She seems to have no energy left in her. Do you think the cow is going to die?

Cailleachdubh did not answer but began rattling bottles about her kitchen. Then she handed John Mór a bottle and said, "Away home

15

with you as quick as you can and put the contents of this bottle down the cow's throat. I hope that we are not too late. I will follow you in a wee while and if the cow is alive when I get there, there is some hope."

John Mór eagerly took the bottle saying, "Thank you for the bottle, I will give it to the cow when I get home and I will send Jack Dub with his car for you to take you to my house."

Cailleachdubh snapped, "Away home with you and give that to your cow; and don't be standing there all day waffling. The cow needs you more than I. Oh and get a few men if we are to lift the cow up."

John Mór made haste to the house where some of his neighbours were waiting for him. In a short while the men had the cow lifted, and tied to the rafters. And the bottle Cailleachdubh gave him was poured down the cow's throat. And Jack Dub with his car was quickly sent to collect Cailleachdubh.

As Cailleachdubh arrived the cow was vomiting and people were wondering if the cow was about to die. When Cailleachdubh came into the byre she was told that the cow vomited. "Is that good or bad?" they asked.

Cailleachdubh cackled, "For you or the cow? Now that is the first thing done, let's see what we can do for the rest." She mixed some black powder that she had with some kind of oil and water and put it into a bucket and handed it to John Mór and said, "Pour as much of that that down the cow's throat as you can. Now the only thing we can do is wait. I hope it is not too late. Now, let us all have a sup of tea, and let's see if this will take effect."

As they waited, each man was looking at each other waiting in suspense, waiting for someone to speak. More water was given to the cow and she drank two large buckets of water quickly as if she was parched of thirst. After a while the cow vomited a little more and John Mór with a worried look said, "Is that bad? Do you think that the cow vomiting is a bad sign? Do you think she will ever survive?"

Cailleachdubh did not reply for a while then snapped, "John Mór, did you survive after you had a bellyful of drink? Can't you see that the cow's got rid of what was poisoning her? Now John Mór have you a bottle of good poitín. Then pour it down the cow's throat, it will put some heat in her hungry body!"

"Aye" I will, retorted John Mór meekly, "Do you think that the poitín will make the cow drunk?"

Cailleachdubh snapped, "If it will, do you think that the cow will sing for you? Have a bit of sense man, the cow is only an animal like you and me. The only way we can get better is when we get rid of what is poisoning us, which is to vomit it out. Your cow should be better in a day or two. As long as she has plenty of water. And give her some mashed turnips with half cooked nettles and a handful of sugar. You know only a little feeding at a time!"

In a few days' time the cow was out in the field eating contently. The news of John Mór cow was the conversation of the parish for the following weeks. There was the usual enquiry from people as to what exactly did Cailleachdubh give the cow.

Naoise Rua who was an inquisitive young boy, began to make inquiries of the men who were with the cow, of what exactly did Cailleachdubh give the cow. One man would pawn Naoise Rua off to another, saying they had been nearer to her. Eventually Naoise Rua came to Danny Bán's shop to enquire what Cailleachdubh gave to John Mór's cow.

Danny Bán replied, "Naoise Rua, the only person that can tell you truthfully is Cailleachdubh. If you ask her the worst she can do is say no. You know in life it is wise to be prepared to be refused. I myself have been refused many times. The only way you can learn is to ask, and don't be put off by a refusal. Naoise Rua you are an intelligent young man; good luck to you. And if you want something, the best time to ask anybody is in the morning"

Next morning Naoise Rua went to Cailleachdubh house and said, "Cailleachdubh I am Naoise Rua and I would like to know what you used to cure John Mór cow?"

Cailleachdubh did not respond for a while, eventually she said, "Would you now, Naoise Rua? And why do you want to know?"

Naoise Rua stuttered, "Well maybe I could be as smart as you if I knew your secrets, then maybe I could become a vet or a doctor. Maybe I should not have asked you."

Cailleachdubh looked at him before replying, "Naoise Rua if you go into the woods and get me ten leaves. Maybe you could start learning."

Naoise Rua raced into the woods and returned with a handful of leaves hoping that would satisfy her.

Cailleachdubh spread the leaves on the table and said, "Now Naoise Rua tell me the names of the leaves?"

Naoise Rua stood stupefied, then uttered, "I don't know the names, maybe someone will tell me."

"Well" snapped Cailleachdubh, "I don't want to hear, it might must be this, or it must be that, or if the devil died. When you get the names of the leaves, then come back to me and maybe we could start learning. I don't know the names they are called now. My names would make no sense to you. But when you get your names I will tell you mine."

Naoise Rua's problem was he did not know where to find a book with names of leaves and he thought that Fr Jimmy would have lots of books. If he would lend him one. Didn't Danny Bán tell him, the worst anyone can do is to say no. After all, Cailleachdubh didn't chase him away, and he thought she might. Walking with confidence up to the door of the priest's house he knocked and waited until the door was opened.

Fr Jimmy stood on the doorstep and snarled, "Is somebody sick or dying?"

"No father Jimmy, I was wondering if you had a book of plants and leaves that I could borrow for a wee while."

Fr Jimmy grunted, "Who are you to be begging at my door, and what do you want with my books?"

"I am Naoise Rua and I am trying to learn about the cures that Cailleachdubh has. She might tell me."

Fr Jimmy roared, "Don't go near Cailleachdubh, don't you know she is an old protestant witch. If you do, you will go to hell and burn in the fires of hell for eternity. And you will never see the bright light of heaven."

"But father" said Naoise Rua, "You are a priest, why don't you go to her and save her from the fires of hell. Isn't that your job to save people from hell?"

Fr Jimmy barked, "I went to her and she had the audacity to question me!"

Naoise Rua stood on the doorstep without speaking a word.

Fr Jimmy snarled, "Now Naoise Rua, what have you to say for yourself!"

"Well," replied Naoise Rua in a hushed voice, "If anyone who visits her will go to hell, doesn't that mean that you too will go to hell for visiting her."

Fr Jimmy hollered, "You young unmannerly brat. Clear away from me and don't come back until you learn some manners. How dare you to question me, a priest of God! I have a good mind to put horns on you."

Naoise Rua was walking up the road somewhat dejected when he met Seamus O'Boyle who had returned after spending years in America. As his father Teague was facing death.

"Good morning Naoise Rua said Seamus O'Boyle, "You are not your usual self that always had a smile on your face. Is something wrong with you?"

Naoise Rua looking up with a frowned face said, "Maybe I am going to hell?"

Seamus O'Boyle smiling replied, "Where did you get that silly idea from?"

Naoise Rua began to tell him about Cailleachdubh curing animals and people with the leaves that grow in the ground. She said that she would help him if he could get a book to show the names of the leaves. "Then I asked Fr Jimmy if he has a book of leaves, and if he would lend it to me. He said that he would put horns on me and put me into hell. Now I am worried."

Seamus O'Boyle laughed and said, "That is all rubbish Naoise Rua! I didn't think that they were sprouting the same old rubbish as when I was young. That is all superstitious garbage to control the people, and collect money. Naoise Rua, when I was fourteen, I left Ireland and went to my Aunt in America. Her husband was an attorney and he said, 'You have a choice of going to high school or digging ditches. If you go to school, then you can stay in my house."

I took the choice of school and with his help and guidance I became an attorney. The only condition he asked of me was to help someone else. Now Naoise Rua you and I will go to the library that has books on herbs. Everything will be under herbs, trees and bushes."

When they entered the library Seamus O'Boyle asked the librarian Finnula, if she could suggest the best books that would be of interest to Naoise Rua, as he was beginning to study curative herbs.

Finnula gave them two books and said, "Perhaps you should speak to Reverend Klasson as he has a keen interest in the subject, and is an amiable person. He has a beautiful garden with a wide variety of plants and could give you both the common and the Latin names."

Seamus O'Boyle took Naoise Rua to visit Reverend Klasson, who shook their hands and made them welcome. They told Reverend Klasson about Cailleachdubh, and how she cured animals and people with herbs.

Reverend Klasson said, "I am pleased that someone has the intelligence to research and to compile an index of the curative value of herbs, before all is forgotten. Naoise Rua you have intelligence beyond your years. Come to me anytime and we will walk through the garden and look at plants and herbs. When you pick a few leaves we will dry them between newspapers and I will give you a book to you to save them in. You know you make an old man happy with your interest.

Perhaps you could think of researching herbs in college. If you will I will give you a good reference."

Naoise Rua was pleased with the turn of events. In the morning he felt that his life was ending, and now everything was fantastic. He was told by Fr Jimmy that he was going to hell. But now Reverend Klasson praised and encouraged him by offering him his books and told him to come to him anytime. The sunshine was coming back into his life again after the darkness of the morning gloom. Now Naoise Rua was scurrying between Cailleachdubh's little house and Reverend Klasson, who at times would send some vegetables to her. Of course this became known and was frowned upon by Fr Jimmy.

Fr Jimmy began to make damning sermons about people who had anything to do with those who practised the work of the devil, or had trappings with the protestant heretics. Without naming Cailleachdubh everyone in the church knew who he was talking about. On one of his tedious rants about those who enter the devil's den looking for cures, Fr Jimmy roared, "I am warning you all! If any of you go near those that who dabble in witchcraft, don't come near me for confessions. The devil and evil must be eradicated from our midst, and those who condone it are as guilty as those who practice it." Con Gusigan stood up and walked nosily out of the church. Con was sitting on the wall smoking his pipe as Fr Jimmy was leaving the church.

Fr Jimmy came over and said, "Con are you all right I saw you leaving the church. Are you feeling unwell?"

"No thanks Father, I am feeling fine now."

Fr Jimmy with a puzzled look on his face uttered, "And what made you leave the church before I finished my sermon. Perhaps you were you feeling a little queasy, were you?"

"No" whispered Con, "It was that I didn't think it was nice to criticize anybody; after all the poor Bishop has enough on his plate."

Fr Jimmy snapped, "It was not the Bishop I was talking about. Don't you know what is happening around you? You are an idiot! It was that thing in the woods; you should know."

Con remained quiet for a while then said. "You know father I don't take part in any gossiping. I remember my poor grandfather, God rest his soul, he used to say 'God gave us two eyes, two ears and a mouth. Use them wisely!' If our good Bishop says he is innocent. I believe him. And if you don't mind me saying you shouldn't have anything to do with them that are blathering."

Fr Jimmy face was red with anger and he roared, "Is everyone stupid? I wasn't speaking about the Bishop, it was about that witch in the woods."

"Aye Father" said Con. "I never knew there was any witches about this place. Did she come here with the foreigner?"

Fr Jimmy growled, "God stand between me and numskulls like you. It, it is that damned devil's disciple Cailleachdubh in the woods. She has the people possessed with her black magic. I hope that you don't go next or near her with her hocus-pocus. If you do, don't come near me looking for confessions."

"Well father! I suppose that rules me out. And suppose that you won't be giving your sister Mary any more holy communion. Didn't she go to Cailleachdubh when she had the ringworm, and she cured her? Didn't she?"

By now the people were gathering around listening to Con and Fr Jimmy palaver. They were chattering and giggling at the tittle-tattle between them. Con could be slow in speech but not in long drawn out wit. The suppressed giggle can always have a long lasting effect, and is endemic on others, and somehow magnifies its effect. The people were trying to muffle their giggling with hands over their mouth. Some bent down with stifled laughter which annoyed Fr Jimmy. He felt that he was now the fool and it intensified his fury.

Fr Jimmy walked away cursing and muttering, "You will all go to hell! How dare you to laugh at me I will put horns on all of you. That is all lies, Mary was cured by the power of prayers, and devotions to the good Saint Anthony of Padua. Not that evil sorcerer who practises black magic in her den of iniquity."

A few days later Seamus O'Boyle's father Teague died, and there were the usual preparations for the funeral. He asked his cousin Mara to see Fr Jimmy and tell him the funeral would be on the third day, Wednesday. Would she explain that Seamus was busy trying to organise the funeral; as it was all new to him, as he was in America for a long time."

Mara with a little trepidation went to Fr Jimmy and said, "Ah you know father them in America don't know anything about funerals, not like us at home. In America you die today and they bury you tomorrow. We were planning the funeral for Wednesday; I hope that is alright with you."

 Fr Jimmy gave his customary grunt saying, "They are all pagans in America! Didn't he already show it by visiting that thing in the woods? Well, all right that is that settled!"

To fulfil his father's wishes, Seamus O'Boyle had plenty of cigarettes, tobacco, snuff and drink in the wake house. Then he went for Cailleachdubh, and asked her if she would be the caointe at the wake. Of course Cailleachdubh obliged and everyone was pleased. Seamus O'Boyle sang the "Old Bog Road" as it was his father's favourite. He was determined that Teague's funeral would be remembered. Others who were in the wake house had their easy start of drink, and they began to sing their songs with Seamus's encouragement. It was becoming the best wake in the area and would be remembered for years to come, with the laughter music, caointe and song.

Then all became quiet as Fr Jimmy walked in the door. Seamus O'Boyle, who was resting in the bed, quickly jumped up to see what was wrong. When Seamus came into the room Fr Jimmy was standing there with a face that would frighten away a banshee.

"Well father, it is nice that you have the time come to Teague's wake. You know everyone is welcome here. Now father! Did no one give you a drop of whiskey to warm yourself up? What would Teague think if he knew that someone was left standing there, and not even have a drink in their hand to celebrate his life? He wouldn't be happy to see anyone standing there with an empty hand."

Fr Jimmy growled, "You might have been in America too long! There is no singing or drinking or witch's chanting at anything that I have anything to do with,"

Seamus O'Boyle smiled and said, "Yes, I respect your choice of funeral to your demeanour when you die. But have the courtesy to afford others the ability to choose, to think and act voluntarily; that is free will. Which God has given all of us? Now father, are you going to give us a song?"

Fr Jimmy roared, "I will not say any mass for Teague if you don't change your ways. You think you know something just because you spent some time in pagan America. I say what will happen here and you will obey the word of your priest! Now do you understand?"

Seamus O'Boyle gave his customary smile and replied. "Yes! When I left here 'your crowd' controlled the people. What I learned in America was the law, and how to utilise the press and the law to expose tyrannical behaviour. I know how to have an injunction served on anyone, and to claim damages. Now as I have said, you have free will and you needn't say a mass for Teague. That is your choice and I accept it. If you do not, I will certainly not force you. My advice is for you to sleep on your decision. I will have to follow my father's wishes by granting him his last request. Oh! By the way, I suppose that could be the end of the new altar we spoke about. I hope that the Bishop will understand. Will he?"

Fr Jimmy waddled away with his usual huff and puff. He was aware that he submitted the plans of the new altar to the Bishop. As he was walking away Seamus O'Boyle began to sing the song the Croppy boy:

> "Good men and true in this house who dwell,
> To a stranger bouchal I pray you tell:
> Is the priest at home, or may he be seen?
> I would speak a word with Father Green."

And soon the wake house was celebrating the life of Teague. With the haunting voice of Cailleachdubh inhabiting a limited space between the living and the world of the dead. It certainly was the best wake in the district for years before or afterwards.

Next morning Teague's remains was taken to the church and the people were speculating how Fr Jimmy would behave. As they entered the church Fr Jimmy with his white robes was standing there with a frosty face as long as a wet day.

"Good morning father!" said Seamus, "It is a nice day for a funeral with the birds singing in the sky. I do hope that you have everything ready for Teague."

"Aye!" grunted Fr Jimmy, "But remember where you are."

Seamus smiling retorted, "Yea, I certainly remember this place. For me it is full of conflicting memories. Sometime maybe we can sit down and calmly discuss the changes that have occurred from the past. Some good and others not so pleasant. But what has changed can't be undone. I suppose that the world will continue to turn in spite of us. We are to celebrate the life of my father Teague. I can remember how he would sing. That was what he loved in life, it is only decent that he should have it in death."

"Ah," grunted Fr Jimmy as he waddled up to the altar muttering to himself. The funeral service was rushed and Fr Jimmy's words of eulogy were minimal. And he was hastily concluding the service.

Then Seamus went up to the altar and thanked everyone who attended. Then he gave his eulogy on the life of his father Teague, and how he loved song and began to sing and asked everyone to join him.

> "Hail, glorious Saint Patrick, dear saint of our Isle,
> On us thy poor children bestow a sweet smile;
> And now thou art high in the mansions above,
> On Erin's green valley's look down in thy love."

To Fr Jimmy this song was bearable as it had a Christian undertone, as it mentioned saints as they began to sing.

Followed by:

> "Donegal the pride of all I oft times think on thee

To my cottage home where I oft times roamed when I was young and
free
Big houses grand on a foreign land I can't compare at all
With my cottage bright on a winter's night in the hills of Donegal
Right well I mind the harvest time that woe and dreary day
When the leaving of Donegal for to wander far away
Can't compare t'all with me, cottage bright on a winter's night, in the
hills of Donegal."

This song was followed by:

"Oh Shenandoah I long to see you,
Away you rolling river.
Oh Shenandoah,
I long to see you,
Away I'm bound away
'Cross the wide Missouri

Oh Shenandoah
I love your daughter,
Away, you rolling river.
For her I'll cross
Your roaming waters,
Away, I'm bound away
'Cross the wide Missouri."

Fr Jimmy was fuming that Seamus was leading the crowd into the
graveyard singing at the top of their voices. Anytime he tried to speak
he could not be heard over crowd, until eventually Teague's coffin was
laid in the grave.

Fr Jimmy now tried to take control of the crowd and began his habitual
litany of prayers. He was going to take control of the people as now his
opportunity arose.

Seamus interrupted him, and said, "Thank you for brief service in
church today. I am sure that anyone who knew my father, wouldn't

want any insincere words spoken about him in death. He would want his memory to be celebrated by song and merriment. Thank you again father. Oh I suppose that was the briefest synopsis of a service that I have heard in a long time. Maybe it could be included in the Guinness book of records. Do you think so?"

Then Seamus began to sing.

> "When Irish Eyes are smiling,
> Sure it's like a morn in spring,
> In the lilt of Irish laughter,
> You can hear the angels sing,
> When Irish hearts are happy
> All the world seems bright and gay,
> But when Irish eyes are smiling
> Sure they'll steal your heart away."

Those present began to join in the singing and the graveyard was like an open air concert, much to the disproval of Fr Jimmy. The people were venting their built up rancour of Fr Jimmy by singing as loudly as they could. They knew that that this was their vengeance on Fr Jimmy as the prospect of money for the altar silenced him.

The next Sunday Fr Jimmy was back at his rants about protestant heretics and witchcraft, and those fools who condone it. Seamus, who was in the church, stood up and walked out quietly.

When Seamus went to America, he wrote a letter to the bishop explaining how at present he was reluctant to fulfil his intention of paying for a new altar for the church. He wrote that he would have to reflect if it was appropriate to support the church from America, or the person who had disrespected his father's wishes. In his letter he used 'ornamentation rhetoric style' to mask his intentions. The letter neither confirmed nor denied that he would give the money.

Fr Jimmy was scheming and contemplating on how he could somehow hinder Cailleachdubh. To add to his anguish the bishop reprimanded him for the loss of the new altar as he had promised his nephew the contract. Eventually he perceived a plan and with some of his cronies in the department of agriculture to issue leaflets on the very poisonous nature of taxus baccata (yew tree). None of the people knew what this was by its Latin name and his cronies were spreading fearful rumours about it.

Fr Jimmy in his sermons, reminded the people of this poisoned weed that was discovered in the countryside. He stated, "That if they wished to get rid of this poisoned weed they should give him the landowners names and he would forward it to the Department of Agriculture."

The people misunderstood the name taxus baccata, as Texas something. And soon everyone was talking about the poisonous weed that came from Texas in America. The rumour, like all rumours, was exaggerated in the retelling. With time and fear myths become facts, which worried the people. And Fr Jimmy knew those that were poorly educated were his catalyst to spread trepidation. He would feed their ignorance with mistruths, fear and distortions.

There was a death on the island of Claiddubh and Cailleachdubh was requested to visit as caointe.

As soon as she left, Fr Jimmy had two men, Jim Boyle and John Boyle who lived at Stakamore, to come to cut the blackthorn and yew trees. As the wood of the yew tree is difficult to cut, their saws were sticking. Then they tried swinging at the yew tree with their axes, when the axe shaft broke and the axe blade struck Jim on his leg. In the commotion of attending the wound on Jim's leg, the good axe was misplaced. John Boyle was tenacious in his effort to have the trees cut and took the axe head and shaft. He went to a few men looking for a saw or an axe. When he mentioned that he was cutting old blackthorn and yew trees for Fr Jimmy, they made the excuse of not having axes or saws, and sent him to other men. Eventually John Boyle came to John Rua's house and asked him if he could fix his axe, or lend him an axe or a saw.

John Rua paused before replying, "Where or what are you at that needs an axe or saw. It is a poor carpenter that hasn't a saw, or can't put a handle on an axe.

John Boyle began to tell him how he came to the area to cut a few old blackthorn and yew trees for Fr Jimmy, and how the axe broke and hit his brother in the leg, and he couldn't find the good axe. And how he wanted to have the job finished for the priest.

John Rua looked at him without speaking and then replied, "My good man, may I first correct you, I don't own that priest. You were on private property without the owner's permission. The trees belong to Cailleachdubh; she can cure you or curse you. My advice to you and your brother is to leave while you can, or you might live to regret ever coming here. If you think anything of your brother, take him to the doctor while he has a breath of life left in his body. Then go to Cailleachdubh on the island of Claiddubh. Tell her what happened and apologise to her, then you might be able to save your brother and yourself. Now take that cursed axe and broken shaft with you. I want nothing of that cursed thing around my house or land!"

John Boyle stood perplex as if he was in a coma then he replied, "But Fr Jimmy told me to clear the field and cut all the trees and bushes in the field.

John Rua snapped, "I don't want anything to do with you! Or that which is cursed!"

John Boyle was surprised with the outburst he received from John Rua. He was told that he was a very sensitive and empathetic person. Now he knew why other people were not willing to help him. He decided that there was no hope of looking for help in this superstitious place. And decided that he and Jim would come back tomorrow with sharp tools. Next morning Jim was unwell and he said that maybe he was getting a flu. So they decided to leave the job until the next day. However, that night Jim's leg began to give him pain and they decided to take him to the doctor. In the morning Jim was in a lethargic state and his answers were not cohesive or sensible. He was slipping into and out of a near coma state. The doctor was called and he gave Jim an injection. Saying if this don't work, we will have to take him to hospital. Perhaps he contacted some infection in the wound.

John Rua's words of warning echoed through John Boyle's head and he cursed Fr Jimmy for what had happened. John Boyle decided that the only hope to save his brother was to go and apologise to Cailleachdubh, and to beg Cailleachdubh to try to save his brother. In his mind he was trying to find words that could mitigate her wrath. If only he could get someone that she was friendly with to speak for him. Perhaps if he could speak with John Rua, he may plead for him. Aye this was the only chance for him, not to be cursed.

Next morning John Boyle knocked on John Rua's door seeking for some salvation.

John Rua opening the door said, "What are you looking for. I thought I told you not to come back to my house."

John Boyle through sobs began telling what was happening to his brother, and how he could die. "If you would ask Cailleachdubh to speak to me. I am ashamed and afraid of going near her. If only she would let me talk and beg her for my brother's life. I will give you anything."

John Rua didn't often see a grown man crying and said, "All right I will go with you and try to explain your circumstances. But don't speak until I try to smooth her anger. It might take me a while. Do you understand? Not one word!"

"Aye thanks" said John Boyle through sniffles, "I am at my wits end with worry. I didn't sleep a wink these last nights."

John Rua coming to Cailleachdubh opening door said, "Cailleachdubh, we have a problem and I was hoping that you could help me as a big favour."

Cailleachdubh smiling replied, "John Rua you don't have to ask me for favours whatever is bothering you can't be that serious. Can it?

"Well" retorted John Rua, "Maybe it could be. But I hope that you will listen to me before you make up your mind if you could help.

Cailleachdubh snapped "John Rua! We have been friends for as long as I can remember. Just ask I won't eat the head of you. What is it man? Forget about your long winded blathering."

John Rua smiling replied, "It is about two young innocent fools that were snared by that Fr Jimmy to do his dirty work. He hoodwinked these two dupes into thinking that they were doing something good. And to make matters worse these two fools are related to me on my mother's side. These two poor boys were sent by that bully to your garden to destroy it. But they did not know what they were at."

Cailleachdubh barked, "And who is this person you have with you!"

John Rua quietly replied, "This person is looking to you for forgiveness and healing. This is John Boyle, and to make matters worse he is my own relation. His brother is at home and is not well. Now if you chase us all away I will understand."

Cailleachdubh replied, "John Rua! John Rua how could I chase you away. That is your turf that is burning in my fire. You haven't an ounce of badness in your whole body. You are friends to all and enemies to none. Now forget your honeyed words and tell me the ugly truth, who is this John Boyle.

John Boyle spoke spluttered with tears, "It was Jim and me, not John Rua who cut your trees. We didn't know and now Jim might die. I am sorry it was my fault, if you could save Jims life I don't care about mine."

Cailleachdubh snapped, "John Boyle you keep your gob shut, and let John Rua do the talking. I am a friend to him, not to you. You go outside and if there is something we want to ask you John Rua will. You know if you came to my door yourself, I would chase you away."

John Boyle went silently outside but could hear John Rua and Cailleachdubh discussing what happened. Sometimes John Rua would come outside to confirm the full extent of what occurred. John Boyle could hear the raised voice of Cailleachdubh uttering "that could be serious."

Finally, John Rua come out of the house and said we must get Jack Dub with his car to take us all to your house. She will need a little time to mix her herbs and whatever else she uses.

Inside an hour they were in Jack Dub's car with Cailleachdubh and they all went to Stakamore. There was muted conversation in the car until they reached the Boyles house.

John's mother Sorcha came out crying with tears on her face, "My child! My child, I think he is going to die. The doctor told me to be prepared for the worst. I would gladly give my life for my child's life."

John Rua put his arms around Sorcha and said," Avic, Let's not talk like that. We have Cailleachdubh with us. Let her look at Jim. You know as long as there is life there is hope. Would we have come all this way if there was no hope? Now dry your tears and we will take Cailleachdubh to Jim's bed."

As they walked into the room Cailleachdubh asked Sorcha to remove the clothes so she could see what the matter was, before she would decide what to do. After a while she said, "John Rua lift Jim up in the bed and put a few pillows at his back, then you put as much of this bottle down his throat as you can. Only sips at a time."

Then Cailleachdubh lifted the swollen leg up and put another pillow under it. And began to look at the leg muttering.

Sorcha said, "Cailleachdubh is there any way we can help you? Anything at all to help?"

"Aye" said Cailleachdubh, "Aye get me some cloth, for bandages, and make yourself a cup of tea."

Sorcha returned hurriedly with the bandages as Cailleachdubh was rubbing some cream on Jim's leg and was covering the leg with moss. Then she took the bandages and wrapped them around the leg enclosing the moss.

Sorcha said, "Is there anything more I can do for you?"

"Aye" snapped Cailleachdubh, "You can make us all a cup of tea. All we can do now is wait."

After they drank the tea, Cailleachdubh went to see Jim with Sorcha following her. Sorcha said "How are you feeling Jim, a stoir mo croi (treasure of my heart)?"

Jim replied lethargically, "I am tired and can't keep my eyes opened, I want to sleep."

Sorcha cried loudly with tears running down her cheeks, "Thanks be to God you are alive! Sleep my child sleep, and get your strength back. And thank you Cailleachdubh you gave me my child back."

"Ah" retorted Cailleachdubh, "Maybe we all should get some sleep it is a long day. Now remember don't take the bandages off for a week. Hopefully his leg will mend, but there may be a mark left."

As they left Sorcha was showering thanks on all through her tears and sobs.

Fr Jimmy heard what had happened and was determined to discredit Cailleachdubh as having anything to do with Jim's recovery. He went to Sorcha O'Boyle's house in Stakamore and gave her a medal. He said it was a relic of the good Saint Anthony of Padua who cured his sister Mary, and he had had a mass said for Jim that he would get better.

"Well!" snapped Sorcha, "That was nice of you but we had Cailleachdubh here and she cured Jim."

"Nonsense" roared Fr Jimmy, "It was through prayers and devotions to Anthony of Padua not that protestant witch."

"Well!" replied Sorcha, "Maybe prayers had something to do with it. But I don't want to hear a bad word said against Cailleachdubh in my house. If you have bad to say about Cailleachdubh, say it outside my house! You were the devil that nearly put my Jim in an early grave. And anyhow I am not in your parish. Now leave me before I say something I regret. Away with you! Away with you, before I scald you with this kettle!"

Fr Jimmy went out the door huffing and puffing, then he roared "Maybe I will see the Bishop and become the priest in this parish?"

Sorcha yelled, "The day you come here as a priest, that is the day I will become a Protestant, you can tell that to your Bishop! Now you can put that in your pipe and smoke it!"

Fr Jimmy was furious that Sorcha chased him. In his mind he pondered how to discredit Cailleachdubh or get rid of her. She was like a thorn in his side that should be eradicated. Finally, in his mind Fr Jimmy hatched a plan of vengeance. He bought a horse and began to ride up and down the road to where Cailleachdubh lived.

John Rua spoke to him one day and said, "Fr Jimmy I see that you acquired a horse. And why do you need a horse. Hasn't Jack Dub a car where you would be kept dry and warm on a bad day. Didn't he always take you wherever you want to go?"

"Aye" replies Fr Jimmy, "But if it is an emergency, the horse would be quicker. And anyhow I must do the lord's work."

John Rua mumbled, "Aye maybe, if that is all it is for. But why can't you stay away from where Cailleachdubh is living?"

Fr Jimmy laughed and said, "Don't you know wherever I go I am doing the work of God. A priest has to root out evil whenever it rises its ugly head."

John Rua slowly retorted, "Is it not God's work to show kindness and compassion?"

Fr Jimmy rode on laughing, he spent more time riding the horse anywhere Cailleachdubh was walking. He seemed to take pleasure harassing her, whenever he could. When Cailleachdubh was away from the house he would go into her garden and trample the ground. One day he saw Cailleachdubh arriving and galloped off laughing. He rode the horse to the strand of Ansilmhór. Fr Jimmy was riding around shrieking and laughing when the horse fell on its side. Where the horse lay he was unable to free himself and now began screaming for help with the tide rising. Eventually some people saw the horse and heard the yelling, and came to help. They were unable to free Fr Jimmy or rise the horse and the tide was rising quickly. John Rua went for

Cailleachdubh and asked her for her help; as the horse and Fr Jimmy could drown.

Cailleachdubh's reply was, "I don't care if that prig drowns! Did you see the state of my field? It is wanton destruction. Why should I care if he drowns?"

John Rua replied, "Aye I suppose you are right, but what about the poor dumb animal, the horse. Could you not at least try to save it? It is always the innocent and the weak that suffer for others."

"All right" replied Cailleachdubh, "You were always a big softie. I will come only because you cajoled me to save the horse. As for that gefrog! (runt) I have put the curse of the O'Boyle's on his shoulders! Let him see how he likes a bit of his own medicine! Now he can go to hell; that is if the devil would take him!"

When they reached the strand the water was rising and the people had already had taken off their shoes and folded up the legs of their trousers. Cailleachdubh walked to the horse and held its head murmuring some mantra while she caressed the horse's head with her other hand. Then she said, "Try to help me lift the horse and pull that ball of sh** away. The horse arose somewhat shaken, but was on its feet. Cailleachdubh snapped, "John Rua, you and four of you, walk the horse into the first field and give it a good feed of oats. And for you gefrog, you prig! You tried to take the food from my table. And you destroyed what could cure you. You hate Protestants but you will die in a Protestant house with food on the table, which you can't eat. I curse you again! And as the horse improves you will decline into your own hell."

Fr Jimmy was shaken with the cold and two men 'oxter' or dragged him shaking to the other side of the strand. This was the first time that Fr Jimmy stayed quiet, as he was shivering with fright. A doctor had a holiday house at Ballytochair and could attend him. Fr Jimmy was unable to stand up as they entered Doctor Pauling's house. The doctor examined him and said, "Perhaps the best thing for you to do is rest and then more rest. I have to go way for a few days and you can rest in the bed in the small room beside the kitchen. Oh yes there are a few bottles of whiskey in the dresser. Aye a few hot punches should help. Maybe someone should come to visit you, and see that you are all right."

With that said they had Fr Jimmy in bed with a hot whiskey. Doctor Pauling went to see him and he was sleeping so he decided to let him rest. The doctor went away for a few days and he said that they should leave the key with John Rua when he was leaving. And perhaps someone would come to visit him, to see that he was all right. Maybe the best thing to do was to take him by car as the walk across the strand would be tiring."

When anyone came to see Fr Jimmy he would roar at them to stay away as he was going to his friends. John Rua went and knocked at the door but there was no reply and the doors were locked. He presumed that Fr Jimmy had left and was staying with his friends, whoever they were? John Mór said with a laugh, "I never knew that Fr Jimmy had a friend. See we don't know everything, do we?"

Doctor Pauling returned and went to John Rua's to enquire if perhaps he had the key of his house as the door was locked. Nobody could tell where Fr Jimmy was and finally they had to break a window to enter. When they entered they found Fr Jimmy lying beside the table that was full of food. John Mór said, "I don't like to be talking, but did not Cailleachdubh say he would die in a protestant house with food on the table?"

On a calm moonlight night with a filling tide you can sometimes see and hear a ghost splashing on the strand.

"Aye life is strange."

Unresolved Grief

Nowadays people seem to be always complaining about bad weather. It is either too cold, too stormy, too damp, too wintery, too hot, or the summers are too wet. When the old people complained about the wet harvests, it was said that they would need to dry the hay on chairs around the fireside. That is if they could dry any turf to burn in the fire!

However, today they never have had it as bad as the terrible weather we had in years gone by. In those years perhaps it was a miracle that more people did not die in the gales, storms, or the cold weather that prevailed. Of course the older people would affirm solemnly that the people in those years were hardier men and woman than the youth of today. They would comment that the young people of today could not survive through those odious conditions that were prevalent in those far off times.

Ferdie and Sadie lived in a small house, close to the sea, with a few acres of what could be described as the best of poor land. They had two of a family: one boy and one girl. Their boy died while quite young, and their daughter emigrated to America, but died some years later. They at times felt the loss of the grandchildren who would never play or shout in their house. They had resigned themselves to the fact that they would die lonely, with no one to watch them in their old age. For the present, they eked out a somewhat comfortable living, surviving by the fish that came from the sea, and cropping the land for what it would reluctantly surrender. In the summer, life was more congenial with abundance of fish, shellfish and sea vegetation. However, in the winter life was harsh, with the strong gales that blew in from the sea. The gales sent sprays of water into the sky, where the salt in the air would hinder growth, and only the hardiest short grass could survive.

One cold night was like the many that had passed, with storms of North West wind howling outside the door. It was a miracle that anyone could survive the cold wind that was attempting to rob them of the little bit of heat that was in their bodies. Ferdie and Sadie were sitting contentedly at their fireside that winter's night, when they heard something knocking at the house door.

Sadie said to Ferdie "What in under heavens is that, or who is that? Surely no person would be out on a stormy winter's night like this. Maybe it is the wind that has blown something against the door, with the night that is in it? Nothing would surprise me, with the wind that is blowing outside this night."

"Ah!" Said Ferdie. "I will put some more turf on the fire. Sure, no person that had a brain in his or her head would be out on a night like this. It must be the wind."

Ferdie was about to sit down on his comfortable chair at the fire when he heard another couple of sharp knocks at the door. Ferdie went to the door and pulled back the large rug that was against it and was keeping out the wind which was whistling through every seam and crack in the house. He opened the door and looked out, but he could see no-one there.

"Who is there?" asked Sadie.

"I can see no one here." replied Ferdie. "Maybe whoever was there went away because I did not open the door quickly enough. Perhaps I will look outside or shout. Maybe they are sheltering in the shade of the house from the bitter wind that is blowing. It could be someone who was shipwrecked and survived the terrible sea. It would be a shame on us if someone died at our door step, and we did not lift a hand to help."

Ferdie went around the house shouting, "Who is there, come on in and shelter from the wind and snow."

He looked up and down but could not see any person next or near the house, and was a little apprehensive to be out on such a dark cold night, and quickly returned to the warmth of the fire. "And?" said Sadie.

"Avic, I could see no person alive or dead next or near the house, I do not know what was making the noise that was knocking at our door tonight". Ferdie with added haste closed the door of the house and put the rug snugly against it, to keep out as much draught as possible.

"Aye" said Sadie, "We would never live it down if someone died and we never as much opened our door to a dying person. Don't you remember, not that many years ago when the fishing boat was wrecked at sea and one of the fisherman Connal Vickie, somehow managed to swim or was washed ashore?"

"Aye" replied Ferdie, "We know what happened to him."

"Aye! I do." replied Sadie, "He was found next morning lying outside John Dubh's house, as cold as ice, at death's door. Poor Connal Vickie only survived to tell them that he was knocking on their door all night. But no one opened the door for him."

Sadie retorted quickly, "Ferdie, if Connal Vickie had taken him into the house that night to the warm fire he would surely have lived. It was a shame on them to leave any of God's creatures to die on their door step."

"Musha: Aye, Sadie you are right. Connal Vickie was a decent man. God forgive them, they never had a day's luck after that night."

"You know Ferdie, "That the John Dubh's was a prosperous house until that night. After that they never had a day's luck. God forgive me but I could never look them in the face after that. Can you imagine the hard heart of any person who would refuse to give shelter to a dying man? John Dubh's own family was left destitute on the streets of London and New York. Now the house is closed and I don't think even a ghost would stay there. From what was always a house of plenty, with its neat whitewashed walls? And not a blade of grass was growing on the street. Today the street is covered with nettles and briars that are climbing up the walls. Pride and arrogance is a curse, and charity is a blessing, if given freely."

Ferdie was about to sit down on his warm chair to enjoy the glowing warmth of the fire when the door was knocked again.

Ferdie hurriedly opened the door saying "In the name of God who is there, are you of this world?"

When the door was opened there was a young girl standing at the side with a distressed smile on her face, shivering, with flakes of show covering her slender body. Standing by the doorstep, with a baby huddled in her arms. This sight had taken him by surprise and he was unsure if it was a person or a ghost. The girls face was pale and her slim figure looked emaciated from the want of nourishment.

Ferdie gasped: "Dia O, avic mo croi! What in under God has taken you out on a night like this? You could be frozen to death with the weather that is in it. Come in before you are frozen into a statue of ice. Come in avic!"

The girl began crying and through sobbing said. "I knew that something was happening to me and I was going to my cousin's house. Then on the top of the brae, I had the baby on the hillside. However, when I knocked on the door of my own cousins the Doltys and asked for help, they slammed the door in my face. They said 'We don't want pups in this house'. I didn't know what to do and I kept walking. Then I saw the light of your house but when you opened the door, I was ashamed and was going to sleep in some byre but I was afraid that my baby would die of the cold. The baby started to cry, I think it was with the cold. I didn't care if I died, but I wanted my baby to live until it was baptised. As for me I don't care if I die and go to hell. Please could you help me, and let me stay at your fire this night for the baby's sake".

Sadie hollered: "Come in, come in mo stoir mo croi! Never let it be said that we would refuse a child the shelter of our house. No one in this house is going to die or go to hell. Come up to the fire. Ferdie close the door quickly before we are all starved in the house. Now who have we here with all the snow on you? Who are you?"

The girl walking slowly up the floor saying through her sobs; "I am Eileen Breann of Mullinard and I had a baby, tonight on the brae face".

Sadie quickly retorted, "Eileen avic, you must be drenched and frozen to the bones on a night like this, come up to the fire. Then we will get you and your baby washed and changed and into dry clothes. First we will wash your baby. Is that all right with you? I had children myself I should know a little how to handle children. Quick Ferdie get the basin and we will have the baby washed as quickly as possible."

The baby was gently washed and wrapped into a small blanket with an old towel and sheets cut for some nappies.

"Now Ferdie take the big bath to the room and put as much hot water into it as you can. Eileen and I will have to do some woman's things. Now Eileen, you will have to do with some of my clothes, which are dry and we will wash yours tomorrow".

Sadie exclaimed; "Ferdie now you hold the baby, Eileen and I must clean up and have her wet clothing changed".

Eileen through her sobs she said, "I am sorry to cause you all this inconvenience. It is my baby that was worrying me. Sure, if I could dry out at the fire, I don't want to be a nuisance!"

Sadie interrupted Eileen's flow of discourse saying, "Do you want me to have a death in my house this night. Wet clothing would chill anyone to the bones; we could have a death in the house this night if we are not careful. Whist avic, and we will have you all washed and changed into something dry. Didn't I have a family of my own! I am well used to handling a person who had a baby. Musha, I must have been present with half of the women of the parish, when they had a baby. I also had a family of my own, so you see it is nothing new to me to attend another birth. Eileen you, poor creatuir! You have the hardest part past you, the birth, and no one there to help or comfort you. Now all we need to do is to clean ourselves up as we all had to do following a birth. Isn't your baby washed and in its clean and warm clothes. Now whist, and we will have a bite to eat, then you will have to rest."

Eileen murmured, "With God's help I will leave tomorrow and head to my own place, I should manage."

Sadie retorted "Eileen avic, you will do no such thing as leave tomorrow. Let's see how things are progressing, now you have the baby to think about. What would the neighbours think of me if I let you into a cold house? Isn't my house good enough for you? It is warm and we have a good stack of turf to keep us nice and cosy. Tomorrow is always a new day, and everything will look different with the dawn of the new day. Sure! Didn't I know your poor mother Theresa, God rest her soul. Aye, when we were young we were the best of friends, many the good jokes we shared. Aye many the good days we spent together, and aren't we somehow related, I think? Anyhow we were the best of friends when we were both young and carefree. Aye God be with those far off days when we could skip and laugh, and the sun always seemed to shine warmly on us. Of course it must have rained, but now I cannot remember any of the wet days. Your mother and I were like the little birds of the air, skipping with joy through those untroubled days of youth."

Eileen whispering in a low voice said; "I feel ashamed to be bothering you. It is great to find shelter for the night and a kind word. After all, my own cousins, the Doltys slammed the door in my face, and refused me any kind of compassion. Yet you give me shelter and dry clothing. And you speak to me in a kind compassionate tongue."

Sadie whispered, "Whist, Eileen mo stoir mo croi. It is a long road that has not a turn in it. Never wish on others, what you don't wish on yourself. God knows how or where we will be next year. Remember the doors of the house of our God are always open to all. God forbid that we should speak a harsh word against anyone. God can open or shut the door to anyone. God gives and he also takes away from those that don't do his bidding. False pride is a heavy burden to carry. Forgive them for they know not the joys of contentment. Now the next thing we must do is get you a bite to eat, you must be famished with hunger. Tell me, when did you last have a bite to eat? I would say you never touched a morsel of food all day. Isn't that right, I should know, didn't I have children of my own".

Sadie hollered, "Ferdie quick, scramble three eggs for Eileen or we will have a death on our hands. This girl has not eaten a bite of food this day, or perhaps the day before".

Eileen sighed quietly and uttered; "It is all right, I am not that hungry. All I want is to see that my baby is warm and safe this night".

Sadie retorted; "My girl! You will have to eat if you are going to take care of your child! Now don't insult my house, by refusing my food. I will see to it that you are fit and well and with God's help, you and I will live for a long time."

When the two women came from the room into the kitchen, the fire was blazing brightly and Ferdie was stirring the pot with the scrambled eggs.

Now said Ferdie: "Sit yourselves down. This will be soon ready, and the kettle is singing a happy note on the fire. I think we all could do with a good mug of something hot drink to warm our bodies."

Ferdie had already put the poker into the fire to have it red hot, as this was the cure for anyone that was foundered with the cold.

"Ah Ferdie, you're a man after my own heart" replied Sadie. "Now Eileen sit yourself down here at the table before you fade away before my very eyes. I often seen more flesh on a sausage than is on your bones."

Sadie poured some milk into a mug and put a liberal dash of pepper into the mug, then taking the red hot poker from the fire put it into the cold milk. There was sizzling as the milk warmed up with the heat of the hot poker in it.

"Now" said Sadie: "That is a cure for a foundered body. This was the old cure for a cold or a starving. Now Eileen avic, drink this milk first and it will put some heat in your body, or drink it with your scrambled eggs, I want to see some heat in your face. You know you looked as white as a ghost when you came in tonight. Now don't let me see you leaving the table until you have a good feed in you. That is the one thing that will make me happy, mo stoir, is to see you eating and your face warming."

Eileen sat at the table eating a little slowly at first. However, as she commenced eating her appetite was returning. It was then that she realised how hungry she was. Sadie continuing putting more bread before her and encouraging to eat more. With the food and the heat of the fire Eileen was beginning to yawn and her head was nodding with sleep.

Sadie put her hand on Eileen and said "Rise up avic! I put a hot water bottle in your bed, now you must lie down and rest yourself. It is a God's blessing to have a new child under the roof of our house this night. Tomorrow is a new day and everything will look different when we all have had a good night's sleep. Don't you remember when poor wee Birdie Vickie and her new born child was refused the shelter in the house of her cousin the Owen Padricks? Wasn't she found with her little baby in her arms when the snow cleared? Both frozen to death at the gable of their house. God forgive me but they never had a day's luck after that. You don't want me to have that kind of bad luck, do you Eileen?"

Eileen responded; "Ah I don't want to cause you any more bother. I could sleep on the chair at the fire. It's too good to me you are, after all my own cousins the Doltys refused me and my baby the shelter of their house".

Sadie interrupted Eileen saying, "Let's forget everyone else tonight avic! Now come with me until I tuck you in your bed, and remember no silly talk about sleeping on chairs in my house. You will need to get your sleep because we don't know when your baby will call you. Ah sure we could all do with a good night's sleep with all the commotion this night".

All went to bed that night with cold squalls of wind blowing and the snow falling outside. Next morning the ground was covered with a heavy blanket of snow that left the place like a Christmas card, without the small birds. It looked as if the cold weather was intending to continue with a vicious mantle of snow falling. It would be difficult to see any distance, or where the road was.

After breakfast Eileen was looking out the window and uttered, "Thank you for the shelter last night. I will leave you and head for my little house in Mullinard".

Sadie gasped: "What in under heavens is wrong with you Eileen avic. You would not let a cross dog out, the day that is in it. Is there something wrong with my house? You have a child to think about. Do you want your child to die of the cold? You are not going anywhere with the weather that is in it".

Eileen faltered before speaking, saying; "I don't want to cause you anymore bother, I was glad to have a place last night. It is too good you have been to me. I think that I should manage on my own now".

Ferdie who was returning from the byre with a bucket of fresh milk uttered, "Only that the byre is at the end of the house, I would never find it. God help anyone who is caught out this day, one place looks like another. God help us because someone is going to get lost and die with the cold that is outside. It would be utter madness to try to travel any distance today".

"Aye" said Sadie: "No one is going to leave this house this day. It is enough to go outside to get turf for the fire. You don't want it on my conscience that we let you and a child die in the cold, do you? Anyway we must have a name for your child, what name have you chosen Eileen?"

Eileen replied; "I am not sure. I was thinking maybe Fionn, or what do you think?"

Sadie retorted slowly with a smile and a tear falling from her eyes. "Fionn! Fionn would be wonderful name: Fionn the fair haired one. I think that that name would be fitting as he has blond hair. Aye and I had a baby whose name was Fionn. God rest him he died when he was young. God is good that he has put another Fionn into this house, what do you say Ferdie?"

"Aye" replied Ferdie in a low whisper, "We must get Fionn baptised as soon as possible. You know I didn't like to be calling him the baby, after all he is a person who is wanted and appreciated in this house. It would be a blessing on this house to have Fionn baptised and sleeping under our roof. Wouldn't it?"

Sadie replied; "Aye we certainly will, but not in the weather that is in it. However, we will do our own baptising until we get someone else like a priest to do a proper job!"

A drop of holy was poured over the baby's head and Ferdie uttered: "In the name of our lord Jesus Christ. I baptise your Fionn! You are welcome to our house, for you are baptised with the water of life. God bless you and your mother Eileen, who carried you to our house. Now I am going to have a hot whiskey to celebrate. I hope you all are going to join me."

Ferdie made them all a hot whiskey to toast the birth of Fionn. Eileen was reluctant at first to drink the toast until Sadie said: "Eileen won't you drink a toast to your son who has blessed this house with his arrival, and of course your presence under our roof of the house, this day? A new child is a blessing to any house and will bring happiness. God's blessing to you Fionn (Dia beannacht do Fhionn)."

"Aye" retorted Ferdie: "We lift a welcoming hearty glass, and toast you Fionn! May your days on this earth be many with good health and happiness!"

The following days it snowed almost continuously, but now not as heavy as before. By the third week the snows were abating a little, and travel was becoming less hazardous. The sky had at last shed all its snow, and now the days were brighter. Some people could be seen walking about, even if it was only for short journeys. One day a man could be seen coming up the fields, riding a horse. Ferdie who was carrying a burden of hay to the byre that was some distance from the house, happened to wave to the man to enquire about his neighbours. As he came closer, the figure of Reverend Boyce became clearer.

Ferdie said: "Good day Reverend Boyce, I did not know who you were in the distance. I am sorry if I disrespected you by shouting at you."

Reverend Boyce replied; "Good day to you Ferdie. This was terrible whether we had these last few weeks. You know I was getting cabin fever as I could not leave the house. I hope that you don't mind I was shooting some rabbits and ducks on your land."

"Not at all, your Reverence" responded Ferdie, "You shoot away and good luck to you. It is not going to upset me one way or another. Wasn't the wildlife a gift from God to feed the people that had to live on the land?"

"Yes Ferdie, if we take the bible literally; man has dominion over the fish in the water and over the fowl of the air and over all the cattle on the land. I have been lucky with my day's shooting. Would you like to have a few rabbits to make a stew, as I shot them on your land?"

"Ah thank you, Your Reverence Boyce. However, there is no need to give me what is after all your hunt. I suppose that you could use it all in your own home."

Reverence Boyce replied: "There are no need for titles on this earth, we are all equal. My name is John. And I insist that you will relieve me of a few rabbits for your table. How many is in your house, I don't want to be skimping".

Well retorted Ferdie: "There is my wife Sadie, me, Eileen and her baby, who is staying with us for the time been. Oh! The baby was born three weeks ago and we only gave him a basic christening. As you are a man of the cloth, maybe you could give him a religious christening. We would feel better if the baby had an official christening. Do you think that you could do it for us? I know that we are not of the same religion. God stand between us and harm, if anything happened the child. I would feel better if the child was christened by a man of God. If you can't I will understand, your reverence."

Reverend Boyce smiled and replied "Well maybe we are of a different sect. However, if we all believe in Christ, therefore we are all the same religion. Certainly I will baptise any child, if that is what the family desires."

"Aye" retorted Ferdie: "Thanks, that would be great and I am sure that we would all be more contented. Come on in your reverence, you are welcome in our house."

As Ferdie and Reverend Boyce entered, Sadie and Eileen were busy tiding the house. Ferdie told them the good news he had for them.

Saying "I have begged Reverend Boyce to baptise Fionn and he agreed. Now, isn't that good news?"

"Thanks be to God" retorted Sadie "Isn't that wonderful Eileen, to have Fionn baptised by a servant of God. The baptising we did was all right for the time, but now Eileen, this baptising will be the real thing. What do you think Eileen"?

"Thank God and thank you Reverend Boyce" cried Eileen, "Since I came into this house they have treated me with respect and kindness. Thank you Ferdie and Sadie for letting me stay in your house. If not, we could be frozen to death. They opened their house to me while my own relations refused me or my child a shelter from the cold."

Reverence Boyce spoke slowly and retorted: "It is nice that people have compassion in their hearts. Remember that Jesus was born in a stable surrounded by animals, as all refused them shelter. Be grateful to God, that he had guided you to where you and Fionn would be safe and wanted. Forgive those that refuse to share the cup of kindness, for bitterness is a bitter chalice to sip. Let's us not dwell on negativity, but celebrate the birth of a new life that was shaped by the love of God. Now where is this new man Fionn, that God has called us to welcome him into our community."

Eileen lifting the baby handed the infant to Reverence Boyce, with tears falling from her face, saying "Thank you Reverence Boyce for your kind words. I felt lost until I came to this door, where the made me and my baby welcome and wanted."

Reverence Boyce smiled and sang,

"Amazing grace,
How sweet the sound,
That saved a wretch like me,
I once was lost,
But now am found,
Was blind, but now I see.
Amazing grace,
How sweet the sound,

That saved a wretch like me."

"We are all lost until we are saved. Have you any water so we can baptise Fionn into the community of Christ. Oh! Eileen would you care to add a second name to Fionn?"

Eileen hesitated before replying: "O gosh, I have not thought of it, I was only interested in the safety of my baby. I am not sure what name I should call Fionn. Maybe Sadie you or Ferdie could chose a second name for Fionn".

Sadie replied "Your father's name was Conall. Don't you think that is fitting that Fionn should carry the name of his grandfather?"

Reverence Boyce replied: "Conall would be a fitting name as it derives from friendship, or a hound. It also applies to a swift footed warrior. It won't be long until this boy will be running around the country. Now have we any water to baptise Fionn Conall into the community of Christ."

Sadie stammered "Reverence Boyce, do you want plain water or holy water of the Catholic Church?"

Reverence Boyce responded with a smile: "Whatever water you feel comfortable with. After all, Jesus was baptised by John in the water of the river Jordan. We are led to believe in Matthew that at that moment the heavens opened when Jesus was baptized. We are merely mortals that follow the pathway of Jesus."

Reverence Boyce took the water, which he poured on the head of the baby saying, "We will ask Jesus Christ to formally accept Fionn Conall into his safe keeping. In the name of the Father and Son and the Holy Spirit, we name you Fionn Conall. May God protect you and your mother Eileen in his care and safeguard, Amen. Unfortunately, we cannot offer you gold, frankincense or myrrh Fionn Conall. Do you know that frankincense is merely an oil to relieve the body and myrrh is a perfume that is sometimes used as an incense or a perfume?"

Reverence Boyce put his hand in his pocket and produced a large silver coin saying "This is my gift to you Fionn Conall, perhaps it is not gold, and it is merely a token of welcome."

Eileen quickly replied: "Reverend Boyce! I can't take your money, it is I that should be giving you money, you baptised my child Fionn."

Reverence Boyce smiled and replied: "I often heard that it was lucky to be the first to give a new born child a little money. Surely you wouldn't ask me to break an old custom and leave me without luck. We all need whatever luck we can get. Anyhow the money is for Fionn Conall. As Jesus was given gifts, shouldn't we all follow the example of giving a little gift?"

There was silence for a while until Ferdie spoke, "Saying shouldn't we all drink a toast to a new member of our community?"

Reverence Boyce laughing aloud retorting "I certainly agree with you Ferdie, that is a sensible decision. After all, it is not every day we have a christening. In twenty years' time Fionn Conall will be a young strong man, and we like last year's apples will be withering or perhaps meeting our maker."

Ferdie had four cups of hot whiskey sitting on the table and all were invited to again drink a toast to Fionn Conall.

Eileen said; "I don't know how but somehow, I intend to repay all of you for your kindness to me. When I came to this door, I was not scorned and detested but you gave me a sympathetic welcome. All I received in this house was kindness."

Reverence Boyce softly interjected: "Eileen you owe me nothing, it is Sadie and Ferdie that gave you their home. Whoever welcomes you into their home they also received the Lord God into their home. And whoever welcomes a little child like this, in his name also welcomes God. Now let's not dwell in the past, it is the future we must all look forward to. Ah maybe it's the drink that is makings me morbid. But in the Bible it says, 'Give strong drink unto him that is ready to perish, and wine unto those of heavy hearts.' Let's not dwell on the past, as we are here today to celebrate the christening of Fionn Conall."

Sadie was now beginning to cry saying: "God took away my Fionn from this house but now he granted us another Fionn. It certainly was God's wish to guide Fionn and his mother to our door, thank you God for your mercy."

"Aye" said Ferdie: "Let's have another drink. This is the first celebration of a birth I had in this house for years. Who is for another drop of whiskey to celebrate? They used to say a child is not properly baptised unless there is a drop of whiskey spilled for the fairies."

Reverence Boyce smiled replying, "Perhaps we should not deprive the fairies of a little drop of drink. My father said he did not believe in superstition, however when we had a celebration he always left a small glass of whiskey outside the door at night. I suppose we are not superstitious, but why deflect away any good luck that may be coming our way."

Following a further drink Reverence Boyce said his goodbyes to all.

As he was parting Sadie uttered: "Reverence Boyce, excuse me for interrupting but do you think that you are all right. You know that perhaps it is not safe to attempt to have the horse jumping any fences on your way home."

Reverence Boyce replied: "Yes perhaps that is good advice. We all of us should be prepared to take advice, and I certainly appreciate your concern. I will return by the road, as for traveling the way I came here there would be little chance of shooting another bird or rabbit. Here take these rabbits, perhaps you can stew them and make a meal for all in the house. A fresh bit of meat will conclude your celebration for the arrival of Fionn Conall."

Ferdie and Sadie protested that the gift was too bounteous, and it was them that should be giving gifts.

Reverence Boyce smiled saying: "He that gives a cup of water in God's name shall surely be rewarded in heaven. And you that have shown what is Christianity, it is your generosity that leaves us all in shame. Sometime events happen in life that may be put there to test us. And this house will surely ring with the joys of laughter and blessings. Now good bye, and God's blessings be with you all in this house."

As Reverence Boyce rode his horse out the gate, all were delighted with the outcome of the day. Sadie felt that it was providence that sent Eileen and Fionn Conall to them and she would endeavour to have the child as long as humanly possible. With the loss of her child Fionn she felt that there was a void left in her life. Now there were the cries and giggles of a baby in the house and especially at night it made her happier. She felt a little as if between a mother and a grandmother. Now if she could use her influence to get Ferdie to ask Eileen and Fionn Conall to stay, if only for a while longer.

That night Sadie spoke to Ferdie about the terrible weather and how God must have sent Eileen and Fionn Conall to them.

"Aye Sadie, I see that you are happy to have a baby about the house again. Wouldn't it be nice if they could stay at least until Fionn is stronger? The cow has plenty of milk, God knows more than we can drink. And a growing child needs plenty of milk to strengthen its bones."

"God bless you Ferdie" said Sadie: "You have taken the words out of my mouth. I was thinking the same thing myself and I didn't know how to say what I was thinking. You know this last while, it felt as a heavy burden was lifted from my back. But we can't be too abrupt in case we offend Eileen. You know that she has her pride to consider. I think that Fionn has given us back what we have lost. Isn't it funny that Eileen would chose the name Fionn, it must be God's answer to our prayers?"

"Aye Sadie, an empty house is a lonely place and only the laughter of a child can make a house a home."

Ferdie and Sadie talked into the night how to approach Eileen on the subject of her staying with them. They did not wish to offend the girl with words that could be construed offensive. "Aye, said Ferdie, "I often heard it said, there are three things in life that never come back: a speeding arrow, the spoken word or a lost opportunity."

Sadie whispered, "Ferdie maybe you could speak to Eileen and say that she could stay here as long as she likes? After all you are the man of the house."

"Well Sadie, let's not trip ourselves over by being unduly hasty. You know a careless word could upset everything, and we could unintentionally upset Eileen. Let's take things slowly, you know with this bad weather, no one is leaving if they have an ounce of sense in their head. By the time that the bad weather is past Eileen will feel more at home in this house."

"Aye Ferdie, you are a shrewd one that never jumped before you look. I will try to keep Eileen happy and wanted, then perhaps she will stay with us, every day is a day longer."

The snows finally dissolving after six weeks but now the cold north winds continued blowing. This was the worst winter for many years, and the news came that Crochar Doyle was found sitting on a log at the lakeside frozen to death. The poor man was trying to get something for his fire as there was not a sod of turf in his house. There were many stories of loss of life in different places, some of the news more drastic than another. It was once you heard a distressing story, someone would tell another equally perturbing account.

By now some people had visited the house, but neither Ferdie nor Sadie would comment on the baby, only that it is healthy, thanks be to God.

One evening Eileen came running into the house saying: "I see Sara Dolty coming up to the house. That is one woman I don't want to see after how she treated me, when she slammed the door in my face. As long as I live I never want to see or speak to her!"

"Ah Eileen avic leave it to me, now she has a guilty conscience. I certainly won't be showing any welcome to that woman, God forgive me. Slip up into the room mo stoir, we will treat her with her own medicine that she dashed out. Let's see how she enjoys it."

Sadie was afraid that Sara Dolty could be the catalyst to cause Eileen to leave the house, and through hell or high water she wanted Eileen and Fionn Conall to remain with her.

Eventually, Sara Dolty came into the house and said, "I see Sadie, that you have a baby in the house."

"Aye Sara Dolty isn't it great that you can see a baby through the stone walls. After all someone could not see a child at their own doorstep. Aye there are none as blind as those that will not see, what do you think? I pray to God that that person will be able to see the light of heaven; maybe God is also blind."

Sara Dolty face flushed and she retorted: "Are you insinuating that that person was me?"

Sadie face lit up and she replied angrily, "Sara if the shoe fits wear it!"

Sara Dolty was fuming with anger, as she knew that all the neighbours must have heard how she chased Eileen and her baby away. She riposted: "Sadie I will not stand in this house and be insulted."

Sadie snapped: "Well Sara Dolty, I suppose that you can always go to another house, to be insulted. I am sure that there are plenty of places that would oblige you, aren't there?"

Sara Dolty was aghast and surprised. Sadie was usually a quiet and refined person that never said a discourteous word to anyone. She expected that Sadie would be easily intimidated, and would be embarrassed to have that tramp Eileen under her roof. She was well aware how easily she could browbeat other people and have them squeaking when she spoke. She headed home fuming with rage cursing Sadie for being so outspoken.

When Eileen came down from the room Sadie was smiling and said. "Well I put a bee under that one's bonnet. If she came here to make little of you or me, we showed her what a cold shoulder feels like. Let her see how she likes to get a little of her own ignorance throw back into her face. That brazen hussy!"

Eileen said "Thanks for saving me from speaking to that one. I dread ever seeing or speaking to Sara Dolty again."

"Musha, Eileen avic, you needn't have any fear of speaking or standing wherever that one is about! Can't you see, she is the one with the guilty conscience? You can walk tall anywhere you like. As long as we are together nobody will insult you or me."

But retorted Eileen; "What will people say about me, staying in your house."

Sadie retorted, "Never worry what people say, believe nothing no matter what they say, unless it agrees with you. You will see that we will have the last laugh; ignorance and arrogance is not in our nature."

But Sadie "Sometime I must think of heading to my house in Mullinard. You all have being extremely kind to me for letting me stay in your house."

Sadie replied with haste, "Eileen avic, don't tell me that you are going to leave me with Christmas around the corner. What are we going to do, if you take Fionn Conall away from me? Don't you know how attached Ferdie is to Fionn Conall, it would break his heart. He looks on Fionn as the son he lost. Can't you at least wait until the sun is high in the sky? It would break Ferdie's heart and mine to lose you and Fionn Conall."

Eileen began to cry saying, "I am sorry, but I thought that we were a burden on you and Ferdie."

"Not at all" riposted Sadie, "Your coming was the best Christmas present we could ever have received. I promise you, we will not keep you a prisoner, and when the time is ready you can leave on your own free will. Can I tell Ferdie that we will have you and Fionn Conall for Christmas? It will keep him happy."

When Ferdie came into the house Sadie said, "I have good news for you, Eileen and Fionn Conall are staying. Isn't that the best Christmas present we ever had. We are all going to be one big happy family."

"Aye great" said Ferdie, "I have started to make a new cot for Fionn Conall. Wouldn't it be wonderful to have him in his own new cot before Christmas?"

They all settled down as a new family and Sadie would proudly refer to Fionn Conall as mo leanbh féin (my own child). Whenever neighbours commented on Eileen or Fionn and how they came to stay with them. Sadie could become annoyed, and lash out verbally at what she considered was a disparaging remark. The neighbours would say you could criticize Sadie and she would only smile. But if you said a word of censure against Eileen she would verbally cut the socks from under your feet. Sadie now looked on Eileen as if she was her daughter and Fionn Conall as a longed for grandchild. Whenever Fionn cried, Sadie would lift and cuddle and nurse him, while chanting some old lullaby she heard in her youth. Anytime Eileen would talk of leaving Sadie would say, it wouldn't be right to leave a child on his own, if someone was not there to look after him. Then when Fionn started crawling Sadie would say, someone would need to keep an eye on him in case he fell into the fire. Sadie always had some justifiable reason why Fionn Conall would remain, like a bad influenza or some mysterious 'flu. As weeks turned to months and years. Fionn Conall was now attending school and Eileen was less curtailed by a demanding child. Besides Sadie was always on hand to attend to Fionn Conall's every need, and Eileen was offered a job in a fish factory. One day she told Sadie of the offer of a job, and if she minded if she would take the job. But she was concerned about leaving Fionn Conall because she would not be home in time to attend to Fionn.

Sadie smiled and hugged her saying: "Eileen avic mo stoir mo croi, good luck to you, take any job you wish, it is your life. Now don't you worry about Fionn Conall, aren't we only too glad to be able to attend to him. Can't you see how Ferdie is always playing with Fionn Conall: it is his second childhood. Sometimes I think if Fionn Conall was ever to leave it would break Ferdie's heart, he is happier now than ever he was. You know Eileen, it will do you good to get out and meet other people your own age. Thank God Fionn Conall is healthy, and is growing up, someday he will be a fine young man."

Eileen slowly replied, "Thanks Sadie, I was unsure of how you would react, after all you were my saviour when we first came here."

"Eileen avic, isn't it time that you looked on this house as your own. All I ever wanted is that you are happy. Musha, it will do you the world of good to have a job where you can earn a few shillings. Ferdie was saying that we are smothering you in the house. You know we only want what is best for you and Fionn Conall."

Eileen began work and her demeanour was brighter, now she had a little money that she could spend on Fionn Conall and herself. With time Eileen became more confident with people and herself. She was promoted to an office job as she had a better than average education and intelligence.

Things changed for all with Eileen working, Sadie could spend more time with Fionn Conall, who he called granny, and Ferdie who was referred to as grandpa. Their home was now a happy and contented house. Ferdie would make a toy wheelbarrow or wooden cars, which were painted in bright colours, for Fionn Conall. When he was mending his lobster pots Fionn Conall was always with him. Ferdie gave Fionn Conall a hammer and a little box of nails to play with. Some of the neighbours commented that the child could hit his fingers with the hammer. Ferdie's reply would be; "If he hit his fingers once he would learn not to hit them again." Fionn Conall hammered as many nails into a plank of wood, that he cracked it. On calm days Ferdie would take Fionn Conall out in his boat, and allow him to steer it. The two became inseparable in their daily tasks.

Sara and Sean Dolty's son Seamus was perhaps a little fond of drink, and on many nights he did not come home until the next day. Indeed, he had a serious inclination to drink, and at times would visit the hills where people were brewing their own poitín. People distilled the illicit alcohol, termed poitín. It was the virtuous good mountain whiskey, if you believed in it. The whiskey bought in pubs which was a little more expensive was described as government whiskey.

However, some people did not take care of their brewing and their product was not good. Some people would say that bad poitín could make you sick or poison you. Seamus was never careful from whom or where he obtained the poitín, as long as he could find a cheap bottle. One day Seamus did not return home and as this was not usual, no one went looking for him. After a few days' people went looking for Seamus but they could find no trace of him. The police were informed and they made inquiries in the various townlands, but to no avail. The search stretched into weeks, without any progress. Eventually a man who was searching for lost sheep found the remains of Seamus's body on the hillside. The police were informed and the badly decomposed body of Seamus was retrieved.

The coffin had to be closed and Seamus was to be interned in the graveyard. The neighbours of course came to offer their sympathy to the Doltys. The usual words at a funeral were spoken; "Ah, Seamus was a decent man who never did anybody any harm; or he would give you the shirt of his back; he is in a happier place now, God rest him a decent honest man".

This loss of Seamus played on Sara's mind as was one of her daughters, Jane, who went to America, and no trace of her was ever found. She wondered if her refusal to let Eileen and her baby into her house had anything to do with her loss. She then dismissed the idea as irrelevant and absurd. However, the reflections played on her mind, as God's punishment. Things settled down a little as life had to continue in the Doltys house. Sara would blame everyone but herself for the loss of her son Seamus. She blamed the people from the mountain and said that the police were not doing their job.

Sara Dolty's husband Sean, like most men in the area, was a fisherman. One blustery morning in the month of March Sean Dolty went out to sea as usual to catch some fish. That evening he failed to return to his home port. However, the people were not particularly concerned because at times he landed in the neighbouring harbour of Poldubh. As the night wore on Sara became concerned and sent someone to see if Sean was in Poldubh. There was no trace of Sean or the boat in that harbour, or the next harbour. By now it was a dark night. With the wind increasing it would be dangerous for any boat to go to sea. The fishermen called the coastguard who made an initial search, but found nothing. Next morning the coastguard with the fishermen conducted a search of the area of sea. Their search was in vain as no trace of Sean or the boat was found. On the third day the lifeboat crew began searching an extended area of sea. Eventually the lifeboat crew found the body of Sean Dolty on the rocks of Tordubh. It seemed that Sean had survived the storm, but died of hypothermia on the cold black rocks of Tordubh.

There was another wake of Sean Dolty, and as is traditional, the neighbours came to offer their condolences. In death no person would mention any wrongdoing of the deceased, or whatever errors they have committed in life. In the country, people would be apprehensive of saying anything disparaging about the dead. They believed that the soul of the dead could return to haunt you, especially at the night of the dead, November 2nd (oíche na mairbh). Those present at the wake praised all Sean's good deeds and how he would share anything with a person. The ritual accolades were spoken about Sean, and how he would never refuse anybody anything if they asked. But aren't all men good men and "the good they do lives after them": and Sean was a good man. Sadie in conversation with Eileen referred to the death of Sean Dolty, and that it would be expected of them, to pay their respect to the dead.

Eileen hesitated before answering saying, "I would be very reluctant to enter that house, as I was refused entry the last time I stood on their doorstep."

"Aye" answered Sadie, "You have a justified reason to stay away; but why lower yourself to her level? Certainly you have a valid reason for staying away from the house. But don't you think that you and I should go to the funeral. That way the neighbours will have no excuse to talk about you or me. You can with your head held high, go anywhere or to any funeral. Musha, if anyone should feel ashamed it would be Sara Dolty. She is the one that is feeling the pangs of grief, agony and despondency. Today and every day of her life Sara's will be weighed down with grief and lamentations. What has she to look forward to but mourning and pungent salty tears?

Eileen slowly replied, "Aye Sadie perhaps you are right. If you are going to the church perhaps I should also go. I certainly respect your guidance, as you were always there to guide me through my bitter days."

Eileen and Sadie went to church laughing and chatting like mother and daughter each comforting the other. Each one was now becoming more confident with the other. Whenever Sadie was speaking to other people, she referred to Eileen as "my Eileen".

Eileen was working in the office while Tom Plunket the manager was away on some business, when a buyer Mr. Guy Carydis from France came on an unexpected visit with the intention of buying fish. Mr. Plunket would communicate with Guy Carydis in French, to finalise their transactions. Mr. Carydis spoke in very broken English and there were uncomfortable muddles by all, as they tried to communicate with each other. The hand gestures were excruciating to all concerned. When Eileen spoke in French to Guy Carydis saying "I am not fluent in French but I remember a little from when I was young. If you will forgive me as I am not fluent, and I have not practiced French for a while. I would appreciate if you could, and correct any mistakes I make"

Of course Guy Carydis was delighted that someone could speak to him in his own language. The awkwardness faded away with laughter as they discussed the products that the factory had to offer. Eileen apologized that she had not the knowledge or the authority to give the correct prices.

Guy Carydis asked her, "Where have you learned to speak French, as you have a better command of it than Mr. Plunket?"

Eileen blushed and replied, "When I was young, Philip and Brigita Macron, who were French, lived close to my house. They had other friends who were French who came to visit. They spoke French to me when I was a child, and when I answered in French they gave me sweets or bit of cake. After years of speaking with them I picked up a little of the language; which is not good."

"A oui" replied Guy Carydis. "Mademoiselle, you have perfect French, don't worry about your pronunciation. Do you know there are twenty-eight different accents or dialects for the many regions of France and that is not including Canada? Don't you know that the dialect that was taken to England is langue d'oïl, or old French. I can understand you perfectly, perhaps better than I can Mr. Plunket."

Eileen's face flushed, as she replied, "Mr. Carydis you are extremely kind to me; but if I can be of any help until Mr. Plunket arrives, I will do anything in my power to assist you."

The telephone rang and it was Mr. Plunket wishing to speak to Guy Carydis. He apologizing for not being there to meet him, but would be back within the hour.

Guy Carydis replied politely, "Mademoiselle Eileen is with me and she is kindly assisting me with all information, barring prices, which she is leaving to you. Perhaps you, Mademoiselle Eileen, and I should meet where can conclude our business, over lunch. Do you agree?"

"Yes" replied Tom Plunket, "That would be perfect and please forgive me for my absence from the office today. I will be there as soon as possible."

"Now Mademoiselle Eileen," said Guy Carydis "if you please; we will we go to the hotel to await Monsieur Plunket."

Eileen replying a little hesitant, "Monsieur Guy Carydis, I am only a menial worker here and I would not have the acumen to talk business."

"Nonsense Mademoiselle Eileen, if you don't accompany me to the hotel then I would be reluctant to meet Monsieur Plunket. Monsieur Plunket and I agreed that you would do the courtesy of accompany me to the hotel; please say yes."

Eileen and Guy Carydis sat in the hotel speaking French. She was becoming more confident and her French was becoming clearer. Now they were laughing and joking about everyday accounts. And Guy Carydis was complementing her on her clear delivery, which left her more relaxed. After a while Tom Plunket arrived at the hotel and began to apologize for missing him.

Guy Carydis with a smile dismissed his apologies saying, "Your assistant Mademoiselle Eileen has been a perfect hostess. You are fortunate to have such congenial staff with your company. There are few companies in Ireland that have staff as courteous and civil as you have Monsieur Plunket."

As they sat down at the table Eileen said, "I hope you will excuse me as I have to attend to my son. Perhaps you men will feel more confident discussing your business between yourselves?"

However, she was persuaded to stay by Guy Carydis and Tom Plunket to take notes of their discussion. The meeting was a success for Tom Plunket as he obtained a substantial contract. As they parted Tom Plunket insisted that he would get a taxi to take Eileen home.

Guy Carydis' parting words were, "If any further phone contacts are necessary, please may I speak to Mademoiselle Eileen?"

Tom Plunket was pleased with the outcome of the meeting as he knew that a lost opportunity was a loss of business.

When Eileen went home she told how everything transpired at work today, and the Frenchman who was a buyer, and how she remembered little bits of French that keep him happy. She was like a little child who was telling about her Christmas toy.

Sadie was equally pleased with the news, and kept asking Eileen, to repeat the story for the benefit of Ferdie. Then Sadie had to tell the story to Fionn Conall, saying, "Your mother is a smart woman: she got a contract that will keep people in work. What do you think of that?"

The house of course was ecstatic with joy as they savoured the good news. And when Eileen went back to her work Tom Plunket praised her for her help. He awarded her a rise in pay and gave her an enhanced position in his company. Whenever Guy Carydis phoned the office he requested to speak with Eileen.

In Sadie, Ferdie and Eileen's house they were delighted and there was a feeling of euphoria that enfolded all. The house for weeks afterwards was riding on the feel-good factor. But people become exhausted in their effort to find themselves, as pride comes before a fall. And Sadie became unwell and had to go to hospital. Tom Plunket gave Eileen time off work to visit Sadie and at times would drive her and Ferdie to visit Sadie.

Eileen was for a few weeks the loving daughter in the house organizing its day to day running. After a few weeks Sadie was discharged from hospital but was reliant on Eileen for support. Sadie would say, "Eileen avic, you are a godsend to me and Ferdie. What would we do without you and Fionn Conall? You made this house a home."

Eileen smiling would reply, "It is nothing to what you did for us, when we were destitute and alone in the world."

With time all was back as normal, and Eileen was working and communicating with Guy Carydis and other buyers.

Ferdie went out each day as usual to fish, this time he intended to set a bottom net for fish. It was a calm day and he considered that around the island of Inishdubh would be a likely place to catch fish. The fishing was good but there was a little fog rising. Ferdie was so engrossed with catching fish that he did not pay attention to the fog. After a while it descended so heavy, that he could not see more than the front of the boat. It was pea soup dense fog. He was aware that it would be madness to try to return home. He was aware that many experienced fishermen were lost through fog. Everything looks out of perspective, a small ball can look like a mountain. A person's eyes can deceive logic. Ferdie headed to the island slowly to sit out the fog. On the island there was an old hut that the fishermen used for a short stay. Ferdie lit a fire to cook himself some warm food and to warm the hut. The smoke filled the hut and made him choke but it also chased away any insects in it. Ferdie enjoyed the warm food and he hoped the fog would lift by evening, enabling him to return home. He was a prisoner there as long as the fog continued.

The fog remained and Sadie and Eileen were getting concerned about Freddie's safety they contacted some friends to enquire if they had any information. The village was anxious as to why the boat did not return. The fog was so heavy that no boat could go to sea. John Rua said that perhaps Ferdie went into some cove, and was sitting at the fire smoking his pipe, as it would not be safe to walk home. John Rua words brought some comfort to Sadie and Eileen, and dulled their fears a little. That night Sadie and Eileen slept uneasily and were awake with any little noise.

Next morning the fog was as dense as it was the previous day. Some of the neighbours phoned houses along the coast to inquire. As the day passed Sadie and Eileen went to the church to pray for Freddie's safety.

Inside the church Sara Dolty was kneeling close to the altar praying somewhat hoarsely. When she heard Sadie and Eileen approach she lowered her voice to a whimper. After a while Sara Dolty with tears in her eyes came to Sadie and Eileen. Saying, "I was praying that the same thing that happened to me doesn't happen to others. I have suffered the wrath and indignation of God for my arrogance and false pride. Perhaps God will listen to a sinner like me and take Ferdie home safely."

Sadie stood up and hugged Sara Dolty saying, "We will all pray together, won't we Eileen? The house of God is no place for envy or old bitterness." Then she reached for Eileen and said, "We will all hold hands before we ask God for his help." With all standing Sadie embraced Eileen and Sara Dolty. Sadie said, "We will not speak, but each of us will ask God for forgiveness for any past wrongs we may have committed. We will all walk out of this church today with no bitterness in our hearts, for envy decays the body and soul."

All were crying with heavy eyes of tears and asking each other for forgiveness.

Sara Dolty begged Eileen to forgive her before she died. Saving, "Eileen I never had a day's luck since the night that I chased you away. God's wrath is on me and he has poured a bitter chalice of indignation for me to sup."

Eileen who was crying said, "There is nothing to forgive, God had guided me to Sadie and Ferdie where I am happy. If you pray for Ferdie to return home to Sadie and me, that is all I ask of you. I have forgiven you a long time ago. The day after your husband Sean was buried I knelt on his grave and asked him and God to forgive me for my bitterness. Then I felt better, for it is not right to hold bitterness against the dead, or anybody."

Sara Dolty hugged Eileen as the salty tears ran down her cheeks muttering words of prayers and thanks for forgiveness. The three woman were now crying and praying for Ferdie's safe return home.

Sadie was pleased that any old animosities were now settled amicably. She hoped that as this had happened in the church, God would look down with compassion and send Ferdie home safe and sound. Each of them left the church hugging and praising each other, all were happy with the outcome from the tranquillity of church. As they walked home each promised each other that they would meet again.

Early in the morning of the third day the fog was abating and Ferdie prepared for his return home. When he entered the harbour some of the boats were about to depart to search for him. The fishermen and neighbours were delighted that he returned. Word was quickly sent to Sadie's house.

When he landed some of the people asked him if he was hungry.

Ferdie laughing said, "I am not hungry for food as I had plenty of fish to eat, but I am dying for a good cup of tea and a good smoke!"

The people who were in the harbour helped with securing the boat. After they had secured everything they advised Ferdie to go home to his wife and family who were waiting for him.

Sadie and Eileen were waiting for him in the house all smiling and laughing. Their happiness was restored with smiles and the table was set with food as Ferdie entered the door.

"God" said Ferdie, "It is nice to see you all again beside a warm fire in our own home. I was worried about you that you were worried about me who was away on holidays."

"Aye" said Sadie, "Eileen and me we were all out of our mouth with worry about you. Musha we didn't have a full night's sleep worrying if you were safe and well. Or could you be lying on the bottom of the sea! You could be dead."

"Ah" replied Ferdie unhurriedly, "God or the Devil would not want me. They would reject me and throw me back to upset you."

Eileen sobbed as she said with tears in her eyes, "Sadie, Fionn and me want you. I for one would be devastated if you were lost."

"Aye" snapped Sadie, "That is enough of your playacting. We were all worried out of our head, and you have to upset poor Eileen, who stood by me and helped me."

Ferdie walked over to Eileen and put his hands around her saying, "Eileen my child I am sorry for upsetting you. You Sadie and Fionn Conall are something that I will always hold close to my heart. I was safe and on the island, but I was always worrying about you, my child, my child."

There were hugs and kisses all around as they laughed and cried. Now there were tears on Ferdie's face and he said, "If I knew this I would have gone to the island long ago just for the welcome home. Sure there were people in America for twenty years, and they never got as good a welcome as me."

Then Ferdie sat drinking a mug of tea and had a smoke, smiling with all in the house.

Tom Plunket's car stopped at the house and he entered with a bottle of whiskey, as he said, to welcome Ferdie home. They sat for a while drinking tea with a good dollop of whiskey in it. After a while Tom Plunket asked Eileen how she was feeling.

Eileen replied, "Never better; I think that I could jump over the moon."

"Well "responded Tom Plunket, "Do you think that you could come with me for a little while. Guy Carydis was on the phone and he will not do business with anyone but you. I will drive you back home again when you have pacified him."

Eileen answered in haste as she put on her coat, "Certainly I will go with you and will be glad to have something to settle me. It will give time for Sadie and Ferdie to talk things over."

When they left Ferdie said, "I am glad that Eileen is at work again. You know that there is something I would like to talk to you about. When I was alone on the island I had time to think. You know that we are not getting any younger. When you were sick I was worrying that you would die. I was thinking, what if the worst had happened to me? Or, if you and I died, what was going to happen to Eileen? We have distant relations but they are not as close to you or I as Eileen."

"Ah Ferdie, you always had a sensible head on your shoulders. Eileen is a daughter to me, and Fionn Conall is my grandchild."

"Aye Sadie, God forbid that you or I would die. But if we did, what would happen to Eileen and Fionn. Would some relations of us start a war to get them out of what is after all their home?"

"What" said Sadie, "God stand between us and harm and danger! I want Eileen and Fionn to have this place when we die. They are my family. What will we do?"

"Well Sadie, maybe we should make a will. You know her old house in Mullinard is now a ruin, and it would be too far away from her work. And Fionn Conall would have to change schools. He wouldn't have any of his friends there. Perhaps we should ask Tom Plunket or Reverend Boyce for their advice for the best way to proceed, and to let Eileen know how she stands."

"God bless you Ferdie you took the words out of my mouth. I would die contented if Eileen was with me when I took my last breath, and to lay me out."

Freddie retorted, "What about asking Reverend Boyce for his opinion, he spent year at university and would have good education. He would know the law, and I am sure he could direct us how to avoid unnecessary expenses on us or Eileen?"

"Ah" replied Sadie "you and I are agreeable on what we will do. I saw Reverend Boyce heading for Loch Wellan for a bit of fishing maybe you and I should try to meet him. What do you think of that?"

Freddie smiled and replied, "Sadie you have lifted my heart with your wisdom. There is no time like the present!"

Ban an Trá

There was mention of a ghost or apparition on Keadue Strand, who would walk in front of people as they traversed the strand.

Before the present road was built around Keadue Strand, people would walk across it when the tide was ebbed, or had to take a longer route when tides were unfavourable. There was a rough-hewn road that was built subsequent to 1801, which is recorded on the OSI maps of 1836-42. This road followed the old cassan (footpath) that skirted the low lying areas, which were full of water holes. There was also the problem of crossing the struthan (river), which was perilous in daytime and unwise to attempt at night.

In 1936-38 the present road was completed, circumventing the inchins (water meadow). This new road was built crossing the Strand's upper end. Years of blowing sand have gathered around its walls, creating land that did not exist prior to the construction of this leg of the roadway. The football field owes its existence to the movement of sand that accumulated on top of mud.

People, some on the Strand's west side including Cloghglass, Arlands and Keadue, would cross the strand to attend church in Kincasslagh, or to communicate with friends or relations on the opposite sides of the strand. It was customary for those crossing the strand to remove their shoes. This action saved their shoes from getting wet, and also from the effects of salt water. People crossing would often say that the salt water was good for the feet and it would also clean them, although in winter it must have been bitter cold, as the remnants of an icy sludge was scattered along the high water mark. People who wished to go to mass in Kincasslagh had to endure this trip across the strand to attend church, and then to return. Those from the west side who crossed the strand, put their shoes at a rock on the Belcruit side, which became known locally as Oilean-na-Bróga; (Shoe Island). To walk across the strand took approximately 15 minutes. However, if you were to walk the road around the strand it would take anything between 100-120 minutes.

Many young people met their partners while crossing the strand. The young men would use the excuse of being concerned and caring, by holding a girl's hand while she walked through the cold water, and the girls would give preference to the boy of their choice to help them. Many young girls feigned frailty while crossing, by holding a boy of their choice's hand, for perhaps an extended period. As with all young men, vanity is easily massaged by the smiling face of a pretty young genteel girl, or by holding her hand.

While the strand had its privations on a cold wet day, it had its remuneration as a place where future partners could be appraised.

However, when folk were crossing the strand at night-time, they sometimes saw a ghost or an apparition of a woman who would appear before them. They referred to this ghost as Ban an Tra. It always walked some distance ahead of them, and over time they accepted it, and they did not regard it as a threat. Regardless of how slow or fast they walked, it was always some distance in front of the person crossing. People, as they crossed, always said a few prayers for Ban an tra that her spirit would find peace and rest. If someone from the area was in church, it was customary to say a prayer for Ban an tra. A local woman, who had to walk the longer road around the strand one night when the tide was high, is alleged to have said "That road is so lonely and I did not have Ban an tra to keep me company. Musha, you never feel as if you are on your own with her before you." The local people perceived Ban an tra to be a benign spirit, but were also a little apprehensive, and preferred to cross with humans as company.

One-night Mickey Shan was waiting for his young son, who had gone to October Devotions in Kincasslagh Church. As was customary Mickey Shan took a sod of turf from the fire and went to the shore above the strand with his dog, which was held by a short rope. The sod of turf was impaled on an iron that was kept for the occasion, which was inserted into the ground. The glow from the sod was a beacon that guided the person crossing the strand, and a comfort that a living person was waiting. While Mickey Shan was waiting, a neighbour John Rua joined him, and they lit their pipes from the sod for a smoke and a chat. Mickey Shan was glad to have John Rua for company as he was a facetious and mischievous person, who was always looking for a laugh. As the waited, the banter flowed from person to person discussing matters that were as diverse as saving the turf, or who had the best harvest, or who was going to be the next to get married.

As they looked out across the strand they could see the outline of a woman approaching them. The person or the image came near and then avoided them, staying some distance away. "Who is that?" said John Rua, "Speak or I will send the dog after you. If you are a ghost or a person you will know it when the dog takes a good bite out of your old ass."

"Ah!" replied Mickey Shan "Leave well enough alone; we don't own the strand; it belongs as much to the next creature as it is to you or I."

"No" said John Rua, "We will see tonight if it is a ghost or a person that is taking a hand of the people. Then John Rua let loose Mickey's dog saying, "Get it! Get it! Get it and we will put an end to this playacting." The young dog, which was full of eagerness for the chase, immediately bounded across the shore in the direction of Ban an tra.

Immediately Mickey Shan called the dog back, saying "You John Rua! You or the next man has nothing to do with my dog! Ban an tra or any other creature have not harmed me or my family, and I will never lift a hand to her, or chase my dog at what causes me no harm. If you are such a brave man why don't you run after her? What you or the next man does is none of my business, and my dog is not your property, to chase your inhibitions. Now away home with you John Rua! I can see the young fellow crossing from Oilean-na-Bróga, I am happy to sit here on my own."

John Rua could see that he had upset Mickey Shan and he knew no excuses would pacify him tonight. It was prudent to let Mickey calm down, as he could be a difficult man to beat in an argument or a skirmish. Mickey Shan was a quiet gentle man but on the rare occasion if he was forced to fight he left the opponents feeling sore and sorry they had upset him. So John Rua took the wise course of action, and quickly departed from his company without saying anything that could inflame or inure his temper. The little incident was forgotten or at any rate never spoken of again by either man.

Sometime later, on a moonlight night, as Mickey Shan was crossing the strand from Oilean-na-Bróga, he saw the Ban an tra ahead of him staying on the land side. The people always stayed a short distance away from Ban an tra, which became the accepted custom. As Mickey Shan was crossing it was as if the Ban an tra was trying to manoeuvre him to the sea. Mickey was beginning to think that Ban an tra was trying to drown him.

He started praying in earnest and saying, "Ban an tra, are you going to drown me? I know it was my dog that chased you, but I did not tell the dog to chase you. I called the dog back to me. In under God and his Blessed Mother, why are you punishing me for something that was not of my making? Have I not always treated every creature on this earth with respect? And the night that the heavy fog fell as my mother was crossing the strand, did you not guide her to safety to our doorstep. Why now must you punish me for the crimes of another silly person, why? Why under the name of God? That surely was a disrespectable thing John Rua did, but he is like a big child that never grew up. I hope that you will find it in your heart to forgive his moronic prank. John Rua is a good man at heart, but sometimes I think there are more brains in a dead chicken's head."

Now Mickey Shan could hear and see the sea which was less than 20 yards away. Mickey Shan could see something that was being washed up on the shore. Looking closer he could see it was a ship's lifeboat. Hastily Mickey Shan ran to claim the lifeboat which was a prize. A good boat was worth almost half a year's wages, and he could do with the money to renovate the house. In the boat he found plenty of rope and an anchor. He secured the rope to the boat and took the anchor, which was tied to the end of the rope, up the strand. The length of the rope would give him at least an hour to get help. And the anchor would hold the boat secure to prevent it from being taken away by the sea, or being claimed by another person. Whoever secures the jetsam on the shore is an indicator to others that it has been claimed.

Mickey was beginning to run to the house to get help, as with a donkey he would be better able to haul the boat to safety. Turning quickly, Mickey said in a loud voice, "Thank you Ban an tra for guiding me to the boat. And please forgive me for thinking you were going to drown me, forgive me for doubting you, Ban an tra. Now tell me how I can repay your kindness. We, the Shan's, were never mean, and we always pay our debts in full. Whatever you want, let me know, and I will do my best to fulfil it, if it is humanly possible."

Mickey Shan arrived in his house somewhat a little out of breath, saying, "Quickly harness the donkey and come all of you to the strand with me."

"In under God, Mickey!" said his wife Sara "Has something terrible happened you or have you seen a ghost?"

"Terrible?" retorted Mickey, "No not terrible Sara, but good. I have seen Ban an tra this night on the strand and she guided me to a boat that was washed up on the strand. You know Sara, I always said that there was nothing but goodness and kindness in Ban an tra. Didn't she take my mother home the night the fog covered all the country. Ban an tra is a good person or ghost".

"Well" said Sara, "Don't stand there all night praising Ban an tra, away with you to your boat before someone else grabs it. You know Mickey Shan, a good boat would tempt a saint to steal with the times that is in it. The boys and I will follow you as soon as we have the donkey harnessed. Whatever slack you get, pull the boat up the strand. You know the tide is rising. Now Bridget be quick and go with your father, it will keep him company until we arrive. With the help of God, we will have the boat up the shore safe and sound this night."

When Mickey Shan and Bridget came to where the anchor was, the tide had risen and the wind direction changed. If Mickey had not anchored the boat it would have been taken out to sea. They quickly hauled the boat further up the strand while they waited for help. With all strands there are heights and lows, and as they pulled the boat it grounded on the strand for a little while, but later it was floating again and they could pull it a little further ashore.

After a while Sara arrived with the family and donkey and cart. Her first action was to take anything that was in the boat out of it, saying there is no need to be dragging what we or the donkey can carry. They quickly filled the cart with whatever accessories were in the boat, from a small barrel of provisions, to a ship's compass and various gadgets. "Now" said Sara, "You boys take the donkey and cart to the house and leave everything in the upper room. We will examine it again without the gawking of begrudging people skulking about us. And remember boys, don't tell anyone what is in the house! Remember, a closed mouth catches no flies. You can call the neighbours for help when you have everything safely tucked away in the house."

The cart was loaded with whatever was in the boat, and taken to the house where it was safely stored in the room as instructed by Sara. Then the boys called the neighbours for help in securing the boat.

The boys, together with the donkey, arrived at the shore followed by the neighbours, who hastily dragged the boat up to the green grass. They all commented how lucky Mickey was to find such a prize as a boat, and how fortunate he was to have found it before the wind washed it out to sea. John Rua commented, "Was that Ban an tra about when you found the boat Mickey Shan?"

"Aye" retorted Mickey "Maybe she led me to it".

Sara hastily interrupted, saying "That is enough of that nonsense from you two, for this night. Thank you again John Rua for leaving your warm fireside to help a neighbour. You are a decent man".

That night when they were on their own, Mickey Shan asked Sara why she did not let him speak about Ban an tra who led him to the boat.

"Ah Mickey, Dia O avic! Do you intend to sell the boat? Tell me who is going to buy a boat if there is any mention of ghosts about it. Mickey, Mickey, we should keep a good distance between our mind and tongue, and what they don't know won't harm them. Now Mickey, say nothing about your travel across the strand this night. We will have the boat blessed before we sell it. Nobody would have anything to do with a boat if they thought a ghost had any connections with it! A stor mo chroi, whist avic."

"But Sara, what about Ban an tra? I promised her on the strand that I would do something that would give her rest."

"Aye we will Mickey, we will! We will speak to Maria Connie, she would be the best person to advise us, and how we can help."

"But Sara! Maria Connie, is she not something of a witch? She never goes to Mass. The priest said that we should have nothing to do with her."

"Aye Mickey, and did anyone ever tell you that Christ went to mass. Did Maria Connie not cure your cow with her herbs? As for that priest, he could not cure herring with all the salt in the county. All that is a bother to him is money, money. We will get that wee priest from Broca to bless the boat. He is a holier man, and a few bottles of the good stuff will keep him happy."

Mickey and Sara went to see Maria Connie, to ask her about Ban an tra. "Perhaps her soul is looking for rest. It is a shame that nobody ever tried to find why she walks the strand. Would you know, Maria Connie, and could you help us give her rest?"

Maria Connie was silent for a while and then replied. "Aye I might know but why, is it because of the boat?"

Sara answered hastily "Aye we had good fortune and we thought that we should do a little good. God knows we would not like our soul to be wandering without rest. Do you know why Ban an tra is wandering the strand. Could we in anyway help in gaining rest for her poor wandering soul? We would of course pay you for any help you could offer."

"Well, well Mickey", Maria Connie replied softly! "I know you are a decent man; you leave me a cart of turf every year without fail. God bless you avic Mickey, we will all die someday, and maybe you will bury me somewhere when I die. Will you promise to bury me when that time comes?"

Mickey was a little unsure of how he was to reply, "Aye Maria Connie you don't need to have any worry about that. But your death is a long time away. You may bury us all! God knows, who will be first to die. But won't your relations be there when you die?"

"Mickey! Dia O, Mickey, there are friends and relations: some relations are no friends, and some of my friends are no relations. I ask you as a friend, will you give me your word or will you at least think of it?"

Mickey replied, "In under heavens Marie Connie! I don't need to think about anything, if I am living after you, I certainly will. I give you my word and I will swear it on a stack of Bibles."

Marie Connie riposted smiling, "Ah Mickey I don't need any swearing from you on any Bible: a word from you, or any one of the Shan's is all I need. Musha you were always good natured, sorry if my words offended you. But Mickey avic, craig na bhais (the knock of death) always comes to everyone's door."

Mickey replied hesitantly "With the will of God that day will be a long time in coming; we all hope to see many a summers' sun. But could you help me in giving Ban an tra rest? Who was she, this unsettled spirit?"

"Aye," Maria Connie replied unhurriedly, "I know: Ban an tra died during the famine on her way to the graveyard. She knew that she was dying, and wanted to be buried in the graveyard in Oilean Mhor. But she died on her way there, and is buried beside Clochmhor. It is the only green spot. People at that time didn't have the strength to take her to the graveyard. You know that those who survived were on the verge of starvation and death. If you want to help her, take your cart and fill it with the soil, and leave it in the old graveyard in Oilean Mhor. Mickey, be there tomorrow morning before the sun rises in the sky if you want to leave her to rest."

Mickey timidly asked, "Will we tell the priest? Maybe he could give her a Christian burial."

Maria Connie responded, "If you ask him, you will never have her at rest. Do what I say. If she is happy she will knock on your door one night with the craig na bhais (the knock of death)."

Next morning before the sun had risen, Sara and Mickey were there with their donkey and cart. They filled the cart with the soil and the bones were gathered and put into a bag. They then took their cargo to the graveyard in Oilean Mhor where Mickey buried all.

One night afterwards there were a few gentle knocks on their door, and when they went to open it, no one was there. Following this, Ban an tra was never seen on the strand again.

Sometime later Mickey Shan sold the boat and had the house repaired with the money.

A Mocking Man

Fiachra was an astute and talkative young youth who always attempted to have what other people had. If he saw something, he would attempt to get it by fair or foul means. While he had a very sociable and talkative personality, there always was that bit of rascality in his mannerism. He always had that teasing grin on his face, but he would be obliging, especially to the old. If he took the notion, he would divert something to a person that was in need. A bit of an honest brigand whose motto was to share with those without. Some people would say that he had giddy fingers, and would lift anything that was not nailed down by two six inch nails. When he visited a house he had a habit of going into any shed that was not locked, without an invitation. When the people of the house would follow him to impede him, Fiachra would praise the building or something inside, and a string of questions would follow. "Where did you get this and where did you get that, and how much did it cost?" The next question was, "Would you lend it for a wee while? It would do a small job for me."

It didn't matter how many times Fiachra was refused or told not to return again, he would always reappear, like an unwanted weed.

Fiachra's mother Mary was from the area, and they had many relations who were living in the district. While the locals were cautious of Fiachra, they were reluctant to be openly abusive to him. Nobody wanted to offend a relation, or upset his mother Mary. John Mór would often say, "You can choose your friends but not your relations. Aye, some of my friends are no relation and some of my relations are no friends."

Some people would say that with Fiachra, God was money, as he was always attempting some scam to acquire it. One year he went to sell donkey cart loads of turf. During the night he would collect other people's turf that was beside the road, or take it from the bog. The closer the turf was to the bog, the more likely it would be to disappear.

Early one morning John Mór saw Fiachra with his donkey and cart in his bog, lifting his turf. John Mór came running up the bog shouting,

"Who the hell gave you permission to steal my turf? When you were born they threw away the wrong bloody thing, and kept the rubbish. Clear to hell with you, you bloody blackguard! You are worse than plague in any country. God help your poor mother that was left with a scoundrel like you. I sometimes think that the fairies took her child, and left you, an old gefrog in its place. You are not like any of your father's people or your mother's people. If I had my way, I would burn you on the fire to get rid of the fairy that is standing in you. Since the day you were born you, gefrog, there was nothing but narking and squawking. God forgive me, if ever I get you next or near my land or house, I will do Mary a favour and kill you. You! An old fairy gefrog."

Fiachra grinned and replied with a demure smile, "John Mór do you want me to take the turf home for you?"

John Mór roared, "Leave everything where it is. And never you or your shadow cross my path again as long as you live. I would rather see the devil standing by my side than you Gefrog! Get away to hell with you, that is if the devil would have anything to do with you. Certainly no one about the place wants anything to do with you. Since the day you were born you have scrounged and stolen. The sight of you is a curse on any townland. Go, and get out of my sight for your presence is enough to sicken me. You are a wicked evil scoundrel, the worst kind that was ever stood on two feet."

Fiachra dropped the turf as he knew it was wise not to antagonise John Mór with further words. He knew it would take little to inflame his boiling temper. He knew that John Mór could be a very hospitable man, but when he was upset he would chew stones and spit the gravel in your eye. On his way home he saw Brian Seán working at the side of the road in his field. And he stopped to give an excuse for having been caught lifting turf.

Brian Seán was not overly appreciative of his company and said, "Good day Fiachra, and what are you at today, with an empty cart this hour in the morning?"

"Ah" replied Fiachra, "I was going to take John Mor's turf home for him, as I heard he was sick with some kind of flu."

Brian Seán nodded his head, but in his mind he knew that Fiachra was never known to do favours for anybody with money. "Well", replied Brian Seán, "That was very kind of you to help you neighbours. I never heard that John Mór was sick; is it serious? Maybe I should go to visit him if he is sick. Perhaps I could do something to help him, as he was always a good neighbour and friend."

Fiachra quickly retorted, "If I was you I wouldn't do anything for now. I was trying to help him by bringing some of his turf home from the bog. And he turned on me and called me for every name under the sun. You know I think that his mind could be wandering. I was trying to help him by leaving plenty of turf left at his doorstep. You try your best to help people, and what do they do but insult you. It is hard to please some people, who don't appreciate when you go out of your way to help them."

"Aye" retorted Brian Seán, "What exactly is wrong with John Mór? Is it a flu or is it something serious? You are the first person I heard speaking about him. I must go to visit him immediately as he would be the most honest man in the neighbourhood. Aye he is always a good neighbour and friend."

Fiachra quickly snapped, "If I was you, I wouldn't go near him today. God forgive me but I think that he could be getting a stroke. Or maybe he had a bellyful of poitín last night and the effects are only wearing off. You know Brian Seán, there is nothing worse than bad poitín to upset the head. Maybe a few night sleep would help him recover from his hangover."

"Well thanks" said John Mór, "Like it or not, I am under an obligation to visit my old and helpful friend. But I will certainly heed your advice and be cautious of whatever I say. Thanks again Fiachra for telling me. Without you what would we do?"

Brian Seán was aware that Fiachra's words could be deceptive, and that evening he went to speak to John Mór. Entering John Mór's house he said, "I met a man today who was enquiring about you. He thought that you may be getting sick. Are you?"

John Mór said, "It is it is the first I heard of it. And who might that man be. Maybe he is waiting to bury me. Is he?"

Brian Seán laughing replied, "It is your friend and mine Fiachra."

"Ah God's curse on that habitual thief and liar. It was lucky that I happened to be up early today. I caught Fiachra on my bog stealing my turf. It is a good job that that I didn't have a spade with me or I would have killed him."

Brian Seán smiling relied, "I know how you feel: only for his poor mother Mary he would be in jail or killed long ago. Her heart must be broken with him with all his rascality; and she has to carry his shame. The police are continuously calling at her door about one thing or another."

"Aye "responded John Mór, "Only for his poor mother I think that he would have been locked up years ago. People make complaints about him to the police, but are reluctant to follow it through into the courts."

"Aye" said Brian Seán "I sometimes think that only for his mother, things would be different for him. There aren't many people around here that wants him about their place. He will either become a rich man or he will be locked up."

"I suppose you are right" replied John Mór, "Aren't all rich men those that have escaped their crimes. Now the richer these thieves become, the closer to the altar they kneel. Jimmy Óg often said, "If you go into any town, you should go to any church, and watch those in the front seats. They are the biggest hypocrites, thieves and liars in the town. And some people said that Jimmy Óg was crazy."

Brian Seán replied, "Aye a lot of people did not like Jimmy Óg for what he said, but if you think, he quickly weighed up people. And if he didn't like you he told it to your face."

John Mór and Brian Seán, sat smoking their pipes, and discussing all the scandal that was happening in in neighbourhood.

Fiachra was not getting much sale, as people were reluctant to buy what could be other people's turf. So he had to try other avenues to get money as his usual avenues had dried up.

Dolty Quinn, who returned from America, was intending to renovate his old home in Scatchdubh. He emigrated when he was a teenager, as his father and mother had died, and his aunt paid for his passage to America. The neighbours often said when Dolty Quinn left Ireland he had his few bits of clothes in an old torn suitcase, tied with a string. And the last few shillings that was lent was in his pocket. He certainly knew what hunger and hardship was. And somehow he became wealthy, by his own cunning manoeuvers leading to his success. The old house was now decapitated and the roof had fallen in years ago. And the walls were destabilized and leaning over, which left the building unsafe and not feasible to restore. Dolty Quinn went to the council's offices and discussed the various options of getting a house built that was comfortable and furnished, over a few meetings and various confabs, with lunches which he paid for. He had the plans of the house that he desired, but he praised the council official for suggesting the type of house, as their design. Dolty began to cut the few trees about the building, and left them to season. He often said, when the house was built, the timber would be seasoned and would be fit to burn. When the house was being built he rented a house in the village. There he could live in comfort with his wife Fanny, and visit the site occasionally to see how the work was progressing.

Now Fiachra had begun to sell bags of timber. Some he sold to Dolty, and told him it had been drying for nearly two years. One day Dolty went to see his stack of timber, which he noticed had now decreased. Dolty thought that he would find out who was stealing his timber. He had purchased a shotgun and cartridges. He opened a few of the cartridges and took out the lead pellets and closed them with butter to keep them dry. Then he bored holes in the blocks of wood, put in the cartridges, and sealed them with soil and grease. Smiling to himself as he thought that whoever puts it in their fire they would get a fright of their life, and that would stop them from stealing.

Fiachra was watching Dolty, and one morning when he saw Dolty going to church he went and collected a load of his timber. Then he put the timber into bags ready for sale to someone. Fiachra went to Dolty's house and asked him if he wanted any more timber, as a man in the next townland sent word to him, looking for timber. He would gladly give him first refusal, as he bought timber before from him. Of course Dolty was pleased to get more timber, and dismissed anyone who said that Fiachra was dishonest. In his mind he knew how hard he had struggled before he made his money, through his hard work and shrewdness. He was pleased that someone so young had the business aptitude to make money, and he bought his own timber from Fiachra. A few nights later he lit a fire and he put the timber into the fire. He was beginning to relax with a glass of beer before the fire, when there was an unmerciful blast, which sent coals and ashes flying around the room. He roared a litany of curses on Fiachra.

Fanny who was outside, heard the commotion in the house and came running in to see what had happened. When she came into the room Dolty was covered with ashes. He was like something out of a ghost picture. Fanny began to laugh saying, "Now you know who is burning your timber, it is yourself."

Dolty roared, "That Fiachra is a crook and could teach the mafia how to rob and steal. That Fiachra is nothing but a goddamn thief and I am going to report him to the police."

Fanny said, "If you do, are you going to tell them that you put shotgun cartridges into the blocks of timber. That could be a criminal offence to set a lethal booby trap. You could be the one that would suffer, not Fiachra. Let that be a lesson to you on who you can trust. Dump the timber into some hole and let them rot. Say no more about it or you will be the fool, and the people will have a good laugh at you. Is that what you want?"

Dolty had to bite his tongue and keep quiet, however much it annoyed him. He would bide his time and hope that he could catch Fiachra somehow.

One day in the shop Fiachra met Dolty and asked him, "How is the timber burning for you, and do you need anymore?"

Dolty knew that this was his chance to impede and replied, "No thanks. That timber you brought to me was green and won't burn. You would need to let the timber season for at least two years. You know that green timber will block the chimney and could cause a fire in the house."

Fiachra quickly snapped, "No, that timber was nearly two years' old. I never had any complaints about the timber from anyone and that is the God's truth."

"Well" said Dolty, "Where exactly did you harvest that wood? If someone sold it to you they were cheating you. If I was you I would take the timber back and get your money refunded. You will never get any custom by selling a dangerous product. To be a progressive business man you must be able to trust your suppliers. Now think who around here could trust you? I was often told that you could sell a million good products, but one bad one could put you out of business. I hope that you will take this as good advice."

"But", retorted Fiachra, "I have burned it myself and it gives the best of heat."

Dolty smiling said, "I hope that you take my advice; however, I don't wish you to think this is a reprimand on your good character. Just be careful of the products you buy."

The people in the shop were questioning Dolty on the safety of timber. And now Dolty had what he wanted and he spun stories about houses in America that were burned to the ground with green timber. Dolty said, "In some states it is illegal to sell unseasoned timber, as it could be a fire risk."

He had what he wanted: a captive audience that would not buy Fiachra's timber. Needless to say Fiachra was not pleased with the outcome, as he surmised that Dolty knew it was his own timber he had bought. But how did he know; did someone see him?

Fiachra would have to come up with another plan if he was to earn some money. One day he was visiting some people in Purt, and he went into Morna Beag's house as she was related to his father.

Of course Morna Beag was pleased to have someone visit her. And as is the custom in the countryside she made Fiachra tea with freshly made boxty bread. Fiachra was pleased with his meal and thanked her for as he said, "That is the best boxty I ever had in my life. Then they began to talk about what was happening, and the conversation came around to health.

Fiachra said to Morna Beag, "How are you feeling? You look to be in good health for your age God bless you."

Morna Beag answering slowly "If that was only was true I would be happy. You know these old bones are wearing out, and I have nothing but pains these days. A new day, a new pain, but thank God for what he has given me. If only I had the strength to go to Fr Gallagher in Ardubh, they say that he has a great cure with his 'office'." (This is an old belief, perhaps pre-Christian, that the salt the priest blessed was panacea for all ailments.)

"But" replied Fiachra, "If I had a car I would take you there myself. Is there no one here that will take you? I will ask them; I don't mind if they refuse me. They won't be the first person to refuse me, my life is full of refusals."

"Ah god bless you Fiachra you are full of goodness, but don't ask anyone; it was never in our family to beg. If you ever happen to be going to Ardubh sometime in the future maybe you would visit Fr Gallagher and ask him for his office. Maybe it might help me."

Fiachra with his charming smile replied, "Don't you know that I would go to the ends of the earth to help you. After all Morna Beag, you are my own relation, and I will make it my business to go to Ardubh. I remember you many years ago in the house with your kindness, you would do the same for me."

Morna Beag retorted, "Fiachra only if you have any other business in Ardubh. Don't go there just for me. I am an old woman and I don't have many more years left in me. It doesn't matter for all the time I have left; I can tolerate a few pains. If you are going maybe, I could give you some money for the priest."

"No!" retorted Fiachra, "Whenever I get the 'office' of Fr Gallagher, then we can talk of money. No don't insult me by giving me money for something you didn't get. What are relations for if we can't help one another? Now that is settled Morna Beag and I don't want to hear any talk about money. Shure wasn't your nice boxty better than any money?"

"But" said Morna Beag, "Please take some money; after all you will have to give something to the priest."

"No" said Fiachra "If ever I get it, then we can talk about money. It is not lucky to take money before you get something. You don't want to take my luck away, do you?"

Morna Beag said, "You are the first person that came into this house that fought not to take money. Everyone else would bite the hand of me if I had a penny in it. Ah you certainly have a good heart without a smidgen of greed in you."

Morna Beag and Fiachra sat talking about all what was happening in the area and who died or who got married. Each extolling the other until it was time for Fiachra to go home.

Fiachra deduced it would be to his advantage to let Morna Beag ponder over a period of time. In his mind he speculated that absence makes the heart grow fonder. Aye anything that is difficult to get must be better. Like good wine, it matures with age. Then he bought a packet of brown envelopes, and put some table salt into one of them.

Next morning, he went to visit Morna Beag, and said, "I suppose you didn't think that I was ever coming, and many times I thought the same myself. You know I had to go to Fr Gallagher four times before I could get him in the house. Fr Gallagher is a little fond of the drink and if he was in bed with a feed of drink, he won't open the door."

"Aye "said Morna Beag, "I hear all about him and the cursed drink that has many a good man ruined. You know that a silenced priest has more power, and their 'office' is better for cures."

Fiachra smiling replied, "Is that right Morna Beag? Well here is your 'office', and I hope that it might do some good to you."

Morna Beag put the envelope on her knee and cried out, "O God bless you Fiachra! I can feel the heat in my knee already. I knew that you wouldn't let me down. The feet must be worn off you tramping over and back to Ardubh. Nobody but you would do what you did; you have a heart of gold. Now I must pay you for the 'office' and your time."

Fiachra retorted, "Forget all about it Morna Beag. It is a bad day it I can't help a neighbour and my own relation. Sure, what else would I be doing?"

Morna Beag quickly retorted, "Ah Fiachra, you must have worn a pair of shoes off yourself. Tramping over and back to Fr Gallagher in Ardubh. Who else would put themselves to such bother for an old woman like me? Your kindness has the wings of an angel."

Morna Beag went to put money in Fiacre's hand, but he refused to take any money and said, "I didn't go to Ardubh for money, it was for you, and only you. Now forget all the talk about money, aren't we related and I remember when you used to come to our house. Didn't you always give me a biscuit? Now it is my turn to pay you back some of your kindness. Wait until we see if the 'office' is working."

Morna Beag stuck some money into Fiachra's pocket and said, "I feel like a new woman already, the pain is easing. Something told me; as soon as I had an 'office' of Fr Gallagher it would cure me. They say that Fr Gallagher has great power in his 'office'. And don't insult me by taking the money out of your pocket."

Fiachra made the usual grandiose gestures of not wanting to take the money. But he did not take the money out of his pocket. He was satisfied with the money he received. He surmised that if speaking is silver, then silence is gold. And he went home pleased he had more money than he did not ask for. He had the few more requests for Fr Gallagher 'offices' from some of the older people and he knew that it was prudent to be seen in Ardubh. If any of the neighbours seen him in Ardubh and asked what he was doing. His usual retort was, nothing much. He knew a closed mouth catches no flies. And he would not hang himself with his own words.

The local priest Fr O'Toole was informed of Fiachra supplying 'offices' to the old people, which was depriving him of the money. He decided he was going to get the bottom of it. One day he met Fiachra in the shop and said, "Fiachra, I hear that you are selling 'offices'."

Fiachra with a sharp rejoinder said, "If I am it is the first I heard of it!"

Fr O'Toole snapped, "I heard that you have a pocket full of 'offices' that you are pedalling for money around the area."

Fiachra replied with a smile, "Perhaps Fr O'Toole you don't like competition. If someone wants an office from another priest, is that wrong? I only oblige if someone asks me to run an errand for them. If you don't want me to help people say so, and I will tell them that you forbid me to help them. If that is what you want, then I can tell them."

Fr O'Toole didn't expect such a quick retort said, "How much money do you get for your 'offices' Fiachra."

Fiachra quickly replied, "Ah now, we see what it is all about is money, money and more money. As of now I am finished helping anyone to get an 'office'. Why don't they people ask you for an 'office'? Don't ask me; I can't speak for those that asked me to help them. I am away home: good day Father.

The sharp cutting and unexpected riposte from Fiachra left Fr O'Toole feeling like a buffoon. How could an uneducated country peasant outwit him that studied rhetoric for years. He was aware that those who had hear their confab, would think that he was only interested in money. In his mind he thought that Fiachra was like a little terrier dog that would 'bite the ankles off you'. Perhaps it is wiser to lose a battle and win the war. He was told at school that it is easier to lecture people than have them airing their points of view in public. He would let time erode away this incident.

Fiachra reasoned it wiser not to let any of his words come back to haunt him. He considered his best option was to hide in plain sight. Fiachra would go to church when no one was attending it. This became known to Fr O'Toole, and he came into the church hopping to snare Fiachra in his trap of prepared rhetoric.

Fr O'Toole said "Good day Fiachra, Perhaps you want me to hear your confession? You know that confessions are good for your body and soul. What you tell in confession is between the person telling it and God. Everyone should know that confessions heal both body and soul."

Fiachra remained quiet for a while then said, "Aye! Is that right? Well father I don't wish to hear anyone's confession. But my advice to you is to go to Fr Gallagher; I have great faith in him because I think that he is closer to God."

Fr O'Toole said, "It is not me, I was talking about, it is you. Do you want me to hear your confession? "

Fiachra with his smile replied, "No thanks. I was at Fr Gallagher for confessions and Holy Communion. I don't think that I would be comfortable with my accuser for a while. Maybe in time I could change my mind, but for now I would feel uncomfortable with you. I hope that you understand my feelings. Oh, and if you don't wish me to attend your masses I will understand."

Fr O'Toole with a stutter said, "Fiachra, God's house is opened to everyone. Come whenever you feel. Perhaps we have misunderstood each other in the past. I am only carrying out God's work."

Fiachra let silence be his messenger and calmly replied, "Aye father. What is not said cannot be undone. Perhaps now we should reflect on what was said and let time erase it from our memory. I am away home to sleep on our little discussions. Maybe we should all ask God for guidance?"

With that Fiachra walked slowly out of the church. Fr O'Toole thought to himself that Fiachra's words 'were as slippery as any eel'. He felt that Fiachra outwitted him with every trap he set for hi: he only caught himself. Perhaps he should let time be his weapon.

Whenever anyone asked Fiachra if he could get them an 'office' from Fr Gallagher. His reply was, "I am sorry that I can't; don't you know the trouble I had with Fr O'Toole. He was upset with me, when I obliged a few people. God forgive me but I don't think that his office has any power."

Fiachra would spend a little time in the church when no one was in it. Lecan Beg who in reality was a pathetic little man was always attending confessions. One day when the priest was away and there were no confessions in the church. That evening Fiachra saw Lecan Beg waddling to the church for confessions. Outside he saw Tuthal, who was perhaps a little more than eccentric, who was going for to the pub. Fiachra called Tuthal over and said, "The priest is not here but he asked me to sit in until he comes back. Would you stay here until I go to the shop and get some cleaning things, I won't be long, here are a few cigarettes for yourself."

Of course Tuthal obliged, and Fiachra guided him to the confessional box saying, "Have your smoke in here, it will be warmer than standing outside."

As Tuthal sat down to enjoy his smoke, Lecan Beg waddled into the church and entered the confessional box. Lecan Beg assumed that the priest was sitting in the box, and began to confess his sins. When Tuthal heard Lecan Beg begin reciting his litany of sins, he yelled in a loud voice, "Shame on you, shame on you. You are a dirty wee fat crook Lecan Beg!"

Lecan Beg knew Tuthal's voice and quickly sprang out of the confessional box. Opening the door to where Tuthal sat he punched him in the face. Now there was a confrontation in the church and an audience gathered as Tuthal was repeating Lecan's sins for all to hear. Lecan Begs tried to outshout Tuthal but to no avail. Tuthal kept shouting all of his sins, and perhaps in the heat of the argument exaggerated them. The people that gathered were enjoying the hullabaloo between them with Tuthal getting redder with anger. Tuthal drove at Lecan Beg with his fists and left him on the ground, crying for help.

Fiachra ran into the church saying, "Leave him alone, he is not worth it. He hit the wrong man when he hit you. You know what kind of man he is to strike someone that was sitting down. You showed him what kind of a man you are today. He is always picking on someone he thinks will not hit him back. But today he knows what it is like to be laying down on his backside with everyone laughing at him. Come on, we will go to the pub; I will have to buy you a drink for putting manners on that wee fat bully."

Fiachra's sweet words and praise had settled Tuthal and now he felt as he was the conquering hero. In the pub Fiachra told the people how Tuthal put manners on Lecan Beg today when he hit him. Fiachra sat quiet while the people asked Tuthal how he chastised Lecan Beg. As always with drink, the retelling of a story tends to magnify the truth out of proportion, and the glorious champion was drinking down the applause from the people. Fiachra quietly slipped out of the pub. He did not want anyone to know that it was he who put Tuthal into the confessional box. Better to let those in the pub manufacture the truth with their own ornamentations.

One day in Ballybreg Fiachra met a man called Arron Fraser, who said he was a member of the AMG (American Protestant Missionary Group) and he was intending to set up a base in Ireland but he could not get a place to rent. Anytime he said he came to convert the Irish, the doors were slammed in his face. All he wanted was to show the people of Ireland the path to Christ our saviour, but he was rejected. Could he somehow help him?

Fiachra smiled and said, "If you don't mind me telling you my advice, are you putting the cart before the horse?"

Arron Fraser said, "What do you mean? I don't understand your Irish ways."

"Ah" replied Fiachra, "You answered your own question. You don't understand our Irish ways. I will ask you one question; when Saint Patrick came to Ireland did he go around asking people to rent a place?"

Arron Fraser looked intensely before replying, "Mr Fiachra I don't know what you mean. How do you propose I get a place to rent? I still do not understand what I am to do in this country. We in America always conclude business as soon as possible."

"Aye" replied Fiachra, "You are now in Ireland not America. If you won't listen to your own words how am I to help you? You must follow St Patrick's example by starting your conversion in the country not the towns. Do like St Patrick did by getting someone to rent you a place; as they say, when in Rome do as the Romans do".

Arron Fraser quickly answered, "Who could find me a place to rent? Would you, and where would the venue be? I could pay you a deposit on the place."

Fiachra with his broad smile replied, "Now I think that you are getting an idea of the way we work in Ireland. I would take time to talk any person around to our way of thinking. It would be better to proceed with caution. You know we in Ireland like to take our time before we commit to anything. You will have to learn the customs of the country, before you start to proselytise people to a new faith."

Arron Fraser snapped "Fiachra, you are the first person that I have spoken to that has given me any words of help. You have a deep understanding of people. You know I learned more from you with your words of wisdom, of how to proceed in my mission in Ireland. I will have to make notes of your wise understanding for the people that will follow me. Do you wish for me to come and speak with you?"

"No certainly not!" riposted Fiachra. "Have you been listening to me, or was I talking to myself? I said I would try to hire a place for you, and when I do, I will hand everything over to you. If you don't like that, then do it the American way, and see how you progress. Now good day to you and good luck because you will need it." And Fiachra began to rise from the chair.

Arron Fraser quickly said, "Hold on a minute Fiachra, perhaps we have our wires crossed. I apologise if I had upset you. It was just that I was hoping to progress with my missionary work as soon as possible. I can give you a deposit of money if you wish now."

Fiachra smiling replied with a laugh, "When you are in Ireland do it the Irish way! Firstly, I will have to find you a building that will be in keeping with your American way of life. Then I will need time to negotiate the price, and the price you are willing to pay. This will take time as we work the Irish way. If you want to do it yourself that is all right with me. I was only trying to help you."

Arron Fraser interrupted saying, "No Fiachra, I see that you are an honest man. Will you be my agent and secure a building? Let me give me a deposit for your time and search. How much money do you need?"

Fiachra quickly retorted, "I don't want to take your money as I don't know how much I need. If I get as much money that will pay the bus fares for me and a few pints to get a person relaxed. You know you can't get a man in Ireland to talk on an empty stomach. A few pounds will do for now until you can trust me, and I can trust you."

Arron Fraser began to smile and said, "It must have been the Lord that guided me to you. As the good book says, 'the cock shall not crow, till they have denied me thrice'. Yet you answered all my prayers, you are truly a man of God. As is standard in America, when you get me a place I will give you a month's rent for your work."

Fiachra had the money in his pocket and in his mind it was time to leave before someone saw him. He put out his hand and said, "Perhaps it is time to begin the Lord's works. I am away home; the sooner we start the sooner we finish. Oh give me your phone number and I will tell you when I have something finalised."

Fiachra went away home. He had more money in his pocket than he could earn for a week's hard work, and if he played his cards right he would get more. Now it was how to play his hand, without telling anyone who it was for.

Fiachra went to Lecan Beg and told him how upset he was with Tuthal that day in the church. Saying, "You know Lecan Beg I think that Tuthal is getting mad, well maybe he always was. You don't know the trouble I had trying to settle him. I had to leave the church that evening, I thought that he was going to turn on me. The way he insulted you; the most honest man in the country. You know I was ashamed to be there, but I had to intervene, or God knows what he would have done."

Lecan Beg was pleased by the words of accolade and said, "I never thought that you had anything to do with it. You only took that mad man away. Do you know where he was? He was in the priest's side of the confessional box. He shouldn't have been there: it is not for him."

Fiachra replied, "I had my suspicions of him for a long while, but I didn't want to say anything. But I think that when the priest is away he has been hearing people's confessions. You were the first person to catch him, maybe that is why he lost the head. The next he would be doing would be to say mass. He has himself shamed that day, I don't know how he can look anyone in the eye now. I suppose it is useless for the priest to talk to him, maybe he would kill him."

Lecan Beg was like a cat with a plate of milk, purring from the praise. Fiachra was the first person that spoke to him of his shindig he had with Tuthal. Now he felt that Fiachra was a man of honour who was on his side and not laughing at him.

Lecan Beg said, "Fiachra did you hear that Frieda Hugh has died this morning?"

"No, God rest her soul, and thanks for telling me, that is a wake I must go to. Aren't we somehow related?"

"Aye" said Lecan Beg, "You are certainly related to the Hugh's, on your father's side, you are fourth cousins. I must go to that wake myself this evening."

"Well" said Fiachra, "If you wouldn't mind could I go with you, as you know all the relations and it would show the people that we are friends. Then there would be no slander or wagging of tongues."

"Yes!" said Lecan Beg, "I would appreciate your company. You are a refined young man who knows your place. There is not one inch of a blackguard in you, or your family before you. It would be a pleasure to have your company, shall we say around seven o clock?"

On the road to the wake, they had to cross the bridge at Scáitdub. Some people say that the ghost of a man who died can be seen there at times. Lecan Beg was glad for the company as he was an over-religious, superstitious man.

As Lecan Beg and Fiachra went walking down the road to Frieda Hugh's house they discussed what was happening in the neighbourhood, like who married and who died and those that emigrated from home. One conversation led to another and they talked about the houses that were now deserted as the family was living in other lands.

Fiachra said, "Tell me, if someone was looking for a house to rent where would you recommend?"

Lecan Beg quickly snapped, "Tell me Fiachra are you looking for a house. Is it that you are going to get married?"

"No" replied Fiachra, "It is nothing. I was just thinking out loud. I suppose it is nothing. I suppose that it will never come to anything. Forget that I ever said anything about it. I suppose that is the best."

"Well" responded Lecan Beg, "What kind of house had you in mind, is it a new house or one that needs a little fixing. You always hold your cards close to your chest."

As they were crossed the bridge at Scáitdub, Fiachra said, "Goodnight."

Lecan Beg said, "Who are you talking to Fiachra?"

Fiachra replied, "The man! Can you not bid him the time of day?"

"What man Fiachra? Don't tell me you are starting to dote."

"Well" said Fiachra, "That is alright if you don't want to speak to him. I always speak to whoever I meet and if they don't wish to speak to me, I don't mind."

They went to the wake and expressed their condolences to the family of Frieda Hugh, and talked of how good a person she was. Fiachra began to make enquiries about Scáitdub Bridge and when it was built. As with all wakes ghost stories were told, and they came to the ghost of a man who sits on the bridge.

"Ah" said Fiachra, "I don't think there any ghost. What do you think Lecan Beg, it is only the reflections from the moon; isn't it?"

Lecan Beg did not get time to reply as Cundy Owen began his tales of ghosts, and how the ghost on Scáitdub Bridge is waiting to pull someone across to join him. Cundy Owen could produce ghost stories until the hairs on your head danced with trepidation. Of course those present were enjoying the flow of yarns until it was time to leave for home. As they were walking home, Fiachra commented on the wake saying it was the best wake he was at, for a long while. "Maybe we should go some night to visit Cundy Owen, I enjoyed his yarns. Didn't you Lecan Beg?"

"No" said Lecan Beg, "That man must be away in the head, did you hear him talking about ghosts, fairies and the devil. He should leave all that to the priest."

"Aye maybe you are right" said Fiachra. And he began to talk of the good night it was with the moon shining. As they were crossing the bridge Fiachra was walking on the left hand side of Lecan Beg. Fiachra caught Lecan Beg's coat with his right hand and passed it behind his back to his left hand. Then he pointed with his right hand to where an old boat was lying and enquired who owned the boat.

Lecan Beg snapped, "Leave well enough alone, that man was lost at sea and his body was never found. It is not right to be talking about things like that. God rest his soul I hope he is happy."

Fiachra said loudly, "Good night" And he gave Lecan Beg coat a thug.

Lecan Beg yelled. "Someone pulled my coat, who was it"

Fiachra answered, "I am not surprised you don't speak to anyone. Why can't you be sociable and acknowledge the man."

"What man?" said Lecan Beg, "There were no one there. I did not see anyone, there is not a living soul out this time of night."

"Well" said Fiachra, "You and I are out! Why in under God can't someone else be out at night, it is a free country isn't it?"

Lecan Beg bawled, "It must be a ghost! Hurry up before it catches us. God stand between us this night of harm or danger. Something pulled my coat on the bridge; it must be a ghost."

"Ah, have sense," said Fiachra, "There is nothing there to harm us. Will we go back again to look?"

"No for God sake" said Lecan Beg, "Let us hurry home before something terrible happen to us. I pray to God that he will put the bad hour past us this night and day."

Lecan Beg hooked Fiachra's arm with his own and half pulled him up the road while reciting a litany of prayers. When they came to the crossroads Fiachra said, "Well Lecan Beg will you be alright on your own now, you only have a short walk home?"

Lecan Beg said, "Fiachra would you ever walk me home this night, I am afraid of what might happen to me. Maybe that ghost is following me home and could get me on my own."

"Ah" uttered Fiachra, "Old Mary Owen would often have said you have nothing to fear, but fear itself. Let's go back and face what you are afraid of and you will never be afraid again."

"For god's sake no! Leave me home this night and I will do anything you ask of me Fiachra. I am afraid that something terrible could happen to me."

"Well alright" replied Fiachra, "Certainly if that will keep you happy; but I think you should not be afraid of shadows."

Fiachra walked Lecan Beg to the front door of his house while telling him he should not be afraid. Saying "The only ghost you should fear is the living ghost, the dead ghost will never harm you."

Lecan Beg quickly opened his door and ran inside and turning to Fiachra said, "Why don't you stay here for tonight, and you can go home in the daylight?"

"No thanks" said Fiachra, "It is a lovely night with a full moon shining in the sky. What could be as exquisite as a night like this? It is great to be alive to dance in the moonlight on a night like this. It would make you believe in a God. Only but I have to work to do in the morning I would walk down to Scáitdub bridge."

As Fiachra was walking down the road Lecan Beg was calling, "For God sake go home tonight Fiachra!"

Fiachra went to Frieda Hugh's funeral mass and he saw Lecan Beg but purposely avoided speaking with him. He calculated that it would be to his advantage if Lecan Beg would make the first move to inquire about the house. He knew that Lecan Beg had renovated his old home, and would be anxious to recoup the money he spent on it.

One evening as Fiachra was coming up the road Lecan Beg met him, and after they had exchanged a few pleasantries, Lecan Beg drew the conversation to the house. Fiachra kept changing the conversation onto some other subject. Eventually Lecan Beg said, "Tell me something. You said on the night of the funeral something about someone looking for a house."

"Aye I did, but I suppose that I should have kept quiet about it. People say that I chat too much and I should keep my gab shut."

"And tell me Fiachra," said Lecan Beg, "Who was looking for the house? Was he from around here?"

Fiachra paused for a while before he spoke, "Well, Lecan Beg I think maybe he was from America. He could be some kind of gangster or a film star. Sure what would an American millionaire do here? They would be in maybe Paris or Rome."

Lecan Beg interrupted Fiachra saying, "There are American millionaires living in Dublin and Kerry. Why can't there be one living here? If you happen to know one, why can't you direct him here before some other place snaps them up? Don't you know that we have the best scenery in the country?"

"Well" replied Fiachra slowly, "But what about a house, where would you get a house?"

Lecan Beg shrieked, "Haven't I a good house that I fixed up! If you have any influence, why don't you go and tell him? Where is he now?"

"Well", replied Fiachra leisurely, "I have an address that he gave me somewhere in the house; maybe there is a phone number on it, but I don't know. But if you think that there is any hope, I will try to meet him. Do you think that I should ask others if they would have a house to rent to the American man?"

"No" said Lecan Beg in a shrill voice, "Keep it between ourselves. If you can get him for me I will put something in it for you."

"Well" replied Fiachra unhurried, "How much rent would you be asking for the house? I must at least know what I am talking about."

Lecan Beg did not answer for a while, but then he replied. "What do you think about £20 a week? Would that sound alright; we could always bargain for a little less."

Fiachra scratched his head before replying, "At least I have some figures to work with. What if I could get more money? What is in it for me for my time and expense? I could always look for another house?"

Lecan Beg, who always had a quick reply, was stuck for words and was slow to respond, eventually replied. "Who is this man? Tell me and I can talk to him myself."

"Aye" replied Fiachra quickly, "Then I would get nothing and you would get all the money. Maybe I should look around for another person's house who would give me something for my time."

"No" snapped Lecan Beg, "If you get this man I will give you whatever I get for a week. And now I will give you ten pounds for your expenses now, isn't that fair?"

Fiachra replied, "In America they always pay by the month. If I can negotiate a higher price per month, will you give me what you receive for the first month?"

"Aye alright Fiachra, you certainly can drive a hard bargain. Let's keep it to ourselves. You know how curious some of the people are around here. Will we shake hands on it?" And he stuck the ten pound note in his hand.

"Aye alright." replied Fiachra, "That is a bargain between you and me."

Early next morning Fiachra went to Ballybreg and made phone contact with Arron Fraser, who was in Dublin. Of course Arron was pleased that at last he could start his missionary work in Ireland. Fiachra said that he wished to have discussions with him to agree a price for the rent.

When they met Fiachra said, "I don't know if we can come to an agreement on the price of the rent, but we can at least discuss the possibilities. This man is away in the head with the price he is asking."

"What is it?" snapped Arron Fraser, "I don't mind as long as I can get a foothold in rural Ireland."

"Well" replied Fiachra, "That man is mad, or is living in cuckoo land. Maybe we can get him to lower the price if we wait. I am ashamed to say what he demanded."

"What is it!" said Arron Fraser, "I am a man of the world and won't be upset at what a person says. What is the price of the house for a month?"

"Well" whispered Fiachra, "We at least can have a laugh! He at first said £100 pounds a week. But I said he was away in the head and he wouldn't get half of what he asked. Maybe we could negotiate something in between, that is if you agree?"

"Yes, you are an honest man!" replied Arron Fraser, "Will you be my agent and secure the house for me?"

Fiachra replied, "Can we say £50 a week? Or, if you were to draw up two contracts for rent, one for £50, and one for £40 week, then if he won't agree with the higher price I can in a few days' time present him with the £40 a week contract for him to sign."

"Yah" responded Arron Fraser, "I see that you are a shrewd business man that will be of interest to us. But don't wait too long: strike when the iron is hot, and seal the lease."

Fiachra and Arron Fraser shook hands on their deal, each complimenting the other on their wisdom.

Fiachra went to Lecan Beg on his arrival home. He said that he had a long discussion on the house, and he was trying to get as much money as possible for him. "You know Lecan Beg, that there are others who have a house and would try to undercut you. However, I told him that your house would be the best and I will go to him tomorrow. Hopefully we can make a deal that would give you the chance of snaring the money."

In two days Fiachra was back to Lecan Beg with the lease for £40 a week for him to sign. Fiachra said, "I have done my best for you, and I only got it because I said that you were looking for £50 a week. And I showed this paper, that I had printed to fool your competitors. But for God sake don't breathe a word of it to anyone or they will have me killed."

"No" snapped Lecan Beg, "My lips are sealed. Thanks Fiachra I always knew that you were an honest man. Now as we agreed, here is the money we shook hands on: £40 with £10 for your smartness."

Fiachra quickly snapped, "We agreed you would pay me what you get for a month. Now are you not a man of your word. There are four weeks in a month, so that is four £40s.

"Aye alright" replied Lecan Beg, as he counted three more £20 notes into Fiachra's hand saying, "Fiachra you know how to strike a hard bargain."

"Maybe I do," replied Fiachra "but did I not twice tell you what I was asking?"

Fiachra went to Arron Fraser and said, "I have your lease signed but I had the hell of a time trying to convince him to sign. Now will you honour our agreement and pay me?"

"Yea certainly, I am a man of my word, here is your money and a bonus for you. The good lord must have sent you my way because no one was willing to give a place."

"Well, said Fiachra "can I give you my advice? Do like St Patrick did, don't jump in until people accept you. If I was you I wouldn't come until they are waiting for you. The longer they are waiting the better they will accept you."

Arron Fraser retorted, "Ah the wisdom of Solomon, behold, a man greater than Solomon is here."

There was the usual handshaking with compliments heaped on each other, and each departed with smiles in abundance.

A week afterwards Lecan Beg went to Fiachra and said, "The person that has rented the house did not arrive yet. I wonder what is happening?"

"Ah" replied Fiachra, "Aren't you getting your money. Is he not paying it into your bank account? You know there are some funny people in America; maybe he will not come, but who cares as long as you are receiving good money. If you don't want the money, I will take it."

"No" snapped Lecan Beg, "I suppose you are right I am getting my money. The Americans are a peculiar lot, more money than sense."

Eventually Arron Fraser came and at first began cleaning and painting the house which pleased Lecan Beg. His continues retorts of 'the good Gaad' was put down to an American expression. But when he started his missionary preaching in catholic Ireland, Lecan Beg was unnerved.

Lecan Beg went to Fiachra and said, "What kind of man is this you brought to me. What will the priest say? I don't think that the priest is happy with him staying in my house."

Fiachra smiled and replied with his usual smile. "I didn't ask him what kind of religion he had, nor did you ask. The only thing I know that he was wanting a house and you were wanting money. Isn't that right? Why don't you ask him to go to church with you, then maybe you could convert him?"

Lecan Beg snarled, "Every time he opens his big gob, you can't get a word in edgeways. There is nothing out of his mouth but what is written in the good book. Can you get him out of the house for me?"

Fiachra was silent before he said, "Lecan Beg, I am not a solicitor. I think that man knows the law and could use it to clean you out of your money. Why don't you ask him to get you a job in America then you could be as rich as he is."

Lecan Beg snarled, "I don't want to go to America. What will the neighbours think of me with him in the house? How can I go to confession with him in my house?"

Well replied Fiachra, "When you go to confession at least you will have something to tell the priest, won't you?"

"But" snarled Lecan Beg, "What will the neighbours think of me with a heathen in my house?"

"Well" replied Fiachra, "Do know that at least two of your neighbours are trying to rent their house to the American: he told me so. There are plenty of people around here who would jump at the chance to rent their house. My advice to you is keep your money, as he is only an old windbag and the wind will die down like a fart."

Now Fiachra planned that he would open a shop; in his opinion this was the way to make money. However, one of the wholesalers, Charlie McGinley, was reluctant to give him credit until he said that his uncle Mickey in America was financially backing him. He had two 10 dollar bills and he cut newspaper strips the size of dollar bills and put them between the dollars. When he was refused he took what looked like a wad of money out of his pocket. Then quickly putting what looked like the money back into his pocket, laughing said "My uncle said that I should test you to see what kind of man you are. Now goodbye and good luck to you, there are more fish in the sea than you. Some have already offered to supply me."

Charlie McGinley followed Fiachra out the door saying, "Hold on a minute, we did not have time to discuss all what you wanted. In business we always have protracted discussions over what you are intending to sell."

Fiachra turned with his broad smile and said, "You are supplying shops longer than I. If you are interested, then send me a list of producers with your best prices. Oh I have been offered credit by other wholesalers. Can you improve on their offers? Send me your best offer and price by post, that way there can't be any misunderstanding. You know that I will have to consult my uncle Mickey in America who may come back when everything is up and running. Now good bye to you mister McGinley."

Charlie McGinley was unsure of Fiachra, but did not want to forfeit a potential new customer. If there was American money behind of him, then he did not wish to lose his custom. From his talk he seemed to know the jargon of business. Perhaps Fiachra was following his uncle's instructions? He decided that he would send him a list of products and their prices with 21 days' credit.

When Fiachra received the letter he went to Maloney's, another supplier of wholesale goods, and enquired of them their prices of the goods which he had copied from Charlie McGinley's letter, and what they were offering. Sean Maloney laughed and said "The credit time I give you is until you pay at the counter!"

Fiachra laughed and put the list of articles on the table and said, "Don't let it be said that I did not give you the chance to compete. If you don't want my business, then that is alright, you know that you are not the only angel in heaven."

As Fiachra turned to walk out he let the letter he received from Charlie McGinley and the letter from America with the American Missionary Group logo shown on it drop from inside his coat onto the floor. He was almost at the door when he ran back to pick up the letters and hurriedly put them into his pocket. Sean Maloney had a quick glance at the letters with the American, stamps and immediately the greed stirred in him. Sean Maloney shouted, "Maybe I could give you credit for 10 days if you pay a deposit in the bank in my name."

Fiachra turned and laughing retorted, "Mr Maloney your generosity knows no limits. Thanks for your joke I will keep it with my priceless treasures." And he walked out the door laughing.

Sean Maloney shouted, "Perhaps we can have a chat and discuss what exactly you need and the letter from your uncle guaranteeing your credit worthiness."

"Aye" said Fiachra, "Mabey you want my birth certificate and my father and mother's marriage certificate. Good bye Mr Maloney and thanks for the laugh. If I hear from you that is alright, and if I don't I won't be disappointed."

Fiachra had a friend he asked to phone Sean Maloney's saying that his uncle Mickey was wanting to speak to him. The mention of Mickey was enough to bait the trap for Sean Maloney, and he went looking for Fiachra. Fiachra was out of sight in a building across the road where he could see all. He was aware that the longer Sean Maloney searched for him the more leverage he would have in negotiation. Eventually Sean Maloney returned in frustration at losing a customer. And he had a cordial letter sent to Fiachra with a list of products and prices, with an attachment of credit for 30 days.

Fiachra duly opened a shop and his relations and neighbours who wanted to give him a start came to his shop. While he paid the wholesaler he kept negotiating to extend his credit period. Then he began to sell his products at a lower price than the other shops. The wholesale merchants were pleased as their money was paid to them, although maybe a little late. Now other wholesalers were coming to Fiachra to supply him. While Fiachra may have been good at handling people, he did not have a business acumen. He acted like 'Oisín who returned from Tír na nÓg, siting on his illusionary white horse'. Very soon his expenditure was overtaking his profit and like Oisín he was lying on the ground. Fiachra could see that he would soon be left without any money. Then he formulated a plan to order as much as he could and sell them close to wholesale price, which brought him many customers. Other shops said that he couldn't survive, but for a short while his business was booming. But now the merchants were refusing to supply him until he paid them their money and the shelves were emptying. One day unexpectedly Charlie McGinley and Sean Maloney came into Fiachra's shop demanding their money.

Fiachra smiled and replying, "Yes certainly you have saved me a trip to town. But before we conclude any business in this part of the country, we always have a drink. Is that alright with you?"

The two men smiled and replied, "Yes that is fine with us as long as we get our money."

Then Fiachra put three mugs on the counter and filled them from a jar of poitín. Sean Maloney said, he didn't drink poitín and Charlie McGinley also said that he wasn't going to drink any of that stuff.

Fiachra produced a shotgun from below the counter and yelled, "Are you two going to take away my luck. If you don't drink to my heath, I will shoot you. You will never smell a penny from me if you don't drink to my luck."

Charlie McGinley and Sean Maloney lifted the mugs of poitín to their lips and started to sup the poitín. Every time the mugs were getting low Fiachra kept filling them up saying good health.

Then he produced a letter he had received from the American missionary group and said, "Tell me how much money will I get for American dollars?"

Charlie McGinley and Sean Maloney were surprised that a man who they thought was broke was asking about American dollars. Sean Maloney retorted, "How many dollars have you Fiachra?"

"Well," said Fiachra "it might be a cheque, but how much will I get for it" and here he paused.

Sean Maloney thought that there may be some way he could be recompensed and replied. "Well Fiachra, if you give me the cheque I will cash it for you."

"Well" said Fiachra, "That calls for another drink." and he filled the three mugs full of poitín again. Lifting them up he said "Cheers!" What Charlie and Sean did not see, was when Fiachra put his mug below the counter he was tipping the drink into another jar with a funnel on top and was lifting a mug of water for himself to drink. Fiachra would at times pretend that he was getting drunk. At times he would jump up saying, "One more for the road!"

Fiachra kept filling Charlie's and Sean's mugs with poitín and every time they made an attempt to leave, he would point the gun at them and yell "If you don't have a drink with me, to wish me luck, I will shoot you." Fiachra at times would look into their mugs and if it was not drunk he would bang the gun on the counter yelling, "Do you think that you are too good for me to have a drink with me? Are you a man or a mouse? If you are a man drink up like a man."

By now Charlie and Sean were hardly able to stand up they were so drunk.

Eventually Fiachra said "You will have to forgive me, I must have a slash." and went out the back door. On his way he turned to Charlie and Sean and said, "Now don't go away until we finish our drink."

When Charlie and Sean saw their chance, they staggered out through the door as quickly as their legs could carry them. Then they went to the police station to make a complaint about Fiachra making them drink poitín, and how he had said he was going to shoot them if they did not have a drink with him. Both of them were talking at the same time and the Sergeant could make no sense of what they were saying.

Eventually the sergeant roared, "You two boys are going to have a sleep this night in my lodgings!" And they were put into a cell in the barracks to sleep their drink off.

Charlie and Sean were protesting their innocent and cursing at the Sergeant for not believing them. Their attitude annoyed the Sergeant as they said that they had friends who would have him dismissed. Now they were roughly thrown into one of the cells to sleep it off.

Sergeant Mick went to find out what had transpired at Fiachra's house and get his version of events. When Sergeant Mick opened the door Fiachra was nailing a chair together and was tidying up the place.

"Well" said Mick, "I heard that you had a bit of a party here today. How much had you to drink Fiachra?"

Fiachra looks at him for a while and then replied. "Well Mick, I would say as much as you had to drink, and that was tea and more tea."

Sergeant Mick replied, "Were Charlie McGinley and Sean Maloney in here today? I heard that you had a bit of a party drinking."

"Aye Mick I always have a party drinking tea."

Sergeant Mick retorted, "I heard that you had a bellyful of poitín with Charlie McGinley and Sean Maloney."

"Well" replied Fiachra, "If I did it is the first that I hear of it. Where did you get that notion from?"

Sergeant Mick snapped, "Did you threaten Charlie McGinley and Sean Maloney with a shotgun to drink poitín. If you did that is a serious offence. Now tell me the truth."

Fiachra looks at him before replying, "Is this some kind of a joke you are pulling Mick. Sure I never had a sup of poitín for a long time. Why don't you smell my breath if you don't believe me?"

Mick smelt Fiachra's breath, and sure enough there was not a trace of poitín about him or the house. Sergeant Mick stood without saying a word for a while, and then snapped. "If them, two f*****g prigs are trying to fool me they met the wrong man! I will put manners on them this night and they will have to explain it to the judge. I am glad that I called on you this night because if I came tomorrow I might not believe you. Now good night Fiachra, and if ever them two f*****g prigs bother you again tell me and I will put manners on them."

With that said Mick went out the door with his cheeks as red as a strawberry, talking to himself.

Fiachra, smiled to himself thinking that the country was too small for him. Perhaps a bigger place would be more beneficial. He planned to be out of the country before any court could request his attendances.

Anyone can have a friend, but the one who would walk in a storm to find you is all you will ever need.

The Curse of the Creel

Years ago, as today, the young people of Ireland were compelled to emigrate from their native land, as the land was unable to support them. The land of the Rosthiar could be described as impoverished, with little patches of soil hiding between the grey granite boulders, or swampy boggy land. All of the work on the little farm had to be achieved with spade, shovel, or by carrying creels. In the patches of bog land that were utilised for cropping, it had to be initially drained. Following the draining, the land was made into alternate ridges and troughs. In the troughs, the water could lie before running off into deeper drains, and so the ridges of land could dry. This land was infertile, and a crop of potatoes or corn could only be achieved with a heavy coating of animal manure or seaweed. This land was reluctant to produce a crop of food. Most of the manure or seaweed had to be carried in creels to the little fields.

Regarding seaweed: the people had to gather the seaweed on the shore and carry it in creels, with the water dripping down their backs. The seaweed was deposited above the shore line until a suitable load was collected. Then the labour of transporting the seaweed from above the shore line was done with a donkey and cart, where it was deposited as close as possible to the little field where the crop was to be planted. If the field was a distance from where the load was stockpiled, or in marshy ground, it was necessary to carry the seaweed or manure in creels. A man had to labour and wrestle with the hungry land, to have as much food that would feed himself and his family. Life in these unfruitful lands was a continuous struggle for food and survival.

There was also the laborious task of cutting turf with a spade, and then working the turf until it was dried. When a suitable time had elapsed, and the turf had become seasoned and fit to be removed from the bog, it was put into a creel and carried to the side of the road for transport home. A person's back would be weary and sore after a day carrying creels of turf, with the hard rods protruding into his or her back. When people were not working with turf or at the sea shore, there was always some other kind of work to do, and the cursed creel seemed to be forever a scourge to the body.

Many young people of the Rosses had emigrated to America hoping to find a new life, away from the hardships and deprivation of their native land. The people who emigrated had a tendency to congregate together in the same districts. They usually would seek employment through family or a friend's good will.

If a friend had a job, he or she would approach the foreman telling him that their friend "could do with a job". He would endeavour to mention all their positive characteristics, like being a good reliable worker and coming from an honourable family. The person seeking a job for a friend would be cautious, because his own character and reputation was dependent on his word.

The person who found a job was cared for by whoever had vouched for him or her. This gave a feeling of camaraderie and mutual protection in a new and strange land. It was as if part of their homeland had been transplanted into this new land. They shared all the news that came from Ireland, like weddings, or those who had died. If someone from home was intending to emigrate to America, the person in America would give him or her a place to stay, and at times secure a job. The emigrants would usually stay with a friend or relation where they could have a little feeling of security. As was the custom at that time, people from different countries would congregate in evenings on the "stoops" (steps to a boarding houses). There could be a plethora of languages spoken; Gaelic, Italian, German, Spanish and more. The talk was usually about their homeland and their people who were at home.

Tuhil was a young man who endeavoured to leave the adversity of life in his native townland of Tullygorm, in Ireland, and emigrate to America. He told his friends that he was tired of working hard for a stale crust of bread, and a cold bed. If ever he could, he would leave Ireland which had nothing to offer except a creel, a sore back and a heavy spade. With courtesy you could not accuse Tuhil of being lazy, although he would attempt to find a method of lessening the drudgery of work. People at times would say "Tuhil could talk the legs off the chairs and the table." He certainly had the gift of the gab and had an amicable disposition. While he would disagree with people at times, he could always present his difference of opinion in such a cordial manner that it seemed to deflect any offence.

Cundy Owen often said, "Tuhil would charm you with his 'honeyed smiles and sweet words' that would charm the birds in the air. Aye, he certainly would thrive where others would die forlorn in misery and despair."

Cundy Owen was described by some people as being eccentric or mad, or a man who was somewhere between being mentally unhinged and a psychopath. His ideas would not conform to the prevailing dictates of church or state. Cundy Owen had a chat with Tuhil and gave him the same advice he gave to others, who did not accept his words.

Cundy Owen said, "Now listen to me Tuhil, I will give you good advice should you choose to heed it. When you land in America, if you want to progress, play GAA football and join the Knights of Columbanus. If you look around in America, you will see that those with good jobs are in one or both of these groups. And another thing Tuhil! You will never make money by killing yourself with hard work."

Tuhil thanked Cundy Owen for his advice saying, "Thanks for your advice, I will certainly pay attention to your words. As for hard work, it was never particularly keen to have someone living on the sweat of my body, while they lived in luxury like slave masters."

"Ah," retorted Cundy Owen, "I am glad to see that you have wisdom beyond your years. It will make an old man happy if you rise above what you were born with: grief and drudgery. If you mind my words you can make your own luck, either good or bad."

When Tuhil went home he told his parents that he had been speaking to Cundy Owen who had given him advice on how to progress in America.

"Ah!" uttered Art his father, "If Cundy Owen is so smart, why is he living in an old house and not a castle? If you listen to Cundy Owen, you are listening to an old fool. That man's head is away with the fairies. I don't think that even the fairies would have anything to with that idiot!"

Tuhil's mother Mary smiling uttered, "Art, don't be too harsh on Cundy Owen, after all, when our cow was sick and the vet said that the best thing to do was to shoot her. Didn't Cundy Owen save the cow? Listen Art, isn't it true that even a fool can see wisdom where a smart man is blinded by his own perception. Everyone should be prepared to listen to all advice, and then decide what is in their best interest. My advice is to heed all, and believe in only what is in your own gain."

Tuhil was fearful of upsetting his parents as it might hinder his ambitions, and said "Well, Cundy Owen is always good for a laugh. Without him what would we do for a laugh? Don't you always say that some of his sayings would make a dying man smile?"

"Ah! mo stoir," said Mary, "Tuhil, you can always make light of any situation, you are a blessing to any family, God love and spare you avic."

Tuhil contemplated how he was to achieve his aim of getting to America. He was aware that his words could procure his achievements, if expressed to his advantage. He was equally aware that a poorly written letter could dampen his ambitions.

Tuhil wrote a long letter to his uncle Thomas who was in America saying that he was old enough to help his father financially, if he could get a job over there. Tuhil beseeched Thomas if he could perhaps stay with him until he found a job. He stated that he would like to earn a little money as his father needed to put a new roof on the house, and his sister was intending to get married, and also the family could do with someone to earn some money for them. "If you could please purchase me the passage on a boat, I would repay you as soon as I earn some money."

Thomas wrote back immediately to Tuhil, stating that he was welcome to stay with him, and he was hopeful that, through his friends, he could find a job for him. He informed him that when he had arranged with the shipping agent to issue a travel voucher, the shipping agent would forward the voucher for the boat to him. Within a few weeks the letter arrived with the travel voucher together with a letter from his uncle Thomas containing a few dollars to buy new clothing. (The system then was a member of the family in America would send a prepaid boat voucher home to Ireland.)

Tuhil immediately had his little case packed with all the clothing that he would need for his departure to America. Until the time of his departure he had to help his father with work on the land, by carrying creels of wet seaweed that were spread on the ground. Each day that passed was another day away from his conceived dread of carrying wet creels that tortured his body. On the day of departure Tuhil was awake before sunrise, contemplating his departure.

The family was sad, yet tinged with delight of his parting, because they knew that his life in Ireland would be one of poverty. They prayed that his departure would bring him satisfaction in a new land of hope and promise. Tuhil was akin to many young people of the area whose hopes and dreams lay in a land over the sea.

When Tuhil arrived in America his uncle Thomas was glad to see him and inquired of the many changes that had happened since he left home in Ireland. Thomas spoke of the families he knew before he had departed Ireland's rocky shores, almost twenty-five years ago. Most of the people he knew then were either dead or living in other countries. There were many people from Ireland who were living and working in the neighbourhood. They would endeavour to find Tuhil the first job that became available.

With a little help from his friends, who were neighbours from his home, Tuhil found a job. The conditions were not as favourable as he had anticipated. The work was arduous, requiring a man to exert all of his time and energy. The hard work was not to Tuhil's expectations or presumptions. However, he was obligated to stay with the job until he found something more favourable. Now he found alternative lodgings with men that were working in his job.

Tuhil found it repugnant that the other men would boast about what good workers they were. There were endless challenges between the workers to see who could lift the heaviest object, or could do the most work. Tuhil found this aspect absurd and irrational as they were all paid by the day. Whenever he pointed out to the workmen how their boss was reaping the benefit from their hard labour, they laughed at him saying that this was a man's job, and that they were the best workers. Tuhil soon recognized that it was pointless to try and induce the men to seek better working conditions. These men referred to themselves as hard-men in work or who could drink the most beer. Tuhil sometimes thought of his workmates as having an overabundance of brawn and a scarcity of brain. Tuhil found it to his advantage to let them bluster and swagger about their strength. He often said, "It is a poor man that claps his own back." So he encouraged these attention-seekers to espouse their opinions of masculinity.

Tuhil would talk and praise the foreman about his intelligence and how smart he was. While in his own mind he was thinking; "Praise is the payment of a fool." He was a master hypocrite of hiding behind flattering words. Yes, Tuhil had the gift of the gab, and could talk himself out of hell and into heaven. His flattering words were his lever to attempt to deflect away hard work.

Tuhil in time found different lodging in a house that kept men who worked where he was employed. In this house there were four men from neighbouring townlands in Ireland near Tuhil's, John Faddie, Paddy Shan, Anthon Maggie, John Varie. There were always deep and long discussions on their new life in America and what was better and what they missed most from home. John Faddie was always commenting on how he, one day was going to make a creel. John Faddie would say that he was a very good creel maker when he was at home in Ireland, as was his father. However, Tuhil was upset whenever anyone mentioned creel making. This was the one subject when mentioned that would make Tuhil's blood churn. John Faddie was a quiet and mild mannered man, who would always attempt to see others people's viewpoint. But he was keen on keeping the old crafts alive. Tuhil would say, "We are now in a land where there are no creels, and less hardships than where we were born. This life would not be possible in Ireland unless we went around with the backside out of our trousers and ate grass. Perhaps we should focus on the positive aspect of our lives in America. If we could have had a decent living at home, we could all have stayed with our families. However, that was not possible. Perhaps we should look to what is good in our new life in America. If little disputes or mini disagreements surfaced at times we should find ways of settling them without bickering."

John Faddie said that Tuhil was an intelligent young man and they should at least listen to his opinions, even if they didn't agree with them. He said that he was willing to pay attention to every man's opinion, and that it was not appropriate to cause censure or blame on anyone. Let everyone chose their own perspective on life and how they live it. His words calmed the discussion on the creel for the time being. Paddy Shan said "Anyhow it is not possible to harvest rods for any work as they are still growing. Let's wait until the sap is lower in the rods. I often heard the old people say that the rods that were cut while the sap was high would not last."

The discussion on the creel had ceased: Tuhil was contented, hoping that was the last of his dilemma being espoused. The conversation now concentrated on the news that was coming from Ireland and new football teams that were being formed.

Tuhil joined the team, and with his eloquence of talk he attracted a large audience of the football supporters. He first began playing for an amateur football team. With his skills at play and talk the people began to take his advice seriously. In the course of time he was elevated to manager of the new club. He was adroit in management of the footballers who played for him. Whenever the opposing team or supporters would lambast him, Tuhil's reply was, "You have some very good players if you utilised them better. I will gladly shake the hand of any player that is in competition with me. However, I can't or will not manage the team that played against my team; you can't have two masters!"

The management of the opposing teams could see how shrewdly Tuhil could motivate players to do his bidding without disrespecting anyone.

While they might oppose Tuhil's team they could never find anything to disrespect him. Whenever anyone said any disparaging words after the game of football, Tuhil would reply, "Let's play our best against each other on the field, but never fight against ourselves!"

Tuhil could turn an insult into a compliment and a laugh. He knew that some of the opposing team supporters were in middle management in certain jobs, some to which he aspired. And if speculation was true, some were in "The Knights of Columbanus". Tuhil came to the conclusion that it would be to his advantage to join The Knights of Columbanus if he was to have any chance of progress in America. He was also aware that the Knights of Columbanus, was a partisan Catholic organisation. He could be described as a lukewarm Catholic: he would show his faith on his arm but not in his heart! "Ah," he thought, "If King Henry of Navarre has said "Paris vaut une messe." (Paris is worth a mass) to claim the kingship of France, then he could follow that example and be seen at a few masses". Of course he would have to bow to a few priests, which he detested. He was aware that Manny Dolty, who was on the committee of the local Gaelic football team, was a member of the Knights of Columbanus. His opinion of this man was that he was a vile, morally reprehensible man and one of his weaknesses was that he thrived on praise.

At a committee meeting, some of the members were criticizing Manny Dolty on how he carried out his task. Some went as far as saying that he was incapable of being in charge and should be replaced. Tuhil stood up and asked the chairman for permission to speak, which was granted.

Tuhil stated, "As you know Manny Dolty and I have had our difference of opinions in the past, but it was never venomous. However, when any of our disagreements were past we could always shake hands, like the good friends that we always were. All dissents or contrary opinions we held were expressed for the benefit of the of the Gaelic football team. We all are in a new country, and we should keep a unified agenda. Let's not have any venomous words be spoken outside this room. Whatever we decide upon here, we all should shake hands and move on, like Manny Dolty and I have often done in the past. We could disagree on the field but after the game we were the best of friends. Isn't that right Manny Dolty, my good friend? I often thought that Manny Dolty and I were like the Fianna warriors of old, who would fight all day, but when the battle was over they remained friends. There is only one proposal I would like to put forward: it is that Manny Dolty should be given an honorary membership for all his tenacious work to the club over the many years."

Manny Dolty was surprised as were others in the room. He was pleased that some words of comfort were spoken about him, even if he did not expect or understand what the eulogy meant.

Manny Dolty replied, "Aye. You are right, Tuhil. We may have had harsh words but it was all for the good of the game. I know that I may have said some scornful words against you Tuhil in the past, but I didn't mean them."

Tuhil rose and walked to Manny Dolty with his hand outstretched saying, "Put it there my old sporting adversary. You know that I always enjoyed our little disagreements. We never had an argument, they were all just heated discussions. Isn't that right my old friend? Now I think that perhaps the best thing for me at least to do is resign and leave, and let the committee select who they think is best for the club."

As they shook hands all present were, if not shocked, then surprised that Manny Dolty was willing to concede to something that was not of his making. There were smiles all round as some of the members were afraid that it could lead to a rift in the club. Most present were pleased how Tuhil had handled what could have been a schism. As Tuhil walked out the door of the meeting Manny Dolty followed him agreeing that he would also resign, if it was for the club benefit. Tuhil and Manny Dolty who were once bitter rivals went to a pub for a chat over a beer.

Tuhil said "Manny Dolty, I admire you for the stance you took; you know that you did not need to resign. I resigned because I did not want the club to suffer from descent or infighting. I think that all of us who are Irish should bury any bickering, and unite for the common good.

What do you think? After all we are all Irish, in a new land, and should keep what is best from our homeland."

Manny Dolty said Tuhil, "I think that I misjudged you. I thought that you were only interested in my job in the club, but you stood up for me when others deserted me. If there is anything that I can do for you. You only have to ask, you know that."

"Well" replied Tuhil, "If you can remain my friend that is all I ask of you. And don't always agree with me, can't we have our little disagreements about something even if it is only about who pays for the drink? Ha, ha. However, I will always take your good advice, for you are an intelligent man. Maybe sometime you could advise me on what is the best for me?"

Tuhil considered asking Manny Dolty if he would sponsor him to join the Knights of Columbanus, but he knew that it would sound be better if Manny Dolty asked him to join. He knew that everyone who joined would require someone to propose them, and another to second the proposal. It would be better if Manny Dolty discussed it with other members the Knights of Columbanus. Then, when Manny Dolty asked Tuhil to join he could sound amazed, and graciously accept.

Tuhil extended his hand to Manny Dolty saying, "Perhaps it is best if we go home now and rest, you know that I am not over fond of drink. Now, let the club decide what is in their best interest. It may be to our advantage not to remain. As you know, there is always someone who could not organize a snowball game. You know there are always people who say that they know everything. There are people who know nothing and would try their best to start a row between you and me. You and I strove for the benefit of the club and all the Irish, regardless of where in Ireland they came from. Isn't that right my friend, Manny Dolty?"

Manny Dolty quickly retorted, "Aye you are right, Tuhil! Sometimes I think that you were wasting your time with the football club. Would you be interested in joining something better, like the Knights of Columbanus?"

Following a pause Tuhil replied, "I don't know if they would have the likes of me. I was told that they don't take everyone who knocks on their door. That is a decision that I would need to sleep on. I wonder if I would be of any benefit to the organisation. Anyhow, let me know next week if you think I would be accepted. Let's not make any hasty decisions while we are having a drink. I am away home now, perhaps you should do the same, and we could meet again later and continue this discussion."

Manny Dolty was aghast that Tuhil did not jump at the chance of joining the Knights of Columbanus. Other people had harassed him to propose them as a member. Yet Tuhil, instead of jumping at the chance, asked him to delay the decision to propose him. The more that Manny Dolty thought of it, the more adamant he was that he would get the necessary backing to propose Tuhil. A man of honour who resigned from the football club to give support and approval to him!

Eventually Tuhil was invited by invitation from the Grand Knight to a special mass, which was attended by the Supreme and Deputy Supreme knights. During the mass Tuhil received his robes and penal cross. This was his first initiation, which he found childish, irrational and immature. He would have to endure many more stupid rituals if he were to progress. As this was his initial admission, he was aware that there would be many more before he could find a job without physical drudgery. He would make friends with as many of its members and find what work they had. He was going to cultivate the person with the most influence and he quickly learned that Father Jimmie, the chaplain or the priest of the order would have the most influence. While he detested him, he would cultivate his friendship in order to have a better job. He knew that Father Jimmie was a supporter of the team he played against. One day Father Jimmie commented on his team saying that they were the best team.

Tuhil replied, "Yes, they may have the best players, however, they could be better placed to win matches."

Father Jimmie uttered, "Would you care to manage our team?"

Tuhil, following a long pause, replied, "Father Jimmie, I don't think that would be advisable for our people, who are now trying to make a life for themselves in America. In my opinion it could open old divisions that would neither benefit you or me. What I would advise is we should avoid anything that would cause dissent or prejudice. Let's show how united we can be by sinking our personal feelings."

"Aye" said Father Jimmie. "I can see that you have a keen insight into people's psychology. Perhaps we have underestimated you: you have the Wisdom of Solomon. I think that you and I will make a great team if we can work together. I have something in mind and you could be the very person to help me."

Tuhil knew that he had Father Jimmie eating out of his hand! Now if only he could use him to better himself. He would certainly help Father Jimmie if it was also to his own advantage, but he would not be his donkey! In his mind he would use Father Jimmie's influence to better himself, but he could not say anything about his discussions to the people in his boarding house.

Tuhil replied, "I will definitely help if we are all working for the good of all our people. But now what can I do, without influence? I have a menial job, and it would not help me to ruffle someone's feathers."

"Aye!" replied Father Jimmie, "Leave it to me, and we will see to it if we can get you a job in one of the city's Municipal departments."

Tuhil was pleased with the progress of the meeting. He would let the proposal for him joining the Knights of Columbanus play itself out. He went to his house in anticipation that at last, he could let the heavy toil of labour evaporate.

One day John Faddie procured a large bundle of willow rods and was in the process of the construction of his first creel. John Faddie had pushed the first rods vertically into the ground and was then weaving the horizontal rods. His new labour, or hobby, was done in a sense of pride, as if holding onto his lost youth which was now only a distant memory. When he had completed his new creel the pangs of pride had surfaced within him. He looked on it as another man would his new-born child. He was showing it to the other members of the house in anticipation of at least some words of encouragement or praise. But no person was impressed with his labour. The other members in the house were unimpressed with what they had once carried on their backs. Tuhil was hostile and disgusted at what was now greeting him, but did not comment if it was either good or ruinous. However, he would rather see the devil standing before him than that creel! He could scald the devil with a drop of holy water, but the creel would scourge his back. The creel was one of the reasons that he left Ireland, to depart from hardships.

John Varie, who was the most senior person in the house, said that if they all calmed down, they could settle the matter by a sensible discussion. Saying that Tuhil was a sensible man and if they all agreed, that Tuhil would settle the matter, once and for all.

They all reluctantly agreed that they should do as John Varie said, and they would go to the local pub leaving Tuhil to come up with a solution. In the pub they debated the work on the creel and how John Faddie could make a creel of any size or shape. There were several uses that the creel could perform, from carrying wood to its use on farms. Paddy Shan said that if they could patent the creel maybe they could make money. John Varie laughed out loud, saying that it would be impossible to patent a creel as, they were in use for centuries in different countries. The more they drank, the more ridiculous their opinions became. Paddy Shan said that maybe they could give a creel to the President of America. This opinion was greeted with laughter by people in the pub who stooped over with amusement. When they returned to their lodgings they enquired of Tuhil as to his opinion, or what conclusion had he arrived at, about the creel. Tuhil said that he was unsure, and he went to the church to ask the opinion of a man of learning, a priest, which every church had.

The men who were flushed with drink were impatient and anxious to know what was his opinion regarding the creel, some saying "Tell us, what are your conclusions? Tuhil you are the genius from Tullygorm."

"Well" retorted John Varie "Could you tell us before our beards grow down to our ankles?"

Tuhil, smiled and replied, "Well" as I have already said, I went to the church to seek guidance."

Paddy Shan who was impatient retorted, "You already said that you went to church; you are repeating yourself. Tell us clever dick Tuhil, what are we to do with the creel. Is it to break it, as you don't like creels? Ha-ha."

Tuhil snapped, "No, I won't do what my heart desires, but will listen to a man of God who has more intelligence than you or me! John Faddie, as I said, you wanted advice on our little quandary and where best to get it, but from a priest! I had a long talk with an old priest of what we should do about the creel. He told me that he would need to look in the Bible to seek an answer of what to do. The priest was going to sleep on his decision, but would only agree to tell me if you all will abide by his decision. Now do you all agree with what will be the priest's decision? I can only go back to him after you are all in agreement. The decision is yours."

There was a prolonged pause without anyone speaking. Then John Faddie spoke saying, "I for one, will not oppose the priest's decision. It would not be right to go against the priest. After all we would be calling for a priest if we were dying. Isn't that right?"

The other men in the house nodded their heads and agreed with the decision. Paddy Shan said, "I may disagree with Tuhil, but as this would not be Tuhil's decision, I will also abide with what the old priest says. After all an old priest must be smarter than a young priest, he would have spent more time speaking to God."

Each man said "Yes", but they did not know what they agreed to. But who could disagree with a man of | God?

Eventually John Faddie could not bear the constant state of suspense. He said. "What is it that you want? Do you want me to make a creel crib for the church at Christmas?"

"No" replied Tuhil, "It is not a crib, it is something better that will give us rest. I have relied on the Wisdom of Solomon. Saying, "John Faddie you are a great man, the best that ever had left Ireland, you know that you and I are related. I would never do anything that would harm you. I hope that you know what I am doing is for all of you. Now if any one of you objects, I will not go next or near the priest. Now! I will need a small contribution from you all as it is only right to give something to prove that you all agree."

One after another they agreed that it would be unlucky not to do as the priest said, for they could go to hell. Each in turn praised Tuhil for his wise decision, to go to the priest for guidance. Now, all of Tuhil's virtues were extoled and he was proclaimed the most pragmatic man who had left Ireland, and they gave him some money which they assumed was for the priest.

Next evening when the men finished work Tuhil said, "Each of you should go to church and pray for guidance for your life in America. I will do your bidding of what was required, if you will do as I say and go to church."

They thought that Tuhil was becoming religious, for he was a man who did not over frequent the priests or church.

When they had departed Tuhil went to the local petrol station and purchased a quantity of petrol which he took home with him. Then he poured the petrol on the creel and the rods that were remaining. He then lit a fire that illumined the evening sky. Tuhil was happy to see his nemesis dissolve into flames that brightened the night sky.

When they came home, Tuhil said that he had found a solution to their problem and would tell them in the morning.

They were all waiting in anticipation for what had he found, but Tuhil remained silent which was unusual, for at times Tuhil could talk for all of Ireland.

The suspense was holding them in anticipation, waiting for the answer to what had happened.

Tuhil retorted, "The answer is, 'you shall shatter the yoke of oppression and never put a burden across the shoulders of any man.' Do you all agree with the words of the men of God; say Yes or No!"

They pressed Tuhil on how he had found the resolution. Tuhil said that the answer was democratic and was through a majority consensus. The answer was in the Bible and was shown to him by the old Irish priest. The Bible clearly stated, "Take heed to yourselves, and bear no burden on your back, but be hallow on the Sabbath day. This is your answer". (Jeremiah 17:21)

John Faddie was lost for words with his mouth wide opened, he was trying to comprehend the rhetoric, which was flowing over his head. It reminded him of a stormy sea; nobody knows why but it is there. But finally he said "Tuhil, the creel, what is it that you did with it, tell us what has happened?"

Tuhil said with a smile, "We all left Ireland to get away from hard work and hardship with little money to look forward to, rather than a life of tiresome drudgery. Isn't that right? Life is difficult enough and we should protect ourselves, and should not show people anything that would make life more difficult. I have burned the creel on the advice of the priest, because we left Ireland to get away from the creel. If our employers see it, they could put something heavy in it and put it on their backs. The few dollars you gave is to give to John Faddie for a good drink. I hope that he never shows another creel again as long as he lives. Which one of you want to carry a heavy creel on your back all the days of your life, with the sweat streaming down your back? If you all agree with the wise old priest, say "Yes". There were some muted words spoken but who could go against the words of the priest or God?

A Contrary Sense of Religion

Daithi Arrigal with his wife Biddy and their family, lived on a few acres of infertile barren land, eking out a living between the land and sea. The land was bleak and rock-strewn, as if some giants had scraped the earth of soil, and cast the rocks about like little children playing with their toys. His home was sitting on the fringe of the Atlantic. On calm days the scenery was tranquil and beautiful with the rising or the declining sunset. However, on stormy cold winter days it would freeze the body and soul of man or beast. The neighbours would jokingly say that those people took the infertile land from the seagulls, which is why the gulls continue to squawk. Canice Mór would teasingly say "They will have to give this barren smidgen of land back to the seagulls, or they will never stop shrieking."

However, the family had to endure, and try to wrestle a living between what the land and what the sea produced. All the people of the area had an arduous struggle to survive and raise a family. It was not that some had more, it was others had less. Daithi Arrigal and his wife Biddy would be in the category of the lesser. Their windswept little farm suffered the many ravages of the north and westerly storms that blew in from the sea. The strong winds swept whatever crop that was growing to the ground. But adversity and necessity, coupled with survival, breeds a stubborn people, who refuse to lie down under continuous hardships. They struggled on with a smile on their faces, and the likelihood of little money to cover the odd catastrophe that life brings. They had a family of five: three boys Danny, Eoghan, and Fergus, and two girls Moirin and Neave. Their family were growing up and Danny was hired in the Lagan. This would provide them with a little flush of money when the season's work was ended.

Daithi worked hard carrying the many creels of seaweed and the shelly sand from the shore, some in bags and creels, to enrich the hungry land. When Daithi was not fishing, he could be seen carrying something from the shore. Other times he was building stone walls around his little fields, which would give some protection to the crop from the ravages of the impervious winds. These hard hearted winds could damage or destroy whatever crop that was growing in the earth. Those winds that blew from the north east were referred to as the (gui gorta) hungry wind, that chilled the body and soul, or as a lazy wind that blew through your body rather than around you. Aye! The bitter wind was of no benefit, neither to man nor to beast.

Canice Mór would mirthfully comment on Daithi's land, "If the cat died, Daithi wouldn't have as much land as needed to bury it in."

Life was a constant struggle. But he and his wife Biddy were managing to keep their family fed and clothed. Not that there was any surplus of money about the house, but the shellfish from the shore would always fill an empty belly. As long as sickness was kept at bay they would manage to survive from day to day. Their attitude to life was, there is no need to fear the wind if your hay stack is tied down. They would often comment on the good health of their family. Nevertheless, troubles have a habit of arriving when least expected; their daughter Moirin became sick and their money was meagre. They had a single pound note with six shillings and two pence in the house. Fifteen shillings was to pay for the rates, which left them with eleven shillings and two pence. Their dilemma was that for their daughter's sickness they would need money to pay the doctor, which would be at least ten shillings and some money for medicine. If the one shilling and two pence was sufficient to pay the chemist for the medicine, Daithi also had to buy salt if he was to cure any fish he caught for the market. Their immediate problem was how to acquire a little more money. They discussed various options: that of borrowing from their neighbours or friends, but each person was as short of money as they were. Biddy suggested that they should ask the priest, after all he should be a man of charity; surely he would help them, after all he was a man of God. Aye said Daithi "I will ask him. Don't we always pay money to the priest every week, and we are only looking for a loan".

Daithi immediately went to the local priest Father Jimmie, to ask him for help to pay the doctor and for whatever medicine was required.

"The priest's retort was, "Get a mass said for her; everything else is in the hands of God."

Daithi replied bitterly "Was it God's will when you were sick, didn't you call the doctor? And was it God's will or the doctor's help, when you went to hospital? Was it God or the people's money that paid the doctors and the hospital? It is my recollection that you had more than one doctor attending you, hadn't you?"

Father Jimmie retorted with a flushed red face as he was not used to any person questioning his perceived superiority. This outburst from a lowly peasant could not be tolerated, let alone uttered by someone to question his perceived authority. And he yelled, "How dare you! You dirty heathen, you pagan, how dare you question a priest! If you don't go! If you don't go down on your two knees and beg God for forgiveness I will send you to hell. If you don't want to send your child to hell, have a mass said for her! Now what do you want?"

Daithi with tears running down his cheeks replied meekly. "But Father I want my child to live, she is very sick and she could die! I love my child, and I wish to God that a doctor could see her. I am sorry that I upset you Father, but it is like this: I am out of my mind with worry all night. All right, will you say a mass said for her, if you think that will do her any good? But you know that my mind is crazy with worry."

Father Jimmie recognized that he had Daithi beaten psychologically, and he stuck out his hand while saying, "Aye, all right I will forgive you this time, I know that you are worrying, but never dare to provoke a man of God again."

Daithi, a little nervously, replied in a low voice "I have no money on me but the pound that was to pay the rates which is fifteen shillings and I could give you a few shillings.

Before Daithi could finish the sentence Father Jimmie had his hand extended and growled "Aye hurry up man! I don't have all day to waste, standing here listening to you spluttering and stammering. Don't you know I must do God's work? You can pay the rates later. Now hurry I have things to do. I can't stand here all day listening to you moaning about money. Money is the tool of the devil, God will provide."

Daithi took the single pound note from his pocket and handed it to Father Jimmie, expecting at least fifteen shillings change, which would pay the rates. However, Father Jimmie turned quickly, went into the house, and slammed the door shut. Muttering," Pray for your black soul that defies the will of God in all his greatness, you heathen!"

Daithi stood at the door expecting Father Jimmie to return with some of the money as he would be very lucky if he got one shilling for a long day's work, that is if he ever got a day's work for pay. But the priest did not return with any money. Eventually Daithi knocked gently on the door but no one answered as he stood timidly waiting for the door to open. Following a prolonged wait. Daithi knocked a second and a third time more loudly, thinking that his first knocks was not heard.

Eventually the door was opened and Father Jimmie snarled, "What do you want this time, don't you know I am a busy man, with all the work I have to do?"

Daithi responded nervously, "The money father, I need money to pay the rates and we haven't another shilling in the house, not as much as to buy salt to cure any fish."

Father Jimmie sneered with a grimace, "Well why don't you ask the shop for credit? I am sure they would give you salt as you are a good fisherman. I don't have salt in my house to give to every Tom Dick or Harry."

"But the pound note!" Said Daithi "Couldn't you at least give me fifteen shillings; it would pay the rates."

Father Jimmie roared "What do you think that I am, a charity or a bank or something; away with you, I had enough cheek from you this day." With that the door was slammed in Daithi's face.

Daithi was upset and angry. He was upset at himself for handing the money to the priest. Didn't Cundy Owen always say that that bucko is a money grabber, and his masses were useless, and if they were salt they would rot fish? Cundy Owen always called Father Jimmie Gaebolga (the spear of death.)

When Daithi arrived home he told Biddy what had transpired and how Father Jimmie grabbed the only pound note they had. "And now we had no money to pay the rates, or pay for a doctor, or buy salt." he said.

Biddy was silent for a while and began to sob saying, "In under God Daithi how are we going to live? We will be driven out of our house and home. That was the last pound in the house. How are going to get a doctor for our wee child is crying with pain, (mo leanbh beag, mo leanbh beag). Daithi avic my heart is sideways in mouth with worry."

Then Daithi began crying with salty tears running down his weather-beaten face, saying, "Biddy don't cry avic, we will think of something. I am a man of my word. If I have to, I will beg borrow or steal, God forgive me. I will plead with Doctor Smyth and ask him to see our wee Moirin. He is a good man, maybe he will wait until Danny comes home from the Lagan. We will have money for Danny's hire, wasn't the money £5 for six months' work? That money will surely pay the doctor and buy the medicine. I will be away now Biddy, I should have thought of this option initially. This will be the first time that the Arrigals begged, but it is not begging if we are going to pay the money back."

Biddy, trying to answer through her sobs, replied, "No Daithi it is not begging, but I would tramp the roads of Ireland to save any one of my children."

"Aye Biddy and I would gladly go with you for the sake of our wee mo leanbh beag! My child, my child, didn't we walk the floors with her after she was born?" Daithi began crying constantly with heavy sobs. Then he rose from the chair hurriedly saying "I am going to Doctor Smyth now, it is better find out one way or another. To hell with that blood thirsty Gaebolga."

Arriving at Doctor Smyth's, Daithi with tears on his face explained his predicament to the doctor, saying how he went to the priest asking him for money to pay you, but he chased me out of the house and he took my money. "Danny is hired in the Lagan and he will have 5 pounds when he comes home, and then I will pay you."

Doctor Smyth said "Hold on Daithi you are making no sense, what are you going to pay me for. Forget about money, don't you know the Hippocratic Oath?"

Daithi babbled "My wee child Moirin is sick, she has a pain in her side for three days and nothing we give to her seems to give her relief."

The doctor interrupted Daithi saying, "Quick man go home immediately, I will follow you on my horse: this sounds serious: it could be appendicitis. Boil as much water as you can. Don't you know the Hippocratic Oath? It's to save life. I pray to God that we are not too late!"

Daithi did not understand and said "Whose oath?"

Doctor Smyth responded with a smile saying "We will explain all again Daithi, we are wasting time talking."

Doctor Smyth rushed to the stable and made his horse ready, and went to Daithi Arrigal's house. Daithi was just in the door ahead of the doctor and had the kettles and pots over the fire, and some were bubbling.

Biddy was waiting for him and had the house clean, saying "God bless you Mr Doctor we do not have the money to pay you now, put I promise to God we will pay you."

Doctor Smyth interrupted Biddy saying, "Scrub the table, and send the children out to your neighbour's houses; this sounds serious, let's be prepared."

Doctor Smyth, with his kind mannerism, was examining Moirin. Speaking gently to Moirin he said, "Moirin we need you to be brave will you? We may have to do a little operation to make you better, is that all right with you?"

"What is wrong with me." said Moirin "Could I die?"

Doctor Smyth smiling said, "Aye, we all will die someday. I remember a little poem from my schooldays, but promise me you will not laugh at me it's

> Doctor, doctor will I die?
> Yes my child and so will I.

Do you think that is a funny poem? We will give you chloroform that will make you sleep and you will not feel any pain. Is that all right with you? I bet you will be the only one in your school to have had chloroform."

Moirin speaking in a low voice said, "What is chloroform, is it some kind of prayer?"

Doctor Smyth smiled and replied, "Well you could say it was a prayer for doctors. It was discovered in 1831 by Johann Jakob Paul Moldenhawer, a German. It is naturally found in seaweed. It is also believed to be produced in the soil by fungi. I bet no one in your school knows that. You will have a big story to tell all your friends when you go back to school. Moirin, you are the bravest girl I met. Now we will put this cloth over your mouth and you will be able to smell the sea. Its first known use on people was in 1847 by James Young Simpson, a Scotch man. Now Moirin can you say chlo-ro-form, for me?"

With the cloth of chloroform over Moirin's face, this caused her to fall into a deep slumber. Doctor Smyth said, "Biddy would you hold the lamp so as I can clearly see what I am operating on?"

Doctor Smyth began the operation on the kitchen table. Where he removed the offending appendix, he proceeded to stitch the opening closed.

With the operation complete the table was washed and scrubbed and the doctor washed his hands and scalded his surgical paraphernalia. Then Moirin was carefully carried to her bed.

Doctor Smyth said, "Now don't let her out of her bed for a couple of days and don't under any circumstances let her lift anything heaver that a spoon for a week or two."

Then Daithi began explaining and sobbing about his predicament in relation to the pound note and the priest, and said you are not even the same religion.

Doctor Smyth interrupted him by gently saying, "Daithi we are all Christian. It is different sects we are, not a different religion, after all we believe in the same God, don't we? As for the money, I know that you are a good fisherman. Perhaps you could take me and a friend out fishing someday? Putting his hand in his pocket he handed Daithi a pound note, saying "This will pay the rates for you, and salt to cure the fish you catch. Maybe you could get some fresh fish for me? Some day when the weather is good let's go fishing, as I would like to have a calm day to shoot a few seals. You know that a sealskin makes a great rug for the house. Aye then we would be even."

Daithi at first was refusing to take the money saying, "That is too much for you. We can't be begging off you, after all you came here and we are without money to pay you, and the priest robbed us."

Doctor Smyth retorted, "It was God that sent you, Daithi! Because the appendix was about to bust, if you hadn't come to me death was inevitable. Now let her rest for a while. And remember don't let her lift anything. It's rest, rest and more rest for a while, with good food and what we have here, plenty of good fresh air. I will call again to see Moirin, she is a good looking young girl, look after her". With that said the doctor departed Daithi's house and went to his home.

Then Daithi began sobbing and said "The doctor is a good man: he didn't charge a penny, and he gave us the money that 'gadai' robbed us of. I can never have faith in that priest, that robbing Gaebolga!"

"God forgive you Daithi," said Biddy "you should not say that about a priest, you could be calling on him if you were dying."

"Ah" retorted Daithi "I would rather call the doctor any day; there is more goodness in the end of the doctor's little finger that there is in all Gaebolga."

"God forgive you Daithi we should not criticise a priest, and don't be calling him names, it is not lucky."

Daithi riposted angrily "Was it not Doctor Smyth who saved our child life, and who gave us the money to pay the rates, and buy salt? Not that fat robbing priest Gaebolga."

In two days' time Doctor Smyth called into Daithi house to see how Moirin was improving. Saying "Moirin, how are you feeling today, have you any pain or discomfort? Perhaps a little discomfort for a few days."

"No doctor, I am all right, it is only when I laugh that it hurts a little."

"Good" replied Doctor Smyth "Can we have a little look to see how it is mending?"

The doctor examined Moirin and smiled, "Good I see that it is mending and you will soon be skipping around the place. Now Moirin can you remember who discovered chloroform?"

Moirin replied, "It was Jakob Paul Moldenhawer in 1831, and it was first used in 1847 by James Young Simpson a Scotch man."

"Excellent" replied Doctor Smyth, "I can see that you are a very bright girl. Now if I give you a book will you promise to read it?", and he thrust a book into Moirin's hand.

Daithi and Biddy went to thank the doctor again, but he said, "Take care of your child, and don't forget we will have a day's fishing when my friends arrive."

Moirin recovered and was running around again like a sparrow jumping from rock to rock with the rest of the family, playing, fighting, and gathering shellfish from the shore. Daithi had a good fishing, and he cured dried fish and sold them. This left the family more content and comfortable.

Doctor Smyth, with friends at times, went fishing with Daithi, but each time he went out fishing he gave Daithi a plug of tobacco, and the children some biscuits. When Doctor Smyth would call he would inquire about Moirin, saying "Where is my brave girl? Now can I see where you had the operation? Now Moirin you are looking as good as God made you. Now tell me the name of the medicine that put you to sleep and do you remember the person that discovered it."

Moirin, replied it was chlo-ro-form, and the man that discovered it was Johann Jakob Paul Mol-den-hawer."

"Very good!" replied Doctor Smyth. " I see that you are a very clever girl. I hope that you are continuing with your reading. Will you continue your reading and writing for me Moirin?"

Moirin timidly replied, "Yes doctor I will."

Doctor Smyth handed Moirin a sweet saying, "This is for remembering the person who discovered chloroform."

Daithi and Biddy, feeling a little embarrassed, would say "It is too good you are doctor, when we had nothing you gave to us, without ever knowing if we would or could ever pay you back."

"Ah! Biddy my good woman," said the Doctor, "No matter how hard your life is, be grateful we still have one. Remember we are all servants of God, and I trust in the mercy of God forever, and whatever he sends for me. I trust you and your family are well. When the world pushes us to our knees, we are in a better position to pray. I remember a little rhyme from my schooldays, it went something like this:

You spend your life in search of wealth,

You strive so hard to get it,

You spend your wealth in search of health,

And in the grave is where you find it".

Years passed and the family was now healthy and strong, some were now in a position to earn a little money for the house. Danny got a job in Dublin through the help and influence of Dr Smyth. Eoghan,

Moirin and Neave were working in Scotland at the herring fishing. They acquired jobs with a fish curer at the gutting. Life was getting more comfortable for Daithi and Biddy, with a slight surplus of money to spend.

Daithi curtailed his visits to the church and only went there for funerals or the odd christening, and when he did, he remained outside until the priest had left the church. Daithi vowed he was never going to be put in a position where the priest could speak down to him again. This upset Father Jimmie and he was determined that he would make Daithi return under his dominance once more.

There were 'missions' which came to the parish every few years. Father Jimmie saw an opportunity to have Daithi back under his control. He had one of the Missionary priests speak to Biddy. When Biddy was at confessions the missionary priest asked her name, and where she came from, and if her husband was with her.

Biddy ashamedly replied. "No Father I came on my own."

"And tell me my good woman, why has your husband not attended? Is he sick, or maybe he is a protestant or something?"

Biddy said meekly "No thank God father, he is not sick, nor is he a protestant."

The priest said loudly "And why is he not with you? Tell him I want to speak to him."

Biddy humbly replied, "I will Father, I will, thanks Father, thanks Father."

When Biddy went home she told Daithi what the priest said to her when she was at confessions, saying "Daithi, you will have to go to the missionary priest: he told me."

"What!" Retorted Daithi angrily, "It was you that was at confessions not me, who the hell primed him? That 'Gaebolga' the bloody hypocrite! Jimmie is not a priest, how dare they bully you. Never go near that bloody mission again. It is all about money and control."

"But Daithi avic, the people will talk about you, maybe he will read your name from the altar."

Daithi snapped, "Read my name from the altar? I will read my own name out on the altar for them if they wish. Those hypocritical devious money grabbing swindlers, how dare they try to extort or blackmail me?"

"Well Biddy I want no dispute with you. It was that bloody Jimmie Gaebolga'! Our daughter Moirin would be dead today only for Doctor Smyth. Gaebolga grabbed the money out of my hand; he could not care less if Moirin lived or died. Now I am not telling you what to do, but if you kneel down before that thing, don't be surprised if you get a kick in the backside."

"But Daithi avic, could you not go to the mission, for at least one night?"

"Biddy! Let's not let this controversy cause us to argue, you and I will speak no more about it. I certainly will not go near them cartans (a small parasite). It is your choice to go to church and if they speak to you again, tell them to see me."

Biddy did not go to church next night, fearing derisory comments from the priest. She let the neighbours know that she was feeling unwell, saying, "Perhaps I am getting a flu."

Next day Daithi was working in the field when he saw two men approaching the house. He was not going to let them enter the house and intimidate Biddy, and shouted "Who are you? And what do you want, are you tinkers or thieves?"

The two men approached Daithi as he continued working saying "Good morning Daithi."

Daithi turning around and looking at them replied, "Do I know you? You know my name and I don't know you, who are you?"

One of the men replied "I am Father John McBride, and my friend is Father John McCormack."

Daithi retorted, "How am I to address you, as John one or John two, and who is John one? Couldn't one of you take the name Shan? It would cause less confusion."

The remark from Daithi disconcerted the priests who looked at each other dumbly as they didn't know how to reply. They were used to asking the questions not answering any to an uneducated country peasant.

One of the priests replied unhurriedly, "Its Father John McBride or Father John McCormack, Daithi when you speak to us."

Daithi riposted, "Its Daithi Arrigal when you speak to me, and how did you know what my name was Daithi, John one or John two?"

One of the priests replied angrily, "Remember when you talk to us, you are speaking to a priest."

Daithi retorted loudly, "You two cartans, remember when you are speaking to me you are speaking to Daithi Arrigal, and answer my question. How did you know that my name was Daithi?"

One of the priests replied "Father Jimmie told us your name and said that you don't go to church."

"You mean 'Gaebolga' that robbing diabhal, you could start your mission with him. He took my last pound note from me, and would have let my child die to feed his fat whiskey drinking face. It was Doctor Smyth that saved my child's life, and saved us from being evicted not 'Gaebolga."

The priest responded dawdling, "How do you know it wasn't Father Jimmie's prayers that saved your daughter's life?"

Daithi retorted loudly and angrily "Because it was Doctor Smyth's hands that saved her life, and he also gave us money to survive! Did 'Gaebolga' not tell you that?"

The priest riposted, "Aye a black protestant! Don't tell me you are starting to believe in them, who are in league with the devil."

Daithi roared in anger, "If you two antichrists don't be on your way this spade will be stuck up your fat backside. You! You two bullies that were sent by another bully, Gaebolga. Clear to hell to where you came from. Clear to hell from where you two came from! You shower of gob manure makers. Clear, and if you ever upset my wife or family, I will personally deal with you; that is not a threat, it is a promise. Clear back to hell where you two devils came from and take that other devil, 'Gaebolga' with you!"

The two missionary priests knew that Daithi was not going to be easily intimidated and made a fast retreat. From their psychology studies, they were aware that if a person is adamant in his refusal to change his mind, then there was nothing to be gained from inflaming his anger. That would only reinforce his conceived opinions, and so they quickly and silently departed, muttering.

Daithi continued his work while talking loudly to himself. His comments were full of obscenities and profanities against the priests.

Daithi was usually a mild mannered man who was slow to anger, but when inflamed he would chew stones into gravel. He was a man of his word, and if you did Daithi a favour, he would never forget it. However, if you caused him disrespect, he was like an elephant who never forgets.

As the years passed Daithi was as reluctant as ever to go near Gaebolga, and the Bishop was as determined to keep the priest in the parish. The Bishop did not wish that any unscrupulous peasant should be the instigator of changing the church's modus operandi. If one person could cause a priest to leave, it would set a precedent that others might replicate. The Bishop considered and rationalised that it was better to let time weaken Daithi, as it enervated others. The Bishop had experienced many disruptions within the church, and he found that the best tactic was to always fudge the issue. From experience he found his best approach was to let time erode away any issue. Having avoided the many scandals in his office, by playing dumb and procrastinating, this was a tactic that had served him well in the past.

Daithi's family were growing up: Eoghan and Neave were in America and they intended to pay for the passage of Danny to join them. Daithi had relations in America who would help find Danny a job. With the help of God, they would be sending some money home. Moirin the eldest daughter was married in Scotland and Fergus was at home.

Their youngest son Fergus had a slight mental disability, and was kept at home where they could care for him. He was an untidy worker on the land, but loved gathering shellfish on the shore. He would gather periwinkles which Daithi would sell; he was also a good swimmer and would dive for clams and the odd lobster or crab which he put into a net bag. Fergus was in his glory with anything to do on the shore. At spring tides or when the tide was low he would gather carrageen, dulce and sloke, and this made some money for the house. Every penny was valuable and helped with the upkeep of the house, and also the many good meals that were gathered from the sea shore. These meals would be banquets fit for a king's table.

Some neighbours would jokingly say that Fergus was like a seal, swimming and diving beneath the sea. It was often said by neighbours in jest that he could do anything but sleep in the sea. Fergus relished the praise and wonder of others; he was like a child glorying in admiration. However, pride coupled with vanity and conceit can cut down the greatest empire. One day Fergus did not return home, and he was feared drowned. The neighbours spent days searching the shore line for his body. Eventually his body was found lying at the bottom of a sea pool, with his bag which he used to collect the shellfish.

Doctor Smyth was on leave and there was a relief doctor in place covering the area, who was nephew of the Bishop. The priest and the bishop influenced the doctor to record the death as a suicide. Obviously this verdict upset Daithi and Biddy. Daithi went to the doctor saying that it was wrong, because Fergus had spent many days diving for clams in that area and he always took a net bag with him for his catch.

The doctor's reply was "Daithi, you converse with the priest, and then maybe he would be able to change the death certificate with the help of the bishop, it is out of my hands now."

Daithi was enraged by the doctor; he knew quite well that it was an accident, and the church was seeking revenge with the help of its puppets.

There were heated words spoken between Daithi and the doctor, neither conceding their opinion. Eventually the doctor asked Daithi to leave saying "I can do no more, it is not up to me now, even if I wanted to. If you bother me anymore I will have the police arrest you, it is a serious offence to threaten a doctor."

Daithi left the doctor cursing and crying until he arrived home. This was awful news to take to Biddy that the doctor had refused to modify the death certificate.

Biddy went to Father Jimmy to discuss the funeral mass, but the priest dismissed her saying, "Your son committed suicide! So there will be no funeral mass for him, he will go to hell. Why don't you bury him in the strand if he liked it so much? Anyhow he is a sinner and will never see the light of heaven! He will have to be buried somewhere, but not in my graveyard."

Biddy was shocked at his retort and told Daithi when she came home crying, saying, "We do not even have a grave for our child Fergus."

Daithi was equally shocked and infuriated and said, "Whist avic, we will have a grave for our Fergus, I know something that that 'Gaebolga' don't know, leave it to me avic."

There was the usual wake in the house, which all the neighbours visited to offer their condolence, except Father Jimmie, whose absence was noted and remarked upon. With the progress of age death is inevitable, but when a young person dies it is especially sorrowful.

Fergus's wake was distressing and the neighbours were aware of the dispute between Daithi and the priest. Especially since the priest asked those in church to pray for those that commit suicide; that forbids them from entering into heaven. When a younger member of the family dies in such an unexpected way, it is particularly horrendous. The people at the wake had to choose their words carefully in case an unintended word could offend. Daithi selected a day for the burial, and had some of the neighbours helped him dig the grave, which they did early in the morning to avoid a confrontation with the priest. They anticipated an altercation if Father Jimmie saw them. They were conscious that Father Jimmy could be as contrary as a bag of cats. So stealth was a virtue and quietness was essential to avoid any confrontation, and they hoped that the priest might not notice a freshly opened grave. As they worked there was little talk or laughter outside the few whispers.

Next morning the funeral cortege proceeded to the graveyard and they began to lay the coffin in the grave, and were in the process of saying a few prayers.

Then they heard the roar of Father Jimmy shouting, "Clear off from here and take that thing with you! He will never be buried in this graveyard, this is my graveyard. Take that thing out of here or I will put horns on you."

Daithi was of course infuriated with Father Jimmie, as both of them began shouting at each other. Daithi was a reasonable quiet man but when he was enraged he could be as ill-tempered as a roaring bull that would go through a stone wall when it smelled a cow in heat.

Father Jimmy was at the grave shouting "Get it out of here; this is my graveyard and I will decide who is buried here."

Daithi shouted, "This is not your graveyard! My grandfather carted the sand from the shore to cover the bare rocks and fill this spot in the graveyard. This grave was nourished with the flesh of my people. It was never yours, nor ever will be. This is the Arrigal's grave and not yours, Gaebolga.

Father Jimmy shouted, "If you don't remove that coffin immediately I will personally throw it out of here, and leave that thing at the side of the road like a dog."

Daithi grabbed a spade and struck Father Jimmy, with it, which left him speechless, with shock and pain. Daithi retorted, "My son will lie in our grave and if you or anyone lifts him, I promise them they will be buried, for I will kill them. Now you Gaebolga! If you disturb this grave, I will personally kill you, and throw you out of this our graveyard. This is a promise on Fergus's grave, and if you or anybody tampers with this grave I will personally kill them".

Father Jimmy was muted, he was used to bullying people and this was the first time that anyone had ever stood up to him, or struck him. His ribs and stomach were in severe pain. The most capacious bully is also the greatest coward, hiding their inferiority complex beneath a cover of coercion and intimidation.

It was the first time that Father Jimmy was silenced in front of company, which wounded his pride perhaps more than his body. He was afraid to speak, contemplating a violent end for him, and would reflect on how he could regain his unredeemed pride and arrogance.

There was little talk as they closed Fergus's grave, each choosing their words that would not upset Daithi. Canice Mór was with his mirthful way commenting on the weather, and how it had rained continuously most of this year. Saying "That people would need to take the hay into the house and dry it on chairs around the fire." Cundy Own wanting to have his own tale said, "My grandfather used to say one year when he was growing up it was so wet, that he could fish from the chair at the fireside. The chitchat was mostly about the weather and how Daithi was right to stop Father Jimmy from upsetting the burial. Some of the people present had relations who had been denied a burial place in the graveyard because someone said they had died of suicide.

However, if those families' had money then they could overcome any obstacle if their relation had died of suicide; that is if they paid the priests a copious financial remittance. Was there a place in heaven for the rich and a separate place for the poor?

Daithi said, "There are drinks paid for all in Cissie's pub and I would be obliged if all would go to have a drink to honour of Fergus's memory. My heart that once knew joy, must now sip the bitter cup of grief alone. For solitude will be my salvation to let the bitterness of sorrow dissipate."

A few people present made the consolatory gesture of not attending the pub, saying he had enough expense to pay for. However, Daithi insisted that anyone refusing a drink to Fergus life, was refusing Daithi Arrigal. Daithi said he was grateful to all who attended and he wished they would remain his friends. Daithi then produced a bottle of homemade whiskey from his coat and taking a swig from the bottle he handed it around saying have a drink at Fergus's graveside.

Daithi began crying and singing the song, 'The Parting Glass':

> Of all the money that e'er I spent
> I've spent it in good company
> And all the harm that ever I did
> Alas it was to none but me
> And all I've done for want of wit
> To memory now I can't recall
> So fill to me the parting glass
> Good night and joy be with you all"

"Now" said Daithi, "If you do not mind I will sit here alone for a while to remember Fergus and perhaps sing him a few songs. But you my friends, go to Cissie's pub and finish the song "The Parting Glass" which was one of Fergus's favourites. I will be delayed as I have something to do".

When they were all departed, Daithi took the spade and dragged it after him to Shaun Mackie, a known alcoholic who lived with his wife Bridget.

Opening the door Daithi said "God bless all here today. Shaun Mackie, and you Bridget and family, I trust are in good health today?"

Shaun Mackie replied, "God bless you too Daithi, you had a misfortune with the loss of your son. I suppose accidents will happen."

"Aye Shaun Mackie, accidents can happen, but some don't see it as accidents, do they!"

"No Daithi they don't, but God can see all things that are beyond our way of seeing."

"No Shaun Mackie, they certainly don't and that is why I am here. I hit the priest with the spade because he attempted to prevent Fergus from being buried in our grave."

Shaun Mackie retorted, "Ah Daithi the priest should not have stopped you. But hitting the priest is a terrible thing, maybe you could go to hell."

Daithi quickly retorted, "If I go to hell then I will have plenty of people to talk to. If I have to I would kill Gaebolga. Then Gaebolga and I will have plenty to talk about when the devil is finished with him."

Shaun Mackie replied in a murmur "God's help to you. There is no need to kill anyone, is there Daithi?"

"Aye Shaun Mackie, which is why I am here to tell you that if you or anybody tampers with Fergus's grave I will personally kill them with this spade I have in my hand. I don't wish to offend you Shaun Mackie. But if you or others should open my son's grave, this spade will be used to send you or any person that has tampered with Fergus's grave, to heaven or hell. Now do you understand what I am saying? Do you? Shaun Mackie if you should consider collecting a bribe from the priest, and then go to Scotland, then you will have to return home for your own family funeral, for I will kill one of your children."

Bridget spoke nervously saying "In God name Daithi, you wouldn't harm a child would you?"

Daithi retorted, "Not if my son Fergus's grave is not touched. But if it is, then that is the consequence! I hope that you understand."

Shaun Mackie answered nervously "Aye Daithi we understand. I wouldn't touch a grave where someone is buried. I would be afraid of their spirit that would haunt me."

"Well" Daithi replied, "You know you would not have to wait for any ghost to haunt you; you or your children would be the ghosts. Now God bless you Shaun Mackie. Bridget, I have the same task with other people, and if you meet anybody, would you tell them the consequences of their actions?"

Daithi dragged the spade around to every house in the parish, telling them the outcome of tampering with his son's grave. Some of the people, when they heard the sound of the spade being dragged, went to meet Daithi, offering him something to eat saying, "Daithi avic, you must be famished. Come in and sit down until you at least have a bite to eat and a rest."

Daithi thanked them saying "I had something to eat this morning. I already had tea and bread at Conal Mór's house. I have a job to do, if another life is to be spared, God bless you all".

Daithi continued walking and dragging the spade until he visited all the houses in the parish, and the next two parishes.

Eventually the Sergeant of the police met Daithi in the village and asked him about his threatening behaviour.

Daithi replied "It is not a threat; I am merely saying what is the consequence of removing my son's body from his grave."

Sergeant Burk riposted angrily "Daithi if you don't go back and apologise to the priest and all the people you upset, you will be taken to court and jailed. Do I make myself clear? If I am asked, I will remove the coffin from the grave. I certainly would. Now Daithi, go home and think on it. I will give you one day to remove the coffin from the church's graveyard or I will, with the help of the police from Dublin I will! Goodbye."

Daithi replied "Good bye to you, sergeant, but remember, I don't make threats! I advise people how they should live their life, and let others live their life in peace".

Daithi went immediately to see the sergeant's wife Alice, and spoke to her.

Alice was a good looking petite friendly woman opposite to the Sergeant in all things, they were like honey and vinegar; it must be that the opposites attract.

"Good day Daithi," said Alice, "let me first of all offer my deepest condolence to you and your wife Biddy on the loss of your boy Fergus. It is a terrible tragedy for you; your wife must be heartbroken."

"Aye Alice, my heart that once danced with delight must now sip the chalice of bitterness alone, for animosity and grief will be my companion until the day I die."

Alice could see the grief in Daithi face and replied, "God is good and he sees all. It is a terrible thing to lose a child. You and Biddy must be distraught with sadness."

Daithi replied with tears running down his cheeks. "We are, Alice; we are, Alice. That is why I am here today. As you know I have told people that if they remove Fergus's body from his grave that I would kill them".

"Ah Daithi, we know you didn't mean it. Often harsh words are spoken in times of grief".

"Yes in grief Alice, but I definitely do mean it. I was speaking with your husband and he said that he and some of his associates would remove Fergus from his grave."

"Ah Daithi" said Alice softly, "You know that he says a lot of things that he doesn't mean, and surely they would need a court order to touch a grave?"

"Well Alice" replied Daithi, "That is the reason for my visit here today to tell you that if he removes Fergus's body or goes to court to have him removed, I will kill him or one of your children. Now! You chose which one of your family you want to die. Alice you know I am a man of my word. I never injured anything or anybody before in my life, and I don't wish to hang, but I will if my son's grave is tampered with! I will. Now God bless you Alice and your family and I hope we will all be alive next year. I never want to hurt anybody, but as God is my witness, if they tamper with Fergus's grave, I will hang for killing someone. I hope that it is not one of yours that I will swing for."

That night when Sergeant Tom was going to bed, his wife Alice told him of the visit from Daithi.

The Sergeant roared "I will tonight go and get Daithi and throw him in the jail. How dares he to come into my house and threaten you. I will see to it that he is given a long time in jail".

Alice began crying and said "Tom if you arrest him, what charges can you hold him on? If they ask me to be one of the witnesses, I will deny all, and I will take the children away with me. Don't put me in a position where I must choose between you and my children. Remember the first day in court will be the last day of our marriage. The day you go to arrest Daithi, that will be the day that I will take the children away from you and from danger."

The Sergeant growled, "I am member of the police who cannot be seen to be intimidated by anybody. I must uphold the law."

Alice re-joined, "Tom, what has happened between Daithi and the priest is not a criminal matter. It is a civil matter; let the priest take Daithi to court where they can settle their dispute. The church has enough scandal on its plate, let them settle this one themselves. I know they would be reluctant to take Daithi to court to remove a body from the grave. What publicity would the church get? The news would go international and you would be a sacrificial lamb in between them. The next time the priest comes to you, tell him to settle it with his own solicitor. Have no hand, part or act in what happens. Wash your hands of any involvement. Be nobody's skivvy."

Tom riposted, "I have a public duty to perform, to see that there is no public disorder or disregard for law and order."

Alice quickly re-joined "Law and order! Tom you and I, and every dog in the countryside knows that young Fergus was drowned. It was not suicide; it was an unfortunate accident. If you were as interested in the public order you would have demanded a Coroner's inquest, which was legally required by law. Would it upset father Jimmie and his nephew the doctor, who was schooled by the priest's or the parish's money? Would it?"

"But Alice, as much as I loathe it I will have to perform my duty".

Alice quickly retorted, "Did anybody come to you to lodge an official complaint about Daithi? They didn't. Tom! Don't fight other people's battles; you are the only one that will be left to suffer. If Father Jimmie comes to you again, tell him it is a civil matter and he can personally have it settled in a Court of law. Can you imagine what the newspapers headlines would be? Tom think for one minute how you or I would feel if we were in the same position. The same thing could have happened to one of our family. I would be devastated, as you would. Let's neither you nor I aggravate a mother or a father's grief".

Sometime latter Father Jimmie went to the barracks to speak to Sergeant Tom to inquire why he did not remove Fergus's body from, as he said, his graveyard. Father Jimmie shouted "Why have you not removed that thing from my graveyard?"

Sergeants Tom casually replied, "What is it that you mean Father, is something upsetting you? I don't know what your problem is. Could you clarify exactly what you want?"

Father Jimmie barked, "You know what it is! It is that sinner Fergus that is lying in my graveyard. Why haven't you removed him, and thrown him on the side of the road like the dog that he is? You are not doing your duty as a member of the police force!"

Sergeant Tom was expecting Father Jimmie to complain at some time, but the arrogant outburst about a dead person was unjustified and inexcusable. Sergeant Tom could at times be overbearing, but he always tried to be impartial in his transactions with people. He was a reasonable man in his dealings as long as a person did not upset him. If they did then he could be as stubborn as any donkey: the more you pulled it, the more it sat down.

Looking defiantly at Father Jimmie he retorted, "I represent the law in this area. If there are any crimes being committed, then report them to me and I will deal with it. As for your dispute with Daithi you can settle it within the Civil Law Court. As you should know, you will need a court order to exhume a body. There are as you may know a few rules governing the exhumation of a body. Firstly, it may be part of a criminal investigation. Or for public health reasons. Or if the family wishes the removal, and there must be an environmental official present. As there was no crime committed, you would be committing a crime if you remove the remains without the approval of the Court. If the body is exhumed, then there would have to be a post-mortem to decide the cause of death. And there is always the possibility that the original cause of death may be overturned. What do you think of that? It could have unforeseen consequences for you, and your nephew the doctor? It may even have your nephew suspended as a doctor."

Father Jimmie was enraged saying, "I will report you to your Superintendent if you don't get that dog out of my graveyard."

"Aye!" retorted Sergeant Tom, "I will write a report on what you said; you described the man in the grave as a dog. I will make sure that your words are recorded accurately, and forward it in my report to the Superintendent. Perhaps! Maybe your description of the deceased man as a dog would make good reading in the press. I am sure the Bishop would be flattered by your description of the deceased, would he not? Now never tell me how to do my job as long as you remain here."

Father Jimmie could see that the sergeant's face flushed red in anger, and he rose muttering, "I will never let one of your family be an altar boy."

Sergeant Tom snarled, "You will never need to refuse them, from what I heard. I would not be looking after my family properly, if I let you have any interaction with them. You know that I heard appalling rumours about what is happening. I do hope that it is only hearsay."

Father Jimmie rose and walked out of the barracks, huffing and puffing like an old steam train muttering, "Those that defy the holy Catholic Church will go to hell where they will burn forever and ever in the fires of hell."

With Father Jimmie's departure, life settled down again and Sergeant Tom did not have any more visits or demands. This he preferred, but for his own security he wrote a report of what had transpired and saved a copy of the incident and posted another copy to himself. He was aware that Father Jimmie was an extremely venomous man. If the worst came to the worst he could easy curtail Father Jimmie with his own virulent words. Sergeant Tom knew that the priest's words would make damning reading, and the bishop would be reluctant to proceed with any litigation. If the press got wind of what had happened there could be unforeseen repercussions for the church.

In the wake of the fracas between the priest and the sergeant an uneasy peace followed. Sergeant Tom forwarded a full report of what transpired to headquarters. This would be his insurance against any underhand attack from the priest or the bishop. He still retained a copy of the report in an unopened registered letter to himself, as insurance to be opened in court.

Following the interment of Fergus, Daithi went most days to visit the graveyard. Daithi was like a cat watching for the rat to move, so he could pounce. Days turned into weeks and month into years. And there was no further hullabaloo from either church or state, and this pleased Sergeant Tom as he wished no kerfuffle in his life.

Eventually Father Jimmie became unwell, with his overindulgent whiskey drinking. He was aware that the people knew that he was stymied. Father Jimmie could not achieve his objective in having Fergus's body removed from the graveyard. He had to reluctantly accept that he could not this time have his way. It played on his mind, and through drink he had a nervous breakdown and was rushed to hospital. The Bishop used the excuse to replace him with another priest, hoping that the negative confrontations he had created would diminish, and life would continue in the village.

However, Daithi never went to the church again, and the rancorous taste of what happened to his son lingered. The memory of his son's death remained a sour and pungent taste in a mother or father's grief.

Fishing Fiadh: The Curse of Crom Dubh

Fiadh O'Baegill grew up in the mountains of Glenneamhe, which open up to a hidden valley and lake. The old people believe that when Colmcille was being pursued by his enemies, he spent some time sheltering in that glen, where he was given fish from the lake to eat. On leaving, Colmcille gave his blessing to the glen, and a curse on anyone who came to the glen to harm the people. No man on the run was ever caught in the glen even through the darkest of times. A fog would descend over the hills and soldiers were either lost or injured. If someone tried to enter the glen the dogs, the animals, or the hens would create such a racket, that it would warn the people of their approach. Or if a car came at night, the lights would be reflected from the cliffs into the people's houses, giving them a warning. With Colmcille's blessing, the lake had always provided fish for the people in the glen. In the landlord's times, whenever the landlords or their agents fished the lake, they returned home often without a fish. Yet a native of the glen with a rod and line could have a fresh fish for their dinner with ease. Some anglers allege that Colmcille told the people of the glen the secret of fishing.

When Fiadh was a young boy he, akin to others, would fly a kite in the valley which always provided draughts of wind. It is an ideal location for flying kites, or today for hang gliding. As kite flying was the predominant sport for the young and perhaps for the not so young, the people in Glenneamhe had perfected the art of constructing kites. They had to rely on what was easily available, and what was cheap. Every family in the glen spent many Sundays when it was not raining flying their kites. They passed many days between constructing kites and fishing in the lake that seemed to have an abundance of trout; while other anglers would at times visit the lake, they never had the luck of the locals. The old people would say, "Never tell anybody the secrets of tying flies for fishing trout, or how to build a kite." When visiting anglers would comment on how the locals could catch fish, and they could not, the local people would say, that it was just luck, and sometimes added that they also had bad fishing days.

A visiting angler who came regularly said, "You could buy the people of Glenneamhe all the drink in Ireland, but they will never will tell their secrets of fishing. Yes, they will tell what is supposed to be their truth, but you can never rely on it." It was often said the people of glen would never tell the truth, even when they went to confession.

Fiadh's uncle Shamie was the most prolific in making flies for fishing. Even the locals of the glen would often comment on how he could construct a fly-hook that would always catch a fish.

Shamie would often say to Fiadh, "I will tell you how to fix this fly-hook for a bright day, if you promise never to tell the secrets of the O'Baegill. One day this secret could be of use to you, but if you give the secret away you will never have it when you want it." Fiadh and Shamie spent many a day fishing, and at night tying flies.

As the years passed the young people of the glen were emigrating, and the old were now being interred in the graveyards in Ireland and abroad. And now Shamie died and Fiadh was left in an empty and lonely house. Emigration seemed as the only venue for Fiadh, as the glen was becoming devoid of people. One day he went to the fishing port of Scalpamore to make enquiries about places to where he might emigrate. He made casual enquiries in the pub about where was the best place to go to. He got talking to an old man, Dan O'Boyle, who said that he had spent many years working in America and Britain.

Fiadh asked, "If you were going to emigrate today, where would you say was the best place to go to?"

Dan paused before uttering slowly, "I have been to many places in my life. But the best place to live is in the country you are standing in. It doesn't matter how many years you are living in another country, you will still be an outsider. Why don't you look for work here? Why don't you look for a place on a fishing boat?"

Fiadh hastily retorted, "But I have no experience of sea fishing. I have never stood on a sea boat, a day in my life. Ah who would take me on their boat? The only experience I have of fishing is in the lake of Glenneamhe."

"Aye" snapped Dan O'Boyle swiftly, "Are you not one of the O'Boyle of Glenneamhe? Are you going to let down the name of the O'Boyle's or the place you were reared in? Your uncle Shamie could catch a fish while others would die of starvation. Why don't you try the fishing and if you are not happy with it, you can always leave?"

"But" reacted Fiadh, "I have never stood in a sea fishing boat one day in my life, and I don't know if I would be any good working at sea."

"What!" retorted Dan O'Boyle. "How can you say you couldn't work at sea if you never tried it? You remind me of certain people who say they don't like to eat something, and they never had tasted it. Remember the old axiom Fiadh, 'suck it and see'."

Fiadh uttered, "But who can I ask? Surely they will be looking for men who have experience, and I have none."

Dan O'Boyle uttered "Mogue is on the pier mending nets, why don't you ask him? All he can do is say no."

Fiadh walked to Mogue saying, "I am looking for a job fishing, but I have no experience working on fishing boats. Would there be any chance that you would give me a try?"

Mogue looked at Fiadh and did not reply for a while and then said, "Well at least you are honest enough to tell me. I had people that would come to me telling that they were fishing on some fictitious boat. After a little chat I could find them out if it was a lie. Yes, I will give you a berth on the boat as you are honest. A crewman of mine is off sick and I will give you a try until he returns, if you accept that."

"Aye thank you!" said Fiadh, "That will be alright with me, thanks again. Will I start working now?"

"Have patience." said Mogue. "I am intending to go fishing Monday morning at 7 O'clock. You will need a sea gear of boots and sea clothing. You can buy all of it in that shop on top of the pier, they will tell you all you need. And another thing: if you come with any drink in you, I won't allow you aboard."

Fiadh again thanked him for the job and said, "I don't normally drink at home. I was hoping that I could get news of where I could find a job: that was why I was in the pub."

Mogue smiling replied, "Don't get me wrong, I was not saying how you should lead your life, after all I enjoy a little drink myself. But I will never allow anyone with drink aboard my boat. Do you understand?"

"Aye, thanks I will do my best." said Fiadh, "I will be here in the morning."

On Monday morning Fiadh was aboard the boat and listened to the instructions that Mogue gave him. He was a quick learner, and soon learned the art of mending nets. He could see if there were small holes in the nets, and he would mend them before anyone else pointed them out.

One day he said to Mogue, "I don't want you to think that I am telling you your job. Maybe we should put the nets on the pier and measure them, maybe one end has stretched."

Mogue replied, "What makes you think that Fiadh?"

"Well," responded Fiadh, "It is because we used to have better catches of fish, and now some of the other boats have better catches than we have. I don't want to be telling you your job as you know more than me. You are the expert."

Mogue hastily uttered, "Anyone who says they know everything, knows nothing. I spent my life learning from other people and will do so until the day I die. I will tell you something; the more you know, the more you know how little you know. Aye we will put the net on the pier tomorrow and check it."

When the net was stretched on the pier and the few tears were mended by Fiadh and Mogue. Then they measured the net, and true to Fiadh's perception the gear was found to be stretched. This was corrected and Mogue was pleased that someone with as little experience as Fiadh could perceive the structure of a net. The next day the net was hauled into the boat it had a good catch of fish which pleased Mogue.

Mogue said, "Tell me Fiadh what made you think that the net needed correction."

"Well" replied Fiadh, "When I was young we used to fly kites, and if they were a little uneven it would not fly as we wanted them to. It would either not get off the ground or dive into the cliff. I always thought that the net was like the kite flying through the sea."

Mogue did not answer for a while and finally replied, "Aye that is the best way to answer the question! You have a good thinking head for a person who has not been fishing for long. I think that you and I will go places."

These words of accolade pleased Fiadh, and he decided that he would endeavour to somehow remain at the fishing as he was pleased with the money he was earning.

Mogue and Fiadh became good friends, and Mogue had begun to discuss and accept his advice. Some of the fishermen would jokingly refer to them as 'dad and the nipper'. However, their friendship grew and Fiadh began to take the boat out fishing if Mogue had to attend to some other business. Fiadh had an excellent memory and could remember the best places to fish, and what was more important where to avoid underwater rocks that could wreck nets.

At times Mogue would say to Fiadh, "My advice to you is save some of your money in the post office, or the bank. Only a fool scatters their money into the four corners of the earth. Remember after every feast there always comes a famine. Save something for the rainy day when you will need it."

Now Fiadh was taking the boat to sea more often than Mogue, and he always returned with a good catch of fish. Some of the fishermen would mirthfully say, "Fiadh could catch a salmon in a bog, where no fish was ever seen."

The weeks rolled into months and into years, and now Fiadh was considered one of the best skippers of a fishing boat. As he was always in the top bracket of money earned by any boat in the harbour. The question in the harbour always was, how much fish did Fiadh catch today, or how much money was earned by the crew of Fiadh's boat? It now became a contagious obsession with Fiadh to have the biggest catch of fish in the port.

An old woman, Crom Dubh, would come at times to the harbour asking for a feed of fish. At times she would state the fish she wanted, and the fishermen would always oblige her with a smile and a laugh. The fishermen believed that to deny anyone a feed of fish was bad luck. This day Fiadh was busy working with his nets. When Crom Dubh asked for a feed of fish, Fiadh angrily retorted, "Can you not see that I am working? Away with you tramp and bother someone else! You have had your last feed of fish from me."

Of course the Crom Dubh was startled and replied, "Curse on you, that you will one day be what you called me. May all my bad luck follow you all the days of your life."

Cundy Rua who was on his small boat was flabbergasted that anyone could refuse an old woman a feed of fish. He shouted, "Hold on a minute Crom Dubh. I have a few fish here and you can take all you want, with my blessings." And he followed her up the pier with the fish.

Crom Dubh stopped and took the fish and thanking Cundy Rua said, "May my blessing of plenty always be with you. And to those who despise and insult me may they also be rejected and reviled. Mark my words before a year and a day has passed the smirk on his face will be changed." And she walked off with the bundle of fish.

Cundy Rua went to Fiadh saying, "God forgive you, whatever came over you chase away poor Crom Dubh? She is an old woman and her blessings or her curse could change anyone's luck."

"Ah" said Fiadh, "Can't you see I was working, and I didn't have time to be everybody's skivvy. Can't you see that the nets are more important than dancing to her tune?"

Fiadh was forever pushing out the boundaries by fishing in turbulent weather. He would laugh when anyone would say, "Perhaps it is to stormy too fish?" He would dismiss their concerns, saying they were 'sunny day fishermen.' But always pride and conceit comes before a fall. One stormy night when the boat was returning home with a load of fish they experienced an unusual storm and the boat was swamped. With the weight of the fish and the equipment aboard, the boat sank like a stone. There were men screaming above the screeching wind. In the dark nobody could see where another was, or if the howling was man or the wind.

Fiadh grabbed a floating board and hung onto it as tightly as he could. He kept shouting for his men but could hear nothing above the shrieks of wind and white water that was breaking over him. Fiadh hoped that his crew had somehow clambered onto something that would save them.

It was a long cold night in the stormy sea as he prayed for salvation, or a miracle. As the sun was breaking at the dawn of the day, he was washed up onto a small strand. Stumbling and falling he made for the high ground hoping that he would find a house or some shelter from the cold. He was tired, but he knew that if he sat down the cold would overcome him and he would never rise again. Fiadh was physically distressed from the cold of the night that was stealing whatever heat remained in his body. He did not know where he was: if it was a deserted island or was it the mainland. He knew that he would need to find shelter and hopefully a fire to warm his shivering body. Fiadh was unaware that he was on Inishnee Island that was surrounded by bare rugged rocks that had wrecked many boats.

Fiadh was almost at his wit's end when he heard a man calling for his dog in the distance. The sound of a human voice gave him a surge of strength and the impetus to walk on. He began to shout and wave his hands high in the air and continued yelling.

Eventually the man on the island who was attending his sheep saw the outline of what could have been a man, or a ghost in the distance and he called his dog back. He wanted the dog with him if it was someone that could be dangerous. He was aware of the storm last night and from experience there had been many ships wrecked on this shore line before. His immediate impression was that it was a man whose boat had been lost in the gale. He could be from this country, or he could be a foreigner. The old people would say, "You should never save a person from the sea, because if you did the sea would claim your life or one of your family. But if the person made it to the shore you should give them succour and a place at your fireside. As the person came closer he quickened his pace of walking to reach the man. Then he yelled out, "Who in under heavens are you and where have you come from?"

Fiadh staggering called out, "It is me Fiadh O'Boyle! Our boat was out fishing last night and we were heading to the harbour when we were caught in the storm. Where am I, and who are you?"

The man replied, "My good man you are on Inishnee Island, and I am Parick Gannon. How in under God did you survive last night? You know not even the devil would be out through that storm. Come on man until we get you into the house before you die in front of my two eyes."

Fiadh was pleased that he had survived, but the next thought that came into his mind was the crew of the boat. He was helped to walk the last distance to the house. There was a morning fire burning and he was delighted with the heat that engulfed him. Parick Gannon had his clothing changed quickly and now he was in dry warm clothing, with a bowl of warm porridge sitting in front of him. Fiadh didn't realise how hungry he was until he started to eat.

Then Fiadh said hurriedly, "My crew! Is there any word of them? Have you any word what happened to them?"

Parick Gannon's wife Aoife looked at Fiadh and mumbled, "What do you mean your crew?"

Fiadh swiftly answered, "You know that our boat was lost last night and I was wondering if you have heard any word about them. I hope to God that they survived. Was there any word of it on the radio? Could I phone Scalpamore to speak to someone?"

Aoife hastily retorted, "My man you will do nothing until you rest. We will send our boy Shamie to Jimmie Hudie's, they have a phone, and they will do all the calling. Jimmie Hudie knows who to contact as he is the best fisherman on the island."

But uttered Fiadh, "I was the skipper of the boat! I am responsible and I must do something."

Aoife with a smile replied, "You rest yourself and let others do what must be done. You can't turn back time, can you! We will do what is necessary. This is not the first tragedy we had on this island of Inishnee. God knows, we had our share of them, hadn't we Parick?"

The news spread through the island with phone calls coming and going to Scalpamore. The islanders searched the shore and the lifeboat was dispatched to search the sea. The search continued for weeks by the lifeboat and the fishermen, but only bits of debris washed up on the shore.

The islanders of Inishnee were reluctant to take Fiadh on their boat to the mainland. They feared the old superstition of the sea claiming a life: that if they carried him in their boat then they or one of their family, could be claimed by the sea. There was always an excuse by the islanders for not taking Fiadh to the mainland. Eventually the lifeboat landed on the island and Fiadh was glad to be taken off.

There were the usual inquiries repeated about what had happened that night. Then there was the statutory inquiry about the night and questions if it was wise to be at sea in a storm? The same questions were asked of Fiadh continuously, 'Did you hear the weather forecast?" or "Was it safe to go to sea?" One of the wives of a man who was lost accosted him and said, "You have drowned my husband and my children's father. I hope that you rot in hell! You bloody murderer."

Fiadh could get no respite from the questions or the verbal abuse that was thrown at him. And he began to drink to hide the distress of that night.

Some people would say to him, "Do you think that it was the curse of Crom Dubh that sunk your boat? If you had given Crom Dubh a feed of fish, do you think that the boat would be sitting safe and sound at the pier today?"

Fiadh could get no respite from the questions or the verbal abuse that was continuously thrown at him. And he began to drink more to hide the distress of that night. In an effort to escape the perceived indignity he went to England where he could hide in a crowd. Here he could hide his distress and his dignity with drink. At times he would recall the day he refused Crom Dubh a feed of fish. This thought was always in his memory when he awoke from a nights drinking. His money was soon spent and then he began to look for work as a labourer.

Whatever money he earned was soon expended, as was his dignity. And now he would go to pubs where he would scrounge for a day's work or a drink. Now his only asset was to tell of the night that his boat and crew was lost. He began sleeping some nights in a hostel, or as they say, rough. This was sleeping on some building site or in a park. At times he made up a fishhook with flies, which he made from scraps. On some of the building sites he would arrive with a fish that was caught in the park lake. He would jokingly say there is no need to go hungry when you can catch a fish. The policemen got wise to him, and some who were anglers would let him off with a warning, if he would make a fly-hook for them. The police were reluctant to arrest him as they knew of his downfall. Some policemen would at times say that if he was in the army he would be described as suffering from 'post-traumatic stress disorder' or shell shock. His reputation of making hook with an artificial fly was known by many weekend anglers.

Some of his neighbours and those from around Glenneamhe or Scalpamore at times would have him washed up and dressed in clean clothing, and found him a job for, hoping that he would reform. He would promise them that he would never drink again. However, the cursed drink had a hold of him and if they met him again, it was the same old story. "If you buy me a drink this will be my last, I promise."

Some people would say, "You are wasting your time trying to reform an alcoholic."

And Fiadh would continue to cadge a drink and cigarettes from the workmen or anyone who would listen to him about how lucky they were to be warm and dry on a cold winter's night. Whenever people spoke about angling or the best place to fish Fiadh's reply was, "In the glen of heaven where I was born that is the best place to fish trout in Ireland, or the whole world. That is where Colmcille blessed it and cursed our enemies."

The barman would sometimes say, "It's a pity that he would not go there; his old yarn will drive us all to hell, listening to him. Fiadh could drive a mill with all of his old guff about fishing. And as he says; 'the night he was drowned."

However, there is always someone who finds interest in what others term rubbish. One man's rubbish is another's person's treasure.

Claude was a freshwater fisherman from London who, on retirement from the army, travelled to various countries to fish. Angling was always his passion, and he sought places that were unknown to other fishermen. Years ago he had been to Scotland, and to his surprise he went to a lonely glen and found a spot on the river where he caught a few large fish. This catch gave him pleasure and he bragged about it in a hotel in London; of the enormous fish which was reported in many of the papers. Before long that river bank was swarming with anglers, and he couldn't find a space for himself to fish. The local anglers were also upset with him for broadcasting about the river they fished. And now they couldn't find a place along the river bank for them to fish. Whenever he spoke to the locals, they either did not reply or referred to him as, "big mouth." Now he could not fish or get a civil word from the people in the area. And to make matters worse, the landlord raised the price to fish on the river. The local anglers did not want him in their company. He swore that if he ever again found a good spot on any river he wouldn't tell another living soul. His sole intention in life was to find a place that was unknown to other fishermen. From experience he knew that local fishermen knew good places on rivers and lakes to fish, but they refrained from telling strangers. The locals would always keep those good spots on a river a secret for themselves. His endeavour now was, if fate favoured him, to find a country man that could lead to his Eldorado.

One night Claude happened to visit a pub that was full of Irish workers. Many of them spoke about upcoming jobs that might start sometime in the future. The men in the pub only seemed to be interested in work, and singing Irish songs of emigration. Any time he spoke about fishing nobody was interested in having a conversation with him. But as he put his hat on his head that had a few hooks sticking in it, the voice of a man who looked like a destitute tramp uttered, "What are you doing with wet flies hooks in your hat on a good night like this? There is no fast flowing water around here."

Claude looked at the man, who had perhaps a few week's beard on his face, and whose clothing was ragged and unwashed. But the remark of a wet fly-hook had caught his attention as few people would know what a wet fly-hook was. Much against his instant dislike of this man, as he was an ex-army man who disliked untidiness or an unshaven face, he decided to play him along for his own amusement and see if he knew anything about fly-hooks. He thought that he would speak to him about a few unlikely fly-hooks to test him.

Claude with a glimmer of a smile on his face retorted, "Ah I see that you know what a wet fly-hook is. Tell me my good man what is your opinion of the 'black zonker'? And tell me, what is your name?

The untidy man replied slowly, "You can call me 'Donegal' or Fiadh, whatever you wish, and I will answer to you by any name you mention! As for the 'black zonker', or the 'klinkhamer' or the 'black head bloodworm', they are only for lazy fishermen who don't know how to tie a fly for the day, or for the pool they are fishing. Do you want me to rhyme off a list of flies that are for sale in shops and all that they can catch is the person that are spending their money?"

The rapid response had Claude captivated with wonder and delight, and he said, "Oh Fiadh, may I please ask you, where did you learn about fishing and flies?"

Fiadh paused for a while before answering, "Where did I learn about tying flies on hooks or fishing? I don't know which I learned first. We always fished and we made our flies out of what we had. There was never any running to shops to buy what could be made in our own home. It was only the amateur fisherman that had boxes full of flies, and nothing in their head."

Claude quickly retorted, "My good man Fiadh, would you tell me how to tie a fly-hook?"

"Not now" said Fiadh, "I am too tired and my mouth is too dry I must leave."

Claude often heard of old men who tied fly-hooks and he was aware that their skill was a dying art, which he would love to learn. If this vagrant had any knowledge in its head, he wished to acquire it. By his looks he was not going to live a long life. If he could talk him into parting with his wisdom before he died, it would be a tremendous bonus for him.

Claude hastily said, "Fiadh, won't you have a pint before you leave, your company is interesting.

Fiadh snapped, "Aye I suppose that one more won't poison us. With another pint maybe I will sleep better."

With the fresh pint in Fiadh's hand he savoured the taste before he drank a large gulp from the glass, smiling as if he was dying of thirst.

Claude said, "Fiadh you must have been dry the way you swallowed that drink."

"Aye" whispered Fiadh, "I was needing that. It is to chase away the ghosts that come to torment me at night. I can't get a night's sleep on an empty stomach."

Claude quietly replied, "What are the ghosts that are tormenting you. Surely you, a grown man, are not superstitious or afraid of anything?"

Fiadh snapped, "Who said I was superstitious? I see the ghosts of the men that I fished with coming at night asking me why are their bodies lying on the bottom of the cold sea. I see the evil that came to other families, and I can't lift my hand to help them. The curse of Crom Dubh is on me and will remain until the day I die"

Claude replying meekly, "I am sorry that you have lost any of your friends. I presume that the loss was at sea. Dismiss any old curses; we are all at times cursed. You are alive and well, that is all we can expect from life, isn't it?"

Fiadh bellowed with tears running down his face, "Alive and well! I am the living dead that should be with my friends on the bottom of the sea. I will have no peace, until the day that death claims me. And I am too much of a coward to end it. But one day, that bright light of death will shine on me!"

Claude was used to seeing men with the horror of death on their face, from his time in the army. And he knew if they could talk about it to others it could at times annul their fear and anxiety.

Claude replied Fiadh, "We all in our life had friends that died. I myself as a soldier had men dying all around me in my work. We must learn how to honour those who have perished, and remember them by keeping their memory alive. We all must pass on through this narrow vale of life's pain and come out of it smiling. The dead are the dead and will never walk this land again."

With this Fiadh left his unfinished glass of beer on the bar and hurried out the door crying saying "Never, never!"

Claude was befuddled and ashamed. He never wanted to upset anyone and he felt that he had stymied his objective of finding out what the man knew. He did not know what the people in the bar would think of him. And he did not want to burn any bridges of information.

Turning to the barman he said, "It was never my intention to upset Fiadh. I wish that I had the time to apologies to him for anything that I may have erroneously said. It was never my intentions to upset or insult him, or any man."

"Ah!" The barman replied, "Leave him alone for a while until he settles down. You know he was a good fisherman. He was the skipper of a boat which sank during a storm. He was the only person to survive by holding onto a board from the upturned boat, through a long cold winter's night. The bodies of the other fishermen were never found.

He could never go to sea again: it must be the nerves that is bothering him. Aye, from one of the keenest fisherman to a broken man. Life is cruel, but life is life, and it is not eternal."

Claude nodding his head saying, "Mabey I should leave him the price of a couple of drinks it may settle him. You know I would love to speak to him again, he seems to know about freshwater fishing."

The barman nodded, "Yes maybe that might help, but he won't come into this pub for at least a day or two. Whenever he comes in here again I will give him a pint and the next night he comes in I will give him another pint. I would advise you if you want to speak to him again never mention the sea or speak about the people who were lost. When he is settled down he will talk all day about nets, salmon or trout. Now my advice to you is to leave immediately before someone with drink in them comes to the wrong conclusion."

Claude said, "Thanks for your advice, and would you tell him I apologise most profusely for my impudent rude manners?"

Claude walked out of the pub and he felt that everyone was watching him. Were the men in the pub thinking that I said something disrespectful to Fiadh he wondered. He quickly hailed a passing taxi as he felt that someone might take retribution for a perceived insult to Fiadh.

After two days Claude returned to the pub, but the barman shook his head saying "Fiadh did come in here since. But I hear that he is back in the area and I would expect him to return soon. He was in the pub up the road and was caught drinking another man's beer. Now whenever you come into this pub, and he is in, don't speak to him. Buy him a drink and leave, and the next night you come in here do the same. He will eventually come over to you, to thank you for the drink. Then you can have a long chat with him, but make an excuse and leave. Then the following nights you can have a longer yarn with him. You know that he can be very temperamental at times, but if you accept and allow for his vagary, he can be the gentleman he once was. A neighbour of his says, "He is now like a 'clocking hen' on her nest".

Claude thanked the bartender and departed. Following two days, Claude returned to the bar and saw Fiadh sitting across from him. Claude bought a small glass of beer and followed the barman's advice and sent a drink to Fiadh. He drank and read the paper, drank his beer and quickly left the pub. The next day Claude came into the pub he followed the ritual of buying a small glass of beer for himself, and sending a pint across to Fiadh. Claude sipped his beer, and had a quick read of the paper and departed.

When he entered the pub again, Claude found a position in the pub where he could see Fiadh, in the mirror. From his training in the army he could read a man's facial expression. Every day the smile on Fiadh's face was getting warmer and friendlier. After sitting down one day Fiadh came over to him with a smile from check to check saying "Thanks for the pints."

Claude said, "Ah that is all right. You know I must be funny: I hate to be drinking alone even if the person is not in my company. People say that I am a bit odd and I suppose maybe they are right in their thinking. But who cares. Maybe the world needs a few head cases like me. I suppose the years in the army were no help to me."

Fiadh said, "Do you mind if I sit down at your table."

Claude with a broad smile on his face said, "Certainly! I would appreciate your company. You know, I have been thinking about things that has happened to me in my life. My granddaughter is in hospital and I must go to visit her. People say that I should not worry, but it is easier said than done."

Fiadh, with a look of surprise responded, "I hope it is not serious. What is wrong with her? I hope it is not bad. She must be very young as you are not an old man."

Claude with his charming smile replied, "It is woman's thing, you know. Some people say I should not be worrying or talking about it. But as a grandfather and a man there are things that are difficult to talk about."

Fiadh with a look of sympathy replied, "With Gods help everything will be alright. I will say a little prayer for her, that she will get better."

"Ah thanks Fiadh. You know your words of wisdom and kindness have made me feel better already. Now I have to go visit her in the hospital. But you have lifted a load of worry of my shoulders. I would appreciate if you did not mention our conversation to anyone. Can we keep this between us? Do you know something Fiadh, I must be odd, because I cannot express my feelings to others. Maybe I hold my torments so tight that they choke me. Now good bye and thanks for talking to me." With this Claude walked out the door and left Fiadh sitting with his pint of beer.

Claude's rapid departure left Fiadh to feeling sorry for him. Perhaps he got the wrong impression of him and all he wanted was a wee chat. In his memory he contemplated about the people he knew. Some would dance on your shoulders when you are down, while others who you thought were selfish and egotistic would come to help when you needed it most. Maybe all that Claude wanted was someone to talk too. And at times when you need a friend there is no one there to listen.

Claude did not visit the pub until the second day as he wanted to give Fiadh time to think. If he was not pressing Fiadh for information he considered, he would be more likely to talk.

When Claude entered the pub Fiadh was sitting with a pint glass with hardly enough beer in the glass to bless himself. He was also attempting to roll a cigarette from the butts that other people cast away.

"Good morning Fiadh" said Claude. "How are you on this fine sunny morning? The sun is bright in the heavens and the birds in the sky are dancing to some merry tune. Barman, would you serve a drink to Fiadh and me and a packet of cigarettes?"

With the pint of beer in front of Fiadh the smile on his face lit up, and was now partly shrouded with smoke.

Fiadh had a smile on his face as he sipped his beer and said, "Claude you are in good humour this morning. Have you received good news?"

Yes, retorted Claude. "It is what you may say is good news, she is been transferred to another hospital to recuperate. You know I must have upset you and every other person I met. I was in such a state of worry that my head was not thinking right. I sincerely apologise to you if any of my word upset you. I am truly sorry."

Fiadh slowly said, "Claude you did not upset me or anyone. All you did was to buy me drinks. I don't know what you are talking about. There is nothing for you to apologise for. You are the most honest man that anyone could meet."

"Thanks for your kind words" replied Claude. "However, I know my weakness. Wasn't it Napoleon that said a general should know his enemy's strength and weakness, but a good general should know his own strength and weakness? My weakness is that when anything goes wrong I panic and let my mouth say things that I am not proud of. I must learn to hold my words because a spoken word can never be taken back."

"But Claude I can assure you that you never insulted me. All you did was to buy me drinks and give me a smoke. You are a gentleman. As long as your granddaughter is getting better that is all that matters, isn't it?"

Claude smiling said, "Fiadh it is you that is the kind gentleman, you sat and listened to me when others would not have me for company, not even for a pension. I know that at times I must have upset some people. They say that big men don't cry, but I was crying inside behind a veil of vanity. Perhaps this sound silly to you."

"No retorted" Fiadh, "We all have some hidden heavy burden to carry through this life, which was not what we wished for. If I could roll back time; I would never be where I am now. I know that is not going to happen, and I will be found dead some morning. The curse of Crom Dubh is on me until the day I die. But I would be happy if my soul could once again return to sit on the river bank above 'the white horses tail' to watch the trout gliding around the dark stones, and if my soul could watch the lark as it darted to and fro, in the clear morning sky.

To see 'the white horses tail' once again, that would be my heaven, because that place is the heavenly glen."

Claude sipping his drink said "Fiadh, I will tell you something. I sat on the river bank with my fishing rod casting a line with a safety pin on it. I wanted to go through the motions of fishing but did not want to catch a fish. All I wanted was peace and quiet, to indulge in my own thoughts about life. Sometimes I seek a place where I can be alone, but this country is so crowded that it's impossible. The place you describe must be heaven on earth. My wife died seven years ago and now I am on my own. After she died I broke my fishing rods and burned most of my fly-hooks, aye, years of gathering burned in a moments of madness. I suppose you could say that I am in an over ground graveyard, seeking someone who will talk to me."

Fiadh felt sorry for Claude and said, "If you give me some trout hooks, a few feathers and a few spools of silk thread. I will make you some of the finest trout fishing fly-hooks that ever you saw, which I guarantee will catch fish. If you find any pheasants or any wild bird feathers, they would be better than all the rubbish that is for sale in the shops. The only thing that rubbish is good for is to make money for the shops. Oh, and remember blue thread and some cobbler's heelball. A little lick of it would help the hooks, and before we forget, some bicycle valve rubber. And if you have a few small boxes to keep the hooks for dry days or wet day, bring them too."

Claude, with a smile of contentment on his face, eagerly agreed saying, "Certainly Fiadh I will get what you have asked for. I would have more faith in the hooks that you tie, as you have more experience and knowledge of catching fish."

Claude again showered Fiadh with salutation and accolade of what a smart man he was, thinking that 'praise is the payment of a fool.' He was happy at how easy it was to manipulate a man with sugary words that they crave to hear. He bought Fiadh another drink and a packet of cigarettes and stuck a pound in his pocket saying, "Will you do me a big favour and spend the money on a good meal?"

Fiadh thanking him for the money and drink and said, "I will go to the café and have a good feed of fish and chips." Fiadh once again expressing gratitude to Claude over and over again, for the money and beer."

Claude knew he could have a fool searching for snow in the summer, if he could make them believe it was there.

The following night they met in the pub and Claude had all the hooks and accessories that Fiadh requested. As usual Claude bought the beer and they were having a laugh when the barman shouted, "There is a phone call for a Claude! Is that person in the bar?"

Claude jumped up saying, "That is me." And went to answer the phone.

When Claude returned his head was lowered and he said, "I hope that you will excuse my bad manners but I have a little problem to attend to. Could we please meet tomorrow night? Then he stuck a pound into Fiadh's pocket and said have a drink on me."

Fiadh came to the pub next night but Claude did not turn up, and the money that he had was spent on beer. Claude wanted to allow time for Fiadh to finish the work on the hooks. If they were not complete in one day, it was better to allowing an extra day.

Fiadh was sitting in the pub the following night hugging an almost empty glass, and as Claude entered a big smile lit his face. The money he had was spent and there were no one in the pub he could solicit a cigarette or drink from.

Claude said, "I hope that you will forgive me Fiadh, but my granddaughter had a little hiccup, however now everything seems fine. I suppose that you know how a little sickness can alter a man's careful laid plans. Before we get a drink tell me, how are you progressing with the job?"

Fiadh with a demure smile on his face handed Claude two boxes: one box had two hooks, and another with one hook, saying "I was unwell and someone must have stolen all the stuff you gave me. There is nothing but crooks around here, they would steal the milk out of your tea."

Claude was disappointed with what he received. He had expected that he would have boxes of fly-hooks. In his head he was fuming: these hooks would be the most expensive that he ever spent money on. He was annoyed with himself for delaying and for not coming to the pub last night. Perhaps Fiadh has made the fly-hooks and as he was not there maybe he had sold them. He was aware that the promise of a chronic drunkard was as lasting as a fire on ice. Contrary to his inner feelings he would hold his tongue and remain calm.

Claude called the barman saying, "Will you please give us a pint and a glass of beer. Oh and a packet of cigarettes this man must be dying for a smoke. Are you Fiadh?"

There was a big grin across Fiadh's face, as the barman put the drink and the cigarettes on the table in front of them.

"Ah thanks!" said Fiadh as he lifted the glass of beer to his lips. "I needed that. I was parched all day. The man I worked for yesterday and today didn't pay me, and now he is gone away on his holidays. Maybe I will never get as much as a penny from him, there is nothing but crooks everywhere you look."

"Aye" said Claude, "I know all about people that steal and lie. As you say they are everywhere. But, what are you doing tomorrow Fiadh?"

Fiadh looked at him and was stuck for words, he didn't expect that question. "Well!" he retorted, "I suppose I will look for work somewhere, but I don't know where. You know that sometimes work can be hard to get."

"Well" uttered Claude quietly, "How would you like to work for me for a few days. I can pick you up in the morning. Will we say at 8 o'clock outside this pub? I am not an early bird. Will that be OK with you?"

"Aye" stuttered Fiadh, "That would be great, what kind of work had you in mind?"

"Well it won't be too hard work." uttered Claude. "I need a man that is trustworthy like you. An honest man like you would suit me, that is if you agree?"

"Yes" declared Fiadh, "That will be fine. I can do all the work you want; I can work with concrete or wood. In my home place of Glenneamhe, the men there could build stone walls or fix a clock."

"Ah" said Claude "I think you are the very man I want! I must go to see my granddaughter; you know how we all have to obey. See you in the morning Fiadh and oh, we will talk again in the morning."

Next morning Claude sat outside the pub until perhaps closer to 9 O clock than 8. When Fiadh arrived he had the as usual excesses about someone stealing his clock and his food.

"Aye" said Claude, "That is alright, you know I am feeling a little hungry myself this morning. Will we go to the café and have a good breakfast? You know an empty bag will not stand up on its own."

When they had a good breakfast Claude said, "Let's see how the men from your area can work." and they went to an empty shed that Claude had obtained. The only furniture in it was a bench and a couple of chairs.

Fiadh was unsure and perhaps a little nervous and said, "What kind of work have you a mind of doing here?"

Claude said, "Sit down and relax and we will do the kind of work you spoke about."

Claude produced boxes of hooks, bags of feathers and yards of bicycle valve tube. When he bought the accoutrements for Fiadh, Claude had purchased a replica for himself. His motto was, always be prepared for the unexpected.

Fiadh was taken aback as he did not expect this and was shocked and surprised, especially by something that he had not anticipated. With a wide opened mouth, he said, "Is this the kind of work you wanted me to do? I thought that you wanted me do something like digging or building walls?"

Claude with a broad smile replied, "Ah Fiadh I thought that digging holes in the ground or building walls was beneath your expertise. You that is an expert fisherman would require something more fitting to your expertise. I would not insult your proficiency to degrade you with a menial task, you that has knowledge that would be equivalent to the best university qualifications."

"Ah" uttered Fiadh "That was in the past, before I lost my boat and crew. Now all I want to do is forget about the past. If only I could go back in time, there would never be the curse of Crom Dubh on my shoulders.

Claude snapped, "What is the story about the boat and crew and the silly curse, you never told me anything about it. What happened? And who or what is Crom Dubh."

Fiadh lowered his head and remained quiet and did not respond.

Eventually Claude asked him again. "What is wrong, you have gone all quiet? This is not like you, who was always a great raconteur. What have I said that has irked you? Let me apologise."

"Leave it alone." muttered Fiadh, "I do not want to speak about it! We all have to carry our own cross and endure our burden our shame."

There was an eerily silence as Fiadh slowly began to tie the feathers to the hooks. Claude was reluctant to speak, as he had what he wanted. The many fishhooks which were decorated with different colours. It reminded him of his Bible lessons, of 'Joseph's coat of many colours'. He was flabbergasted at his dexterity. Those rough unwashed coarse fingers were weaving the spools of thread around his fingers like a musician playing a piano. The fingers moved so fast that he could follow or learn from him.

Eventually Fiadh spoke, "Is there anything to drink. I am parched with thirst; my mouth is as dry as the Sahara Desert."

Aye responded Claude, "I also could do with a drink. I think that there is a kettle here and I will brew us up a nice cup of tea. They say that tea was discovered in China in 2,737 BC by the Emperor She Nung. What do you think of that legend Fiadh?"

Fiadh in hastily riposte, "I hope that I don't have to wait that long for a drink." And remained silent.

Claude did not reply, but the kettle was soon boiling and he made tea. He had milk, sugar and some buns. His army training of being always ready was now paying dividends. He was not going to run the risk of leaving and going to a cafe, fearing that Fiadh would want to go to some pub. In a short while he had two mugs of tea ready which he presented to Fiadh.

"Now what do you think of that Fiadh! You know I was getting a little thirsty myself. Ah, there is nothing like a nice mug of tea to relax a man."

Fiadh with his head lowered replied sluggishly. "Aye, I suppose you are right."

"Well," replied Claude, in an attempt to try to talk him out of his melancholy. "You can certainly do what you say. How many have you made now? I would say that it must be dozens, what do you think?"

Fiadh nodded the head and replied, "Aye, whatever you say yourself."

Claude was aware that his enquires had somehow upset Fiadh, and did not wish to exacerbate the situation or frustrate him further. From his bag he produced a small box of cigars and said, "I think that I will have one, it must be years since I had a cigar. Some doctors say that cigars are better for you than cigarettes, but I suppose that it is all tobacco!" He opened the box of cigars and slowly lifted one out and was sniffing it.

Fiadh snapped, "Are you going to smoke it or snuff it? You remind me of an old priest saying mass with all your antics."

Claude was pleased that his shenanigan had stirred Fiadh out of his melancholic anguish, and he handed the box to him saying, "Sorry I must have been spaced out of it, living my youth. Here man, let's have a puff."

Fiadh had the cigar in his mouth and the smoke rising out of it like a haze of mist. He began to recite a poem,

"I pray we reach the land of Erin,
We who are riding upon the great, productive, vast sea.
That we be distributed upon her plains, her mountains, and her valleys;
Upon her forests that shed showers of nuts and all the other fruits,
Upon her rivers and her cataract,
Upon her lakes and her great waters,
Upon her abounding springs.
That there we may hold our fairs, and equestrian sports, upon her territory."

Then he lowly cried. "I will never see it in this life!"

Claude said. "Where will you not see Fiadh, are you alright?"

"Aye" responded Fiadh, "It is that my mind was wandering back to my childhood. I know that the 'white horses tail' is now in darkness, and I will never see the sun shining on it again."

"Where is this place Fiadh? And why do you say that you won't see it. We can always change our life if we wish to."

Fiadh promptly replied, "It is where Colmcille blessed the people and the glen, and cursed our enemies. Whenever anyone comes to the glen with evil intent, the curse will fall on their shoulders and bring them down. From this I know what is ahead of me, and the scourge that is on my soul from Crom Dubh."

"Ah!" uttered Claude, "that is old wife's tales. Whoever told you that! There is nothing in it."

"Ah" replied Fiadh, "I need no Druid to tell me my future. When I came to this country on the boat I was drunk out of my mind and didn't know where I was. You know if I step aboard a boat something terrible could happen. The sea was claiming me as its sacrifice and I escaped; but I am a wanted man by the sea."

"Ah" cried Claude, "That is only a fallacy, I wouldn't believe it: there is no proof. That is only old superstition."

"Well" snapped Fiadh, "Do you believe in God?"

"Yes," cried Claude "there is a God, we all believe that. Everyone should know that there is a God, it is written in the Bible."

"Aye" exclaimed Fiadh, "Written by the hand of man, but not a word written by God. Did you ever think perhaps your God is superstition? Is one person's superstition not as valid as another's? Before you criticize one belief, you should look at your own blemishes."

"Well" replied Claude jovially, "I didn't know you were a philosopher. Your well thought out reasoning could have learned men arguing for years. I can't disagree with your viewpoint, even if it upsets me. But if you had lived when the Roman Church had control, then the Inquisition would have had you burned on a damp fire. Isn't it great that now we can sit and discuss everything in a reasonable manner?"

"Aye" said Fiadh, "Let no man laugh at what they do not know. And, I know what is ahead of me. There is a geasa (obligation) on me."

Claude with a puzzled look on his face said, "What is this geasa. That is one word I don't understand. And I don't wish to be rude by my ignorance or arrogance."

Fiadh was silent for a while and then replied, "The only way I can explain it is that there is a claim or an obligation on my life. I hope that you will forgive me, but I never want to speak about it ever again."

"Aye that is alright" said Claude, "I understand." Claude knew how easy it was to upset Fiadh, and he considered it best to let him alone. If he did not wish to talk about his mental torment, that was his choice.

The two men sat drinking tea, and chatted about football and the price of groceries. After a while Fiadh began to recite or partly sing:

"Up the airy mountain,
Down the rushy glen,
We daren't go a-hunting,
For fear of little men,
Wee folk, good folk, trooping all together;
Green jacket, red cap, and white owl's feather!"

Then he included some old poems in Gaelic.

Is é an trua ghéar nach mise, nach mise,
Is é an trua ghéar nach mise bean Pháidín,
Is é an trua ghéar nach mise, nach mise,
A's an bhean atá aige a bheith caillte."

Claude was fascinated with his ease of switching from English to Gaelic and back again, but he did not wish to upset his contentment by speaking. Claude opened a cigarette packet and lit one for himself and left the packet with a box of matches before Fiadh, without speaking. He was contented to listen to those that were in the English language, some he had never heard before. Those in Gaelic sounded like a mantra to him with their lilting rhyming sounds. At times Fiadh would use the lit end of the cigarettes to burn the thread. Claude was content to sit silently as the work was progressing.

Finally, Fiadh said, "You know my eyes are getting tired looking at the spool of thread. I don't think that I can do any more to day. Maybe tomorrow we could try again."

"Aye I suppose that you are right." replied Claude. "I think that if we do as good tomorrow as today, we can go into full production. Can I pay you tomorrow Fiadh, then you will have a good wage?"

Fiadh hurriedly retorted with an angry look, "I need the sub! What am I going to do for money? I am not a charity. This is not what we agreed!"

"Oh I am sorry Fiadh, it is that I thought that you would want to build it up for a week."

Opening his wallet, he produced a £5-pound note and handed it to Fiadh, saying, "I will pay for the meal in the café, we need to be fed for tomorrow."

Fiadh was quietly raging and said, "I need to go to the toilet."

In the toilet he found two bottles of surgical spirits which he hid under his coat. He tasted it and he thought that tasted like poteen that he had at home. As he left the toilet Claude went in as he said, to wash himself. Fiadh was standing over his work and the fury in him boiled over. Then he poured a little of the spirits over the hooks, and opened the door. When Claude came out of the toilet, Fiadh was standing holding the door open.

Fiadh said, "I don't know what they were at outside, it smells like Jeyes fluid. It is choking me."

Claude nodded his head and replied, "Aye perhaps they were cleaning the drains with disinfectant. The smell will be away in the morning."

They went to the café and Fiadh horridly swallowed rather than ate his meal and uttered, "I will see you."

"Aye" said Claude, "The same time tomorrow, is that all right with you?"

But Fiadh was out the door without waiting to reply. He was upset with Claude, as he thought he was trying not to pay him.

In the pub he told of how, as he said, that partan (crab) was trying to cheat him. It was the story in the pub for the night, and with alcohol and retelling the story expanded. The men in the pub felt sorry for Fiadh and bought him drinks. With the retelling of the tale to each other the story was, that he had not been paid for his work.

Next morning Claude was outside this pub from 8.O clock until after 12 O clock. He assumed perhaps Fiadh was full of drink and he would come back tomorrow. Next morning Claude was as usual outside the pub, but there was no sign of Fiadh that day or the next. Eventually he went in to the pub to enquire of the barman. The barman looked at him and said, "You! You are barred from this pub, get out before someone kills you."

As he was going out the door shaking his head an old man flung his beer at him and said, "You ****** you have poisoned Fiadh."

Claude thought it wise to disappear, as the looks from the people in the pub left him in no doubt that a careless word could inflame a fire of hatred. He made enquiries to the police of what they knew. He was told that Fiadh died of alcoholic poisoning, in the park. They said that they found empty containers of industrial alcohol beside him. When asked what he knew about it his reply was, "At times he made a few fly-fishing hooks for me. But he always lost most of the hooks. I know he pilfered some of them. But whatever money he was getting for hooks he stole from me, or who he was selling them to, I don't know. I did not like to upset him by questioning him too closely; you know the way it is with drunkards."

Fiadh was soon forgotten by the police as another statistic to be filed away and forgotten.

However, his neighbours from his home place did not forget. The stories they received were dramatized about a man, who gave him poison. Anyone with the name Claude would always be suspect and unwelcomed in Scalpamore or Glenneamhe.

Sometime latter Claude decide he would come to Ireland for a little angling. He remembered how Fiadh was always talking about a lake in a glen somewhere, which was good for fishing trout. He knew that it was in County Donegal, but Donegal was full of glens. He travelled to many places with a glen in the name. He would follow the rivers or streams to their source but could not find this elusive lake. Whenever he spoke to anybody about Fiadh he was answered with a multitude of questions. Like, "Who are you and where did you meet Fiadh, and what is your name?" The demeanour and facial expression of the person changed when he said that he knew Fiadh, or that his name was Claude. People would say they did not know of any such place and tended to send him on a wild goose chase. He knew that he had to change tactics if he had any hope of finding this mysterious lake.

One night Claude went to a quaint old pub on the outskirts of Derry to have a quite drink and lament his failure. While in there he met an old man and they got talking about generalities, and in the conversation he said that he did a little angling. And he told him that he met a man who came from Donegal and he always spoke about a place he called the glen of heaven. "Ah" he said, "I suppose wherever a person was reared in their memory it was heaven. We all recall places of our youth as heaven. I am sure there is no place named heaven."

"What!" said the old man, "There is a place named Glenneamhe. If you take the English translation, it is the 'glen of heaven', and it is in Donegal."

"What!" retorted Claude, and looked surprised. "I could have put money that there was no such place. Let me buy you a drink. When I go home it will be easy for me to win a bet on that. Nobody will believe me. Where is it, I will have to go there to say that I was in the glen of heaven when I was in Ireland. Who would believe me? I will have to buy a camera to show them the place, and say, heaven is in Donegal."

"Aye" exclaimed the old man, "and there is a lake in that glen." He began to give him instructions on how to get there if he followed the Breagmor River. Claude began to write down the instructions and would repeat them to make sure that he was correct. Claude bought the old man another drink as he praised him. It was his intention to leave before someone asked his name. Eventually the old man said, "Tell me, what is your name, sir?"

Claude said, "Some people call me Coalan, Con, and some Clod. I don't care what name they call me, if they don't call me too early in the morning. I must be going if I am to meet my boss or she will kill me, ha-ha."

Claude departed out the door as quickly as he could, playing the part of a fatuous tourist. From his experience in other places his impression was that Ireland was a small place, where everyone knew someone that knew someone. He hoped there was no one who would recognise him from his enquires in the pub.

Next day Claude followed the instruction he was given and he headed for the bridge on the Breagmor River.

The bridge was, as he was told, partly obscured by rocks and shrubs. He had obtained a good large scale map of the area, where he could drive into an area that was closer to the opening of the glen. He hid his car in a sheltered spot that would be obscured from view. Claude had all that he needed, including food and rain gear. This trip would be a scouting expedition. He did not want anybody or anything to upset his carefully laid plans. He followed the river up to the valley until he found the lake of Glenneamhe. It was as Fiadh said, with a towering rock face hidden from view in plain sight. The lake reflected the sky and the cloud, in a multiple of dazzling colours. The peace of the place was broken when he yelled, "Fiadh! You are right this is heaven." The echo reverberated his voice across the valley as if it was hollered by many people out of harmony. Aye, he thought, what Fiadh said: the voice of the people lives on in the glen. Then to amuse himself, he would shout "Fiadh are you here?" and listen to the fading voice. But a sheep farmer who was on the hill and heard the voice, hid and whispered, "Aye, I am here."

Claude heard the whisper but dismissed it as the dying echo of his own voice.

When he was returning to his car, he saw a very old stooped woman close to his car, and planned to speak to her. Perhaps she wanted a lift to some village. He thought that if he could get talking to her he could get some comradery. However, when he looked again there was no one to be seen. It was as if she vanished. Ah he thought, she must have been some silly odd shy country eejit.

What Claude did not know that the sheep farmer was a brother of the man who threw the beer at him in England, and his wife was a sister of the barman in Derry.

Early next morning Claude was on the river bank all geared up for his day's fishing. As he went up the river he fished in the many pools. He caught a few fish, but they were not to his satisfaction, and he proceeded up into Glenneamhe. Here he caught a few nice trout and was determined to keep this spot a secret for himself. He did not want anybody to know of what he found; only he knew this place. He would not tell any other anglers of this place; this was to be his secret fishing spot.

The sheep farmer knew who he was, and thought that he would play a trick on him. He like all mountain sheep farmers had a well-trained dog, which would follow his instructions on a silent dog whistle (which uses high frequency which humans cannot hear).

When Claud caught a nice fish he cried lowly, "That is a nice one Fiadh, are you here?"

The sheep farmer again whispered "Aye, I am here."

Claude was unsure and shouted again, "Who are you?"

The echoes of his voice again rebounded across the valley, then all fell quiet, and only the singing of the small birds could be heard. He assumed that what he had heard was only the whistling of birds. He continued to fish but the nagging doubt of someone else being in the valley was playing on his mind. Owing to the lack of concentration he had a few hooks fowled, which he lost, but he had other hooks which he attached to his gear. Then he caught another large fish and as he was playing the trout into his net he yelled, "That was another nice one Fiadh."

The sheep farmer again whispered, "Aye, that is a nice one."

Claude shouted, "Who are you? Show your face; do you want a nice fish?"

But there was no reply, and the glen again became peaceful, and the only sound he could hear were the small birds that were wheeling and diving in the sky. Then he thought what he heard was the sound of his own voice. He knew that when he caught fish he was in the habit of talking to himself. Aye this is what he heard, the echoes coming off the cliff. He had a little to eat and a smoke and again took the fishing rod to continue fishing.

After midday a dog came to the river bank and sat there for a while before crossing the river. The dog sat on the opposite river bank before wandering off into the bushes. Then the dog returned and sat on the ground for a while before swimming across the river and walking off. Then it returned and sat on the river bank for a while before strolling off again.

This amused Claude and he came back to the same spot on the river next day to see if the dog would return. After a few days the dog came to the river bank and sat down before it swam across the river, and disappeared into the bushes. Then the dog returned and performed the same ritual of sitting on the river bank and then disappearing.

Claude was intrigued as he heard no human voice, nor heard anything that could be construed as the voice of person. He began to wonder if it could possibly be a ghost dog. However, he dismissed this idea as superstition, but the thought remained in the back of his mind. He returned to the same spot in the river for a number of days but all remained tranquil with no sign of the dog. Then he assumed the behaviour of the dog was merely an isolated incident of a stray dog, and began to cast his line hopefully to catch a big fish. He, akin to all zealous anglers, had his scales and camera which were to record a mighty fish. As he cast his line into the water, the dog came back again and sat on the bank. He thought that the dog could frighten the fish away and went to the dog saying, "Nice doggy come here."

The dog bared his teeth and growled and now Claude was fearful. He was aware that wild dogs could be vicious, and he slowly backed off as quietly as he could. When he was at his spot on the bank of the water he yelled, "Who are you! Could you please control your dog? Can we have a wee chat?"

There was a prolonged silence for a while and then a low murmur, "Aye, I am here."

Claud yelled "Can we talk? I would like to have a chat and a smoke with you." But there was no reply no matter how many times he cried out. The only voice he heard was the echo of his own voice. Claude began to think that there was some madman of a hermit living in the mountains and that this was his dog. He knew that barmen know all that was going on in the area, and next evening he went to the pub.

Claude went into a local pub and ordered a drink and said that he was on holidays and enjoying a spot of angling.

"Aye" said Andy the publican, "This is a good country for angling with all the lakes and rivers.

And where have you tried?" asked Andy, "There are plenty of lakes and rivers all around this area."

Claude replied "I followed the river Breagmor up to a nice lake sheltered in the hills. It has beautiful scenery and I don't know what I enjoyed the most, the fishing or the specular view of the lake."

"Aye" replied Andy, "That must have been Glenneamhe you were in; was it? Years ago many families were living there, but now it is deserted, not even a living soul is living there now. Only the ghosts of the departed are left there. There is plenty of scenery there, if they could eat it nobody would have to leave the mountains."

Claude said to Andy, "I was up the hill, but there was a strange dog on it and I don't know if it was cross or wild. Who would have a dog on that hill? Is it some sheep farmer's?"

Andy was naturally careful about strangers asking any questions about his neighbours, and would always be cautious about them. Andy was going to ascertain why the stranger was inquiring about dogs. Was it that he was inquiring about dog licenses, or was it that he wished to take court proceedings against some of his neighbours? Or was he that man who poisoned Fiadh in England?

Andy replied, "And what kind of dog are you interested in. Are you intending to buy a dog, or are you selling dogs?"

No responded Claude. "I saw a dog up in the hills and I was wondering if you knew where the dog came from, or who might know who the owner was. The dog seemed to be cross and could bite someone."

Andy retorted, "That is sheep country, and anyone who has sheep would have a dog to help them handle the sheep. You know this is not like a city. People don't keep dogs as pets. In the hills they keep dogs to work the sheep. But no sheep farmer who is worth his salt would have his dog straying, they are too precious."

Claude replied quietly, "I saw a dog that sat on the river bank and swam across the river, and swam back again and disappeared into the bushes. The same thing happened on a few occasions.

"Ah" retorted Andy, "There is nothing remarkable about a dog swimming. All dogs can swim. I suppose that those who live in a city have never seen a dog swimming."

"Nonetheless" said Claude, "I never saw any man with the dog or heard any human voice. It is strange that a dog would be running around on his own."

Shamus Mór was in the bar drinking his pint, smoking his pipe and listening to the conversation without speaking. When Andy gave him a sly wink and said, "Shamus Mór do you know anything about a stray dog on the hills."

Shamus Mór replied, "I heard no mention of any dog running wild on the hills. If there were, it would be shot before now. Maybe that man can't hold his drink."

Claude was ruffled by the answer, as he got no positive reply. In a city people don't know their neighbours. But in this country where the land is devoid of people, they seem to know more people. Claude endeavoured to be persistent like a detective and said, "Oh I like dogs and I have one myself, but I was concerned about any dog without an owner."

"Aye" said Andy, "And tell me did you see anything unusual on the hill?"

"Well" replied Claude, "I didn't see anything out of the ordinary. There were the small birds in the sky. Oh, only a big black bird or raven, that looked as if it flew out of the cliff."

Shamus Mór sluggishly uttered, "And what kind of croak was the raven making. Was it 'gradh gradh' or was it 'grob grob', or was it 'err err'? Think man before you answer!"

Claude responded with a look of disquiet, "What is the difference of the quacking of that ugly black bird. It looked as if it flew out on the cliff face, with its squawking of 'gradh gradh."

Shamus Mór blessed himself and said, "God save us, was it the black macha, the bringer of death, that always comes to claim its prize of death."

"Aye" snapped Andy, "It is not a good sign. You know the day that is tomorrow, it is Samhain."

Claude, with a look of curiosity on his face said, "What is this Samhain, and what do you infer from it?"

All in the bar was quiet until Shamus Mór cleared his throat and uttered, "O God forgive us: you don't know the night that is coming! It is All Soul's Night."

Claude quietly responded, "I don't know what all the fuss about. It was only a big black ugly bird."

"You certainly don't know." snapped Shamus Mór, "That is the night that the dead can come back to help us, or extract vengeance. I heard that the banshee was in the hills, perhaps Fiadh's soul is returning, God save us."

Claude gave a forced laugh and said, "I don't believe all that old rubbish! It is only superstition."

Shamus Mór barked, "You won't believe it until the black macha or raven of death is perched on your shoulders. Now I am away home! I don't want to be in your company when the old hag of death calls for you." And he slammed the door behind as he left the pub, blessing himself.

"What is all that about?" said Claude. "I don't understand what all the fuss is about."

"No" said Andy, "you don't. God help and forgive those that don't know. Now I am closing the bar, you take your drink with you that is dammed, and don't come back under my roof again. The curse of Colmcille is on you!"

Claude was somewhat annoyed and shaken. He was not going to believe it, neither could he dismiss it. His only concern was how to leave this place as soon as possible and never return again.

Claude went home to England, and as the winter lapsed, he would reminisce about his time spent at the lake in Glenneamhe. The more he pondered about the enchanted lake it seemed to cast an invisible spell on him. He was a grown man and in his life, death was a part and parcel of his job. Over the winter he began to analyse his fears. It was not like a sword was hanging by a single thread over him and was ready to fall. The Irish may be superstitious, but he was a man of learning and logical reasoning. Everything has a logical answer and he would follow his cognitive psychology and dismiss any irrational thoughts.

However, Claude had to return to the enchantment lake of Glenneamhe which held him entranced. He knew that the salmon begins to run in February, and he hoped to have his first catch of the year.

When Claude arrived at the lake there was a tree partly on the shore and in the water. He tried to pull it onto the shore but it was heavy, so he pushed it into the water and the wind carried it away from him. He was pleased that now there were no more hindrances to him, and he fished the lake for four days without a bite. Then on the fifth day he hooked a salmon. The salmon was large and like all good fishermen he was letting the line run, and reeling in and walking along the shore. If he could land this fish it would make his holiday. He thought to himself that angling or fencing required both physical and mental dexterity. The salmon was now getting weaker and he was about to land the fish when the line snagged in the tree he cast out into the water. Now he had to pull the tree on to land to get his fish. As Claude cursed and pulled the tree with one hand and the rod in the other, he did not see where he was walking. He slipped on a mossy stone and hit his head and was killed instantly.

Was this an accident, or was the curse of Crom Dubh being transferred to Fiadh's flies? Or did the angry ghost of Fiadh come back to haunt

Claud? Who knows? Perhaps the locals will embellish this story and it will eventually enter into the realms of legend.

Ardnagadai

On the lonely hillside of Ardnagadai, stands a forlorn large house. People say that this house is haunted, as neither man nor animal wish to use it for shelter. The house was not always an eerie place that people avoided. In former years it was an Inn /halfway house that was thronged with folk who stopped there or resided there for the night. At that time 'carters' would transport goods from Derry to the west of Donegal. The 'carters' would stop at various houses for a bite to eat and to water their horses. There was a field connected to every Inn, and for a nominal fee the animals would be enclosed therein for the night. Travelers could buy hay or meal for their animals; the water was free. These Inns had a thriving business as the people who traversed the roadway for business or emigration used it. They usually had to walk to Derry to emigrate, or upon returning from America would generally stop at the Inns for a night's rest. The few people who returned from America or Scotland generally had a little flush of money with them. The wise would dress in sometimes clean but always haggard clothing and refrain from drinking. The unwise would dress in new clothes and brag about all the money they had saved from America. People who were careless could and were robbed by someone who frequented the Inn.

John Sweeney and Paddy Cearnaigh emigrated to America around 1840. John initially worked in New York, in a hotel bar, and envisaged the day that he would own his own pub or perhaps even a hotel. Paddy got a job with a drapery firm and observed the price of tweed clothing. He imagined that if he could send the tweed from home to America, he could make a fine profit. However, the clothing stores would only deal in bulk buying, and required a sample of the tweed before committing to any business. A person would have to invest a lot of money before there was a return on their expenditure, which was beyond his ability. John Sweeney and Paddy Cearnaigh would at times meet and discuss how they might gather the finances required to set up a business. They were aware of the 'gold strike' in California and headed west to hopefully make their fortune.

They worked in the goldmines at Sutter's Creek, California around 1848-55, and struck it rich. They often spoke of how some of the prospectors who struck gold and were careless of their company and how they were robbed and killed. Some people became rich if they refrained from boasting about their wealth. There were those who became fabulously wealthy as a result of their gold find in California. While many people lost whatever savings they had amassed by being luckless, others lost their life to the malefactors who would befriend those who struck gold. The villains would murder anyone who was not cautious. The majority of the people that made money were those that supplied commodities to the prospectors, or murdered those that found gold.

Before their return to Ireland, John Sweeney and Paddy Cearnaigh, purchased a revolver for protection. When one slept, the other stayed awake for protection, until they returned home. They dressed in frayed clothing to disguise the fact that they had money. They were aware of the number of people that were relieved of their wealth and life on their journey. On the voyage from America to Derry they were discreet about mentioning where they had worked in America. On the boat home, if anyone asked them to join them to have a drink, they refused saying that they had joined the Temperance Movement in America, which was formed in 1826. They often said "Only for the Temperance Society they would be unable to pay their passage home". John Sweeney and Paddy Cearnaigh often said, "If you worked as hard at home as in America you could be as well off. In America you were expected to work on the Sabbath if you were to have any decent money".

On the arrival of John Sweeney and Paddy Cearnaigh in Derry, the next problem they faced was how to cross the hills to Scalpamor. They each had a trunk and they wanted to get a 'carter' to transport their luggage home. They met with an elderly carter and enquired the price to transport their luggage home. When he gave them a price they refused, saying that they were not wanting to buy the horse and cart from him, but for the money he quoted they would consider buying it. A young man, Seamus Joe, who was a carter from a town close to their home said that he would sell them his horse and cart for a ticket to America which cost £5, and £25 in cash.

Eventually, after a lot of negotiation on the condition of the horse and the cart, and who was robbing who, the money was to be paid. The deal was made for £10 plus $10 and Seamus Joe would give them two stone of oats for the horse.

The three had a meal in an Inn, shaking hands and wishing each other very good luck. John Sweeney advised Seamus Joe to refrain from drinking until he was in America and had secured a job. Paddy Cearnaigh asked Seamus Joe if he had any schooling and how well he could write.

 Seamus Joe replied: "I was taught by Paddy Anna, and he said that if my family had the money to send me to College, I could become a priest, or a teacher".

"Good" replied John Sweeney, "Have you any preference as to where you are intending to go in America? I will give you some advice if you wish to take it. Remember when you land there, get a job and attend night school. You will need an American school certificate before a potential employer would have any trust or confidence in your educational knowledge. One occupation you should consider joining is the Police. But, to join the Police you would need to be cautious and not get into any trouble with the law. As for luck, you will have to make your own luck, by being cautious and working your brain. You may be aware Seamus that Paddy and I have joined the Temperance Movement in America. We would strongly advise you to consider desisting from drink, as there is always someone praying on people's weakness".

Seamus Joe thanked them for their recommendations and said that he would carefully consider their judgment. He was intending to go to Bayonne, where his uncle John was working. He was sure that his uncle would give him a place to stay and help him find a job.

Seamus Joe retorted "Thanks again for your guidance, but if I may advise you, beware on your journey home. I always travel in a convoy of 'carters'. Maybe you should join up with them, they will be going the same way. And be especially aware when you come to Ardnagadai. There are men in those hills who would pillage or murder anyone who travels alone. I have a good whip under the body of the cart; it is yours. Aye, a couple of hard whips across their back should deter any gadai".

"Ah" replied John and Paddy in unison: "You needn't worry about our safety. In America we had many experience of the charlatans and people who would kill for the pennies in your pocket. We would caution you Seamus to look on everyone as a potential cheat. We had our experience in America, but we are going to try to make a living back in Ireland. We have been homesick and would like to die in the land of our birth. But good luck to you Shamus Joe".

With all their goodbyes said, John and Paddy loaded their belongings into the cart and purchased some bread and cheese for their journey home. They joined with a group of 'carters' who were traveling in their direction of Scalpamor. They would journey with ease, as they had only purchased the minimum of goods in Derry. When asked why they did not purchase a good load and sell it at home, their reply was, "It is better to see what the people want before we spend our money. We will have to wait until the Bank in America transfers our money home. This could take perhaps a week or two and we may have to go to Derry to get our money. We will manage to survive until our money is sent".

The 'carters' were unsure of John and Paddy. Some of the 'carters' said that they must have little or no money. Others replied, "When did you ever see a yank without money. Aye and not even having a good drink when they land in Ireland. The only money they had was spent on a horse and cart". Each of the carters had their own opinion of John and Paddy.

Eventually Paddy and John set off from Derry, heading across the hills to west Donegal. The convoy of carts made steady progress into the hills, until John and Paddy's horse picked up a stone under its shoe. They decided to take the horse to the blacksmith to have the shoe secured. They said that the job should only take a while and they would be able to catch up with the others as they had only a light load, and they would not have to double back to pick up the half load at the bottom of the hill.

The system the carters employed was to carry home the maximum load. This involved unloading part of the load at the bottom of every steep hill. They then progressed up the hill with half the load and would leave it there, and go back down the hill with an empty cart to collect what they had deposited. They had a system that there a few carters always remained at the top and bottom of the hill to protect their consignment. This system was time consuming, but it enabled the 'carters' to transport the maximum load.

One of the 'carters' Neil Frank said, "You will hopefully reach Cannon's before nightfall. We will wait for you there. Old Cannon is a bit of a Bible chewer, but he is as honest as the day is long. He will take the last farthing from you if you owed it. But if he owed it to you he will insist in paying it in full. Aye honest to a fault!"

Cannon sold certain bits of merchandise, perhaps a little cheaper than the next shop, but when he quoted a price it was almost impossible to get him to change it. One day a man was buying a turf spade and shovel from Cannon. The haggling was down to a half-penny and Cannon would refuse to change his price. When the man paid Cannon, the conversation focused on his boy.

Cannon asked the boy a few questions like, "What is your name and age?"

The boy replied "My name is Brian and I had my appendix removed on the kitchen table by Doctor Smyth!"

Cannon replied: "Doctor Smyth is a good God fearing man, you were in safe hands. Were you afraid, Brian?"

Brian replied a little hesitantly, "I was afraid a little until Doctor Smyth said that he read his Bible that morning and quoted in it was, you will arise and walk. Then I was not as afraid, as they say Doctor Smyth never lies".

Cannon smiled and replied: "There is truth in the Bible, it never lies." and handed Brian a silver sixpence saying, "Trust the written word!"

When his father said that was too much to give, Cannon replied, "My deal was with you and my deal with Brian was with him. That boy knows that the truth is in the Bible!"

"Aye" said Neil Frank: "Old Cannon is a peculiar but honest man. Try to make it there for the night. As for Ardnagadai, it is a strange and weird place and as to the owners Mary and Davie Trimble, I wouldn't trust them at the end of a six-foot pole!"

Some people say that, "The house is haunted, but in my opinion it is the living ghost that I would worry about. They used to have quite a number of travellers staying there until Jimmie Maggie disappeared. The last place poor Jimmie Maggie was seen was in Ardnagadai. After that night poor Jimmie Maggie was never seen alive again. Some people contend that his ghost haunts the place. Ah maybe that is all talk, but personally I would not stay in it on my own. However, you should not be delayed too long by the blacksmith to attach a single horse shoe."

When Paddy and John went to the blacksmith's forge, he looked at the horse and said with a grunt, "The shoes are worn and the horse would need a new set of them. I don't do half jobs."

Paddy and John agreed with the blacksmith saying, "It would be as well to have a new set of shoes, as we intend to keep the horse to work for us."

The work on the horse's shoes took up more time than they had anticipated. It seemed unlikely that they would catch up with the convoy, but they headed west across the hill anyway. Paddy opened his trunk and produced a rifle saying, "This will be our insurance. It might be better than a box of St Christopher's medals."

As they were ascending the hill they could see what looked like some men waiting to ambush them. They had many experiences of ambush in America and knew how to avoid them.

Paddy said to John "Stop the cart a minute. I see a rabbit in front of us, if I kill it we will have a meal and it will panic those hiding behind that rock".

Paddy discharged the rifle and the rabbit fell dead. Then he shot at the rock where his would be ambushers were hiding. As he went to collect the rabbit. John began to laugh saying, "Those men that were behind the rock must be the fastest men in Ireland. They are running and scurrying like rats that were set on fire. Aye I don't think that we will have to worry about them this day."

The two shots from a rifle had more persuasion than an argument, or twenty whips.

As they proceeded up the hill they laughed and joked about the incident. However, the light was fading and they knew that they would have to stop somewhere for the night. They could see the outline of Ardnagadai in the distance. They were well aware of its dire reputation, but needed somewhere to stay for the night, as it was beginning to snow.

They inquired about the price of staying for the night and were given a room with a fire where they took their belongings. They then put their horse into a stable after giving it water and oats and buying a handful of hay.

They put their damp clothing around the fire and lay down for the night. They continued their system of one staying awake while the other slept. They each had obtained a pocket watch that was used to divide the time. One would sleep while the other continued to watch. In the early part of the night no creature moved, not even a mouse.

John relieved Paddy, and he continued his lookout for the rest of the night. That night would hopefully be their last night on guard, before they arrived home. The night all was quite except for the hail which was now dancing on the windows. John was reminiscing about their journey home and the villainous people that they had encountered. He was recollecting about those vulpine cunning characters who would smile to your face while attempting to stick a knife in your back. Ah, he thought, he was glad at last to be in the land of saints and scholars, not the land of thieves and robbers. Then John heard the door squeaking open and slow footsteps approaching them.

John reached for his revolver: If it was someone who was attempting to rob him, then they would get a hot bullet as payment.

A hand tapped John's shoulder and he produced his revolver and yelled "Stop! Or you may not live to see the sun rise!"

Paddy, who was sleeping, was woken by the yelp and produced his revolver and struck a match to see what all the commotion was about. He lit a candle that was beside him. However, as the light of the candle illuminated the room there was no one to be seen. Paddy asked John what all the commotion was about.

John replied, "I heard someone opening the door and walking up to me and putting their hand on my shoulder. It definitely was someone or something. I could feel a hand pressing on to my shoulder".

"Ah" retorted Paddy: "Maybe you fell asleep and were dreaming. You know we haven't had a full night's sleep this last few weeks. I put my bag to the back of the door when you dozed off to sleep. The bag is still lying where I left it. If anyone entered the room it was not from that door. This was a precaution so they would hear if someone was attempting to enter the room. "Perhaps John, you should get your sleep I will take the watch for our safety".

There was a little banter between them on who would stay up and guard them for the night. John finally convinced Paddy that he would continue his watch. John took a ball of string from his bag and tied it to the door knob and around the leg of a table. Then he tied the string to his leg, saying, "If anyone opens the door tonight they will have to move me. If anyone pulls my leg tonight they won't be smiling when they receive a bit of hot lead from my 45!"

Paddy eventually settled down again to have his night's rest. John arranged the string so he would be made aware of any intruders. Paddy was now snoring like a saw cutting wood. The hours ticked slowly by as he continued his sentry duty. John began to be dubious of himself.

Did he really find someone attempting to rob him? Or was it that he snoozed into a sleep, and had been dreaming? Then he heard the door opening and the string began to tug his leg. He waited until the person was a few steps into the room when he lit a match with one hand and produced his revolver with the other. He shouted "Stop or I will shoot." As he lit the candle the owner of the Inn became visible, standing there with a knife in his hand. By now Paddy was awake and had his gun pointing at the Inn keepers, Davie and Mary Trimble

Paddy said, "If you don't have a good excuse for entering this room with a knife, I will send you to meet your maker."

The Inn keeper's wife Mary was standing behind Davie, with another knife in her hand, and she cried out. "Don't shoot, we were only seeing if you were warm, and if you wanted an early breakfast."

Paddy shouted: "If the pair of you don't drop those knifes that are in your hands, my pet, the 45, will drop the both of you."

There was a clatter of knives as they fell on the floor. Davie and Mary were shaking with fright. They never had to look into the barrel of a gun before and were trembling with fear. The unexpectedly rapid response to their entrance left them stuttering with profound trepidation. The Trimble's were unaware of anyone who had ever pointed a gun at them before.

Mary Trimble stammering uttered "For god sake don't shoot, we meant you no harm. I was going to cut some bread for your breakfast; I swear."

Paddy bawled: "What were the two knifes for? Are you going to cut bread for an army? Perhaps that is what happened to poor Jimmie Maggie. Did he get his throat cut instead of the bread? Maybe you were going to give us the same treatment that Jimmie Maggie received!"

"No" retorted Mary: "I swear we never intended to harm you, it is that we are early risers. The day will be breaking in a little while. We were going to get you an early breakfast, we know that you have a long road to travel to your home."

Paddy interrupted their excuses and said: "Davie go and get our horse ready. You harness the horse to the cart. Get everything ready or I will shoot you and put this place on fire."

"Wait" snapped John. "Could we trust this man to harness the horse? I don't think so. Perhaps we should tie them up and we can harness our horse ourselves. Now where is your hurricane lamp? We will need it to get our horse ready for the road."

David and Mary were securely tied up. Then John and Paddy went to the stable and harnessed the horse and yoked the cart. They gave the horse a decent feed of oats as they knew it was still a long distance to home. With their belongings secured in the cart they untied Davie and Mary before heading away. John left a half-crown on the table saying, "This is for the hurricane lamp. We, unlike you, don't steal,"

Taking the hurricane lamp John walked before the horse as it was still dark. John said, "It is only right for me to walk, as you Paddy had a disturbed sleep".

After an hour or so the dim light of dawn was rising from the east, and John could extinguish the hurricane lamp. Now he could sit on the cart and rest. In the distance they could see the outline of Cannons house. It was a welcome sight to see as they could get a warm breakfast. They were hungry, but couldn't stay at Ardnagadai a minute longer than necessary.

On arrival at Cannons, 'the carters' were only stirring from their rest, and were surprised to see them.

Neil Frank who was eating a bite of breakfast said "In under God! Where were you since we left you? Don't tell me that you were on the road all night? Or were you trapped by the fairies and only now escaped?"

"Well" retorted John, "What we experienced last night! The fairies would be an improvement on the anguish we endured. Perhaps it is better not to talk about what transpired at Ardnagadai, but I would not wish it on my worst enemy. Neil Frank! I thought that you were a little sore on that place. However, I will never set foot inside that door again as long as I live. Mr. Cannon, if you would be so kind as to give us a breakfast of anything, for we have not eaten this day. We shall not speak evil of those things which we do not know."

"Aye" said Cannon: "Let not judge any man, for one day we will all be judged for our transgressions. Now sit down at my table and eat, but thank the Lord that has given us food and good health. Disapprove of no man while you are under my roof for evil begets evil, and kindness brings the blessing of God on man."

John and Paddy were aware that Cannon was a man of his word. If he said he didn't want any discussions in his house he meant it, and he would quickly evict anyone who disregarded his convictions. No man who was under his roof or who would wish to return would upset him. None at the table wished to incur the wrath of Cannon, so there was only small talk around the table. It was wise to be cautious and frugal with unkind words if you ever wished to visit this house again. Cannon served as much porridge and bread as a man could eat for breakfast. The house was known for its value for money. So only family discussions were aired at the table.

All 'the carters' were making ready their horses for the final trip home. The road from now would be getting easier, as most of it was downhill. There were only three very steep hills to climb and they would with ease reach their destination. The 'carters' again asked John and Paddy about what had transpired at Ardnagadai. However, each time John said that they had given their word to Cannon that they would not speak about Ardnagadai until this day had passed.

With a light load John and Paddy did not, like the other 'carters', have to unload their load at the bottom of the hill. They continued uphill and guarded what the 'carters' unloaded on the top of the hill. They had privacy to talk as they waited for the 'carters' to carry out their work. They discussed their night in Ardnagadai. Was it that the ghost was warning them about the danger they were in? "It was bizarre John that you were tapped on the shoulder before the Trimbles entered the room."

Paddy said to John: "Why are we keeping it a secret? Couldn't we tell a little of our experience?"

John replied, "If we are to buy some business it is better that we keep something for their appetite. People will find a reason to visit us if they think they can get a bit of juicy scandal. Perhaps it is best for us to say that we think that the house is haunted. You know what some people say: less is more."

"Aye" responded Paddy: "We will certainly need an advantage if we buy some business and encourage people to visit our business. John have you something in mind."

John answered slowly and said, "Perhaps a pub or a hotel. They say that the train will soon be coming. What have you in mind Paddy?"

"Well" replied Paddy: "As you know my father and my uncles are weavers, however the people that were buying the tweed from my father were making all the profit. Perhaps I will get a market in America or England. Then I could sell wholesale weaving and knitting to the market and cut out the middlemen. Working for a living is a mug's game. However, when we arrive at home, I suppose we will have to go our separate ways."

"Aye" John replied: "What you say could be right. It would not be to our advantage to divulge too much of our life since we left home. We will have to take some of our secrets to the grave: loose tongue, tight hangman's noose knot." The banter between John and Paddy continued until they reached their little village of Scalpamor. They discussed the options of how they would build a business.

On arrival at Scalpamor there was a large gathering of locals, with questions about America. Was it the land of milk and honey, and plenty of money there, where everything is there for the taking? Were they going to buy drinks for all the village? Was it only a holiday they came home for? Were they going to America again, to get more money?"

When they said they were going to bed for a good sleep as they had not slept well these last nights. The neighbours were surprised and baffled until the story of the ghost was told by the 'carters'. It was to become the conversation of everyone in the locality, and some added their bit to make the story more intriguing.

The next night John and Paddy went to the pub and each bought everyone in the pub a drink to satisfy the preconceptions of what a returning yank should be. They remarked on the night they spent in Ardnagadai, and how they were upset at what may have happened in that house. Was it the wind that had rattled something outside, or was it something supernatural? They were reluctant to embellish on Ardnagadai fearing that they would upset any potential customers.

Eventually John bought a house that was the landlord's agent's residence, which included a substantial farm of land. He also purchased many small holdings and began farming. He could afford to pay men to all the laborious tasks. He built a new hotel to cater for the arrival of the train. His business thrived when the train eventually arrived in Scalpamor.

Some families who were emigrating to America required a quick sale of their house and land. He would purchase their property and in time sell it with an enhanced profit. Eventually he became an auctioneer, and captured most of the business in the area. John became a wealthy man, and the neighbours were of the opinion that all a person had to do was go to America to get money.

Paddy built weaving sheds and employed men to weave for him. From his family background he knew all the skills that he could utilize to his advantage. With the experience that he gained in America working in the clothing store, he was aware of the price of wholesale goods. Paddy also built a mixing shed with large baths to dye the wool. He was well aware of the difficulty to have all the wool with the same coloured threads to give a consistent tinge to the tweed. If his product was constant, then he could command an enhanced price. He had utilized his knowledge and the contacts he obtained while working in America. Periodically he would take a trip to America to search for new customers. The neighbours often spoke about the two returned yanks and the gold they had, and how every so often there was a packet of gold being sent home from America.

Paddy and John were now becoming wealthy business men, with men and women employed at the various jobs that were needed to be undertaken.

Paddy employed Barclay Beag to deliver sample boxes of tweed to Derry, which were for customers in America or England. Barclay Beag, was a small burly man, but in a fight he could floor the tallest. He considered himself a hard man, perhaps with some justification. The neighbours referred to him as "the Mule", as you could hit him until you were sore and he would still rise to knock a man down. He was never known to lose a fight, so no man cared to pick one with him, and with good justification. What he lost in size he gained in arrogance and self-confidence. Paddy was used to sending Barclay Beag with his supplies knowing that he would defend his merchandise and also his privacy, which was paramount.

Whenever he would be crossing Ardnagadai, Paddy would say to Barclay Beag, "If you think you can't make it to Cannon's, stay in Derry."

Barclay Beag would laugh saying, "I don't care for man, beast, or ghost, but I will always stay in Cannon's if it is not possible to cross the hill before the night. You needn't worry about me; I haven't met the man that will get the better of me."

"Aye" replied Paddy, "Maybe you are right, but be careful. You are the main man in my business, you know good men are scarce."

The practice of sending Barclay Beag occasionally to Derry continued for years without any difficulty. Sometimes he went with a horse and trap, or by horseback if it was a small package.

On one occasion Barclay Beag left Derry in the early evening, as a slight shower of rain began to fall. The ship's agent advised Barclay to cancel his journey until the next day and stay in some lodging house until morning. The agent would keep his parcel safe in his office until the next morning.

However Barclay Beag laughed saying, "I often sweated more than this little dribble of rain. I have a good horse that will not be long crossing the hills. Anyhow there is a bright moon in the sky this night. Ah, it will be nearly as bright as daylight for the last part of my journey." Disregarding any advice, he proceeded to cross the hill, but now the night darkened with black clouds roiling across the sky, and the heavy snow began to fall. The evening quickly changed from a drizzle to a cloudburst of snow that made it difficult to see. The snowflakes, silver and dark, were obscuring his vision, and all the country was bathed in white snow. The hopeful moon was concealed behind heavy black clouds and visibility continued to decrease. He was obliged to seek shelter against his better judgment in Ardnagadai. He was of the opinion that he could handle the vilest of men in a fight. He was given a room with a fire so he could dry his clothes. He put the packet under his shirt thinking that was the safest place for it. And God help the man that would try to get it.

Some neighbours who lived close Ardnagadai tried their best to find out what was in the packet, but to no avail. Barclay Beag enjoyed having people guessing and coming up with their own interpretation. Some of the men present would ask if it was gold. Barclay would laugh and respond, "I could tell you but then I would have to kill you". Speculating on what Barclay carried had people enthralled by the unknown.

Next night Barclay's horse arrived in Scalpamor without a rider or saddle. There was a search of the hills but there was no sign of Barclay or the harness. Men were sent as far as Ardnagadai to enquire about Barclay. They also enquired of the men of the hills who confirmed that Barclay was in the Inn at Ardnagadai that night. The owner of Ardnagadai, Davie Trimble confirmed that Barclay was there but left early next morning.

Davie Trimble said that he did not see in what direction he was going, and perhaps he fell off his horse, or went to America. Following weeks of searching and enquiring of all the men who were in Derry and the ships agent, there was still no trace of Barclay. The Police were involved but their enquiries came to the same conclusion; no Barclay. It was as if he had disappeared from the face of the earth.

Weeks turned into months and months into years, but no one had seen sight or hair of Barclay. There was a myriad of speculation about what happened to him. Was he lost in the mountains or did the fairies take him away and needed the harness for a fairy horse? If he was in America someone was sure to see him sometime. Others said that he was murdered in the Inn at Ardnagadai and buried in some bog hole. Also the police failed to find any trace of Barclay in Derry, or any other town. The disappearance of Barclay was the talk of the neighbourhood for a while, but yesterday's news is masked by today's occurrence. Now he was only discussed occasionally with the same conclusion: he was murdered by the Trimbles.

As the years passed, Ardnagadai was becoming dilapidated, as most transported goods were now using the railway. There were only the odd few travellers who passed on that road, or those who were living in close proximity to the Inn. Mountain men were used to brewing their own homemade whiskey which they drank in their own houses. The mountain men referred to their home brewed drink as real whiskey, and what was purchased in the pubs as government whiskey.

Consequently, the profit that could be realize in a mountain pub was negligible, and an empty pub chases men.

Mary Trimble died, some say of old age, but others contend it was by the ghosts that haunted her for murdering them. Less than six months' later Davie closed his Inn at Ardnagadai, and bought a little house in Scalpamor. His reputation preceded him, and most of the village were reluctant to have any empathy with him. Whenever he spoke to any of the community they would reply cordially, but never fully engaged his friendship. Some people were his distant relations. Neil Jonny was his nearest relation but if someone pointed it out his reply was, "Some of my friends are no relation and some of my relations are no friends. Now leave me, and don't mention that man's name in my presence."

It was as if an invisible barrier stood between Davie and the community and Davie was lonely in a crowd, which is the worst kind of loneliness. The people blamed him for the disappearance of Barclay. The few times he visited the village pub the locals would often comment about Barclay, on one occasion when he visited John Sweeney's pub.

John Sweeney asked Davie. "Did you ever wonder what happened to Barclay or Jimmie Maggie? It is strange how these people vanished into thin air. Aye, and the last place they were seen was in Ardnagadai. Did you ever hear that there were fairies in them mountains?"

Davie became agitated and replied: "Why ask me? I am not God, who knows everything."

"Aye" replied John, "Whatever you are you are certainly not God, nobody could accuse you of that. There is not a man that ever came into this house who would accuse you of being a God. Whatever else they may say about you. I never heard anyone referring to you as God."

Davie became frustrated, swallowing his drink he walked out of John Sweeney's pub muttering, "You don't know how to treat a customer, just because you got a bit of money in America. I know you and your kind who was reared with nothing."

The people in the pub laughed as Davie slammed the door behind him. The people were pleased that Davie had departed, as they felt awkward with him in their company. John Sweeney was waiting for an excuse to exclude Davie from his premises, as when he entered his pub most of the customers departed as they hurriedly drank their drinks.

Davie was becoming unwell, and was spending most of the day alone in the house. He had the house full of crosses, holy water bottles, and a multitude of holy pictures to all the saints in the calendar. Now he began to pay to have masses said for himself and Mary. It was as if he was trying to conceal a terrible secret. As time progressed he became more reclusive, with rosary beads hanging around his neck and everywhere in his house. Now the light was kept burning constantly during the night. Then he purchased two hurricane lamps; which were primarily for use outside and could withstand a gale. Of course the neighbours drew their own conclusions for the use of the hurricane lamps. Their assumptions were that the ghosts of those he murdered were coming back to haunt him by blowing out the light.

Davie's health was failing and the doctor was called; however, the doctor's prognosis was that he should go to hospital. The doctor said that he could do no more to help him, and his advice was that he should go to hospital for a second opinion.

Davie decided that he would go back to Ardnagadai as he considered that he would be better off there. However, when he went to enquire about a 'carter' to take him and his belongings to Ardnagadai, all the carters had some excuse such as the horse is lame, the cart is in need of repair or they were already booked up to take turf from the bog. Eventually he asked his relation Neil Jonny if he would take him back to Ardnagadai. But he also refused saying, "I intend to build a shed, and between quarrying and carrying the stones I wouldn't have time this year."

Davie through desperation went to speak to John Sweeney and ask him to take him to Ardnagadai.

John Sweeney paused before speaking; "Can't you get one of the old carters to take you to Ardnagadai?"

Davie retorted: "If I could there would be no need to ask you. I am going to die and I can't get peace here, they followed me here, maybe I can leave them behind me."

John Sweeney replied "Who followed you here, I have never seen anyone about your house. Is it the neighbours?"

No snapped Davie: "It is them, if you take me I will pay you well. It will be me and a light cart load of clothing and some groceries."

John Sweeney hesitated and slowly replied; "All right I will take you if you pay me £5. That is for me and a man to keep me company going home."

"Aye, alright snapped Davie, and thrust the £5 into John's hand saying, "Anything to get away from here. Can we go away now?"

John Sweeney replied unhurriedly: "First thing tomorrow morning. Can you be ready at 9 AM? Do you want to get your things together?"

Early the next morning John Sweeney and Neil Jonny had the horse and cart ready, and Davie jumped in to the cart. The trip to Ardnagadai was without many words, the weather was commented upon. However, empathy was lacking between those on the cart. Davie merely mumbled the single syllables of yes or no. In time the outline of Ardnagadai house came into view. John and Neil Jonny were glad to see the house to dispose of Davie and his goods. They quickly unloaded the cart as the horse was shying away from the house. Could the horse sense someone or something at the house? John Sweeney had to hold the horse while Neil Jonny unloaded the cart load on the doorstep.

The first thing that Davie did was to light the lamp. Then he carried his scant belongings which was mostly rosary beads into the house, without saying thanks.

John Sweeney had to hold the horse back as it attempted to run or trot away.

When Neil Jonny was safely in the cart he blessed himself and said, "I know I need the money, "But I wouldn't wish to go near that house again for any money, did you see how upset the horse was, it must have seen something".

John Sweeney nodded, "Aye as he pulled a bottle of whiskey from under his coat. Taking a swig from the bottle he handed it to Neil Jonny and said. Swallow a good mouthful of that to settle the nerves."

Neil Jonny sluggishly replied: "They say that if you look between the horse's ears you can see what the horse has seen. But I was afraid to look in case I saw something that I did not want to see."

"Aye!" retorted John, "There is no benefit in looking at evil".

On their way home they spoke about their experiences and questioned how would Davie survive. They decided to inform the police in the area that Davie was in Ardnagadai.

Sergeant John looked at them in surprise saying, "Someone must be in Ardnagadai1" for he had seen light in the house and reported hearing a turmoil of noise from it. "We may be passing that way tomorrow and will have a look into it. Perhaps it was thieves or blackguards that we heard."

In two days' time Sergeant John and two police men were passing, and decided to call to enquire if anything had been stolen. Knocking and opening the door the sergeant made inquiries if anything was stolen or was there anyone in the house.

Davie replied: "Yes there is someone in the house but neither you nor I can chase it away."

Sergeant John replied: "Who are they, can't you give me a name and I will have them locked up for interfering with you. I will call back this evening and I will sort everything out."

Davie retorted: "If only you could. I can't get peace here they followed me from Scalpamor, and now they are here."

"Who followed you" retorted Sergeant John, "I will have them arrested if they broke the law."

Davie pondered before answering and replied; "Neither you or all the police in the country can catch or arrest what is bothering me. Now go away and leave me with my own botheration!" That evening Davie asked for the priest to come to him as he knew that he was dying. When the priest came to Davie, he enquired as to what he could do.

Davie answered slowly: "The weight of years and strife is a heavy burden on my shoulders, and is pushing me into the ground."

"Aye" replied Father Tom; "If we live a long life then old age is the price that we all must pay. However, you are looking good for a man of your years. I too am getting pains and aches with old age."

Davie said; "Father Tom, you can't banish them out of my house?"

Father Tom replied: "Who are them that you want me to banish? I can't see anyone in the room but you and I. Who or what is bothering you Davie? Tell me what it is that is bothering you. If you ask for forgiveness, tell me what you want to be forgiven for."

Davie bellowed: "It is them! Can't you see them? They are laughing at me, they won't leave me alone."

Father Tom replied quietly, "Tell me Davie who they are. A secret is a terrible burden to carry, it is the heaviest weight on any mortal's back. Cleanse your body of any sins by confessing the drudgery of life. If you want God to forgive you tell him of any transgressions you have committed in life. You know that I am a priest and I can't tell anyone what you tell me. Confession is good for the soul."

"But" retorted Davie, "I can't tell anyone what it is. Can't you see them? They were pulling the clothes of my bed all night. They won't leave me in peace for any length of time."

Father Tom was befuddled by the rantings of Davie and did not wish to upset him so he said. "I will pray for you. Perhaps we should pray together that God will give you peace of mind. Now do you want me to hear your confessions that is between you and God?"

"No" retorted Davie: "I want you to chase those evil spirits out of the house! They are tormenting me day and night. They will not leave me alone!"

Father Tom uttered, "Do you want me to perform an exorcism?"

"Yes Father. Chase them away, exorcise them so I can die in peace. I want rest from those who are tormenting me."

Father Tom speaking quietly replied, "Yes I will perform an exorcism, but first let's hear your confession. Then all will be well and you will find peace".

"All right Father, it seems that you are the same as the others. All right, I killed them! Now are you satisfied? I suppose that you will tell the police."

Father Tom speaking slowly replied: "No I can't tell anyone what you or anyone says in confessions, it is inviolable and must be kept sacrosanct."

Davie lay down in bed murmuring, "All right you do your thing, I am getting tired, now perhaps I can get a night's sleep. I hope that you don't mind if I close my tired eyes."

Father Tom replied, "That is all right I will continue with the prayers. Have you any relations or neighbours that I could contact so they can look in on you from time to time?"

"No" Davie retorted, "No friend or relations wants to see me, and those that do I don't want anything with them."

"All right" replied Father Tom, "Then maybe I will contact the police and they can look in on you from time to time."

Davie closing his eyes fell into a deep slumber as Father Tom closed the door. As Father Tom was walking away he looked back, thinking this man at one time had money, but now in his last days he hasn't contentment. It's an awful shame that no matter how much money a person had in life it won't buy them peace of mind.

Two days' later sergeant John and two guards were passing and went to check on Davie but when they went to knock at the door it was locked. Looking in one of the windows they saw Davie lying on the floor. Forcing the door opened they examined Davie and found him dead.

The police and a few neighbours laid him out to wake him. That night when the moon appeared in the sky the rattling began in the house. It was if someone was pulling the chairs across the floor. One person after another jumped up and went outside fearing the reputation of the house. No person was prepared to sit in the house that night. The commotion of rattling furniture was frightening even the bravest man in the parish. Sergeant John and his entourage were not prepared to stay in the house. They met people who quickly departed as if they were about to be scalded. All the people went scurrying to their homes while reciting the Lord's Prayer, and praying that some evil spirit would not follow them.

Next day Sergeant John with two guards and Father Tom went to the house while some of the neighbours were standing to see who would be the first to enter the door. They found the house wreaked with furniture flung in all directions. Davie body was lying on the floor as if he had been cast about the house. There was a discussion between the priest and the sergeant as what they should do.

Father Tom said, "Perhaps we should take Davie outside where we can put the body into the cart for burial. It was decided that Davie's body should be taken to the church and buried. Father Tom began his prayers of exorcism, with all looking on in wonder and fear. As Father Tom began the prayers of exorcism, there was a racket of noises coming from upstairs as if chairs were being thrown about.

Sergeant John turning to one of the guards said, "You go upstairs and see what is causing all that racket"

The young guard whose body was filled with trepidation quickly replied, "No way! You can go upstairs; I would resign before I would take a step up that stairs."

Father Tom exclaimed, "Could you all stay quiet until we say our prayers?", and continued with his ceremony in Latin. This had the effect of somewhat easing the tension that was in all present. When Father Tom concluded his ritual ceremony he asked for volunteers to put the coffin in the cart for removal to the graveyard. As Father Tom put his hand on the coffin to lift it, it somehow calmed the fear in the men present, thinking that if the priest could lay his hands on the coffin then it must be safe for them.

They quickly had Davie's corpse moved to the church, where there was a somewhat hurried requiem mass said for him.

Then a grave was quickly dug and the corpse was interred with a minimum of accolade said about Davie. In a country area it is considered unwise to say anything disparaging about the dead, in case the soul would come back to haunt them. What was said was, "God rest his soul; he was not bad. God is good and I hope that now his soul will find rest."

Now no person who is traveling on that road would shelter beside the house. Its reputation is acknowledged by all. And if you happen to be passing on a moonlight night, you can hear the cries as if someone is being killed. Forever after, no man or beast will go next or near that lonely building. The local people often say that not even a rat can be seen scurrying around the house. Some of the people were of the opinion that the devil himself was in in that ghost house.

Looking through the Veil

All of his life Parthalan was a cantankerous old man, and as a boy he always found some reason to disagree with others. Following the many years of hardship, Parthalan became unwell and made many frequent rancorous trips to the doctor. Parthalan never told the doctor his honest medical symptoms, believing that if he denied his problem it would disappear. It was his belief or blind arrogance that if he did not divulge his poor health, it would vanish. Nevertheless, bad health has never been known to vanish by wishing the problem away. So the bad health remained, regardless of what medication the doctors would prescribe. Parthalan consistently complained about the medicine saying, "It was no better than a chew of old tobacco." The constant drip of years has worn away at his weary body, which was in younger years robust and supple. It was akin to the drips of rain that had eroded away the mountains. Parthalan was getting stiffer with old age, and with every grey hair there was also a new pain. Death would be a welcome relief from the anguishes of this life. It was the unknown that he feared. It was his belief that religion was an anathema to God. He often said that, "All religions were man made, not God created."

One day as Parthalan was coming home with his weekly shopping he collapsed on the road. The neighbours called the ambulance and he was rushed to hospital. In hospital Parthalan remained his usual self, complaining about everything or anything.

In hospital the cause of Parthalan's condition was still unclear to doctors, following the many tests and various scans. He began to worry that he would die, wondering if he would he go to heaven or to hell. There were certain people whom he disliked for what he considered justifiable reasons. Some of the people he detested saying, "They would steal the hair off your head. Aye that scamp Patsy Neil, if he was in your house he would have to steal something, even if it was only a six-inch nail. Aye! Patsy Neil knew how to lock his own doors, but did you ever know of a thief leaving their door unlocked?"

One night Parthalan fell into a deep slumber that bordered on a coma. He could see a very dark tunnel with a faint light at the end of it. Somehow he was slipping or falling into the distance that seemed to take a long time to reach. But on and on he went until at last he reached the end, from where the light was emitting. As he stood there wondering where he was, or what he should do, he saw that there were two roads leading from it, with a signpost on each of them in some kind of alphabet that he could not understand.

He was alone for a while wondering what road he should take. Then he saw a figure in the distance sitting on a chair, and he went up to speak to it. As he neared the figure, he saw it was dressed in a white robe, seated on a seat that resembled a large cathedra (Bishop's throne). The figure was motionless; neither it, nor the white robe moved, to give any indication if it was male or female.

Parthalan was unsure how he was to address the figure and he did not want to upset any being or thing that was sitting there, and did not wish to give what could be construed as an offence. Parthalan presumed that he was dead. If this was Saint Peter, it would be unwise to give any effrontery. Or was it a woman, he was aware that women were insisting on equal rights while he was living, and perhaps they would also insist on equality in death. He was aware that some grouchy women wanted equality in everything but a day's work in the bog.

He remembered how Hanna Boyle was always spouting on about equal rights for women, and how women could do anything that a man could do. But when Shaun Mór said that a woman could not do what a man could, Hanna Boyle asked him to name something that a man could do, that a woman could not.

Shaun Mór replied laughing, "Could a woman have a pee while standing up, and if she can, prove it."

Hanna Boyle replied in abhorrence "You stupid ignorant gulpin, how dare you sprout your vulgar ill-mannered filth to me or anyone."

Shaun Mór riposted with a loud laugh, saying, "Well Hanna, now you see how a man can do things that a woman cannot."

"Aye but Shaun Mór, can a man have a baby? Now you see what a woman can do, what a man cannot!"

"Aye Hanna Boyle, perhaps you have a point there, but tell me could a woman have a baby without the help of a man?"

Hanna Boyle flew into a string of obscenities whenever anyone could outwit her, and said "Shaun Mór you are good for nothing, neither you or your old family ever was. You came from a long line of thieves, liars, good for nothing swindlers, and scroungers."

That day certainly was a day to remember, and Parthalan considered it would be wise to conserve his tongue, as he was in new surroundings. He pondered on how to avoid any discourtesy. As he was nearing the outline of the figure on the cathedra. The figure became no clearer; was it masculine or feminine? Was it God or St Peter? Or was it St Patricia or something in between?

He reflected on how to address the figure as he considered it would be a discourtesy to use a name that was inaccurate, or could give offence. Perhaps the best approach was to ask the figure. Yes, this should avoid any discourtesy. Parthalan stood in front of the figure on the seat. It wore what looked like a type of poncho blanket, with a hole in the centre for the head and a long scarf over its head. Parthalan, with a little trepidation, approached the figure saying, "I do not know if I am alive or dead and who might you be, and how am I to address you, are you God or one of the Saints?"

The figure looked Parthalan in the face, and after a long interval replied, "I am that I am. And who are you, that don't know if you are alive or dead; why do you say you are dead?"

Parthalan was now unsure how to answer this question. Following a long pause, he replied, "I was in hospital and unable to walk. Then I travelled or fell through a long tunnel with a light at the other end, and now I can walk with ease or without pain."

The stern subdued figure replied slowly, "What is your grievance? Do you want a wheelchair? We don't do pain here."

Parthalan responded with unease, and said "Am I going to heaven or hell? I don't think I committed many of the seven deadly sins."

The figure replied "What do you consider deadly sins? Was it that you were one of the lucky ones that knew everything? Bad health, awful temper, never having enough money, unwanted chastity, unwanted family bonds or blindly believing in religious fanatics?"

Parthalan was hesitant of how he should reply and said; "The seven deadly sins I was taught about in school were, pride, greed, covetousness, gluttony, envy, anger and sloth. I think I did not go overboard on many of these sins. And how should pride be described? I never thought that anyone was better than me, nor that I was better than anyone else. I was proud of myself but seldom derided others. As for greed, I worked hard for anything I ever got in life, and if you included gluttony between working the land for what it produced, I was too busy working to have time to indulge in gluttony or laziness. And for coveting anything that did not belong to me, I had my own wife to contend with. If she found that I was fiddling with another woman, I would be dead before now. You of all should know this without me having to explain anything to you. You never told me how I should address you?"

The figure waited a while before speaking, and said, "Parthalan you are a little like the Kerry man Socratic, answering a question with a question."

Parthalan was getting confused, perplexed and bewildered by the use of the reply from the Figure. And said, "Am I for heaven or hell or will I have to stay here until judgement day and if I am could you please tell me what is your name?"

The figure responded quickly saying, "Parthalan, do you expect to be a judge, or be judged, or is it that we would judge ourselves, or should we not be judged?"

Parthalan retorted in a trembling voice saying, "Are you going to say what your name is or have I to talk to a spectre?"

The shrouded Figure replied "Parthalan, don't you know that people choose their own name when they speak of me. If you feel comfortable with the name spectre, then use it, I don't mind. I have been called many names including Dubhlain. No one upsets or gladdens me more than another. Well! Have you any money for your journey from here?"

Parthalan retorted "I died in hospital and there were only a few coins that lay in the locker, if those thieving scroungers in the hospital did not lift them."

Dubhlain retaliated quickly "Didn't you know that you are obliged to pay the ferryman, or you must walk the bank of the Sruthan to your journeys end?"

Parthalan was unsure of who the figure was, or of how to get any positive answers to his questions. He said "What is the name of this river and where will it flow to?"

Dubhlain did not speak for what seemed an eternity and it eventually muttered "As I have already said, this is the Sruthan. Don't you know that all rivers flow to the sea?"

Parthalan replied, "The river is so slow moving. I can't tell what direction the sea is. Which way should I go if I am to reach heaven and what way is hell?"

Dubhlain sluggishly replied, "I do not wish to discuss philosophy. I don't profess to be Buddha, Confucius, Averroes, Kant or John Manny. I have no personal belief or concern about how you live, or how to deal with your situation."

Parthalan quietly replied, "If I follow the river, which way will this river flow to the sea?"

Dubhlain, with his usual mannerism responded, "Whatever route you take will eventually lead to you to a sea".

Parthalan quickly countered, "How is this coherent to take both options and arrive at the same place? Surely it is not possible to travel in opposite directions and arrive at the same place?"

Dubhlain paused for an extended time before replying, "I do not wish to discuss logical philosophy, or what to you is a coherent logic."

"Well Dubhlain" retorted Parthalan, "Am I alive or dead? If I am dead where will I go to?"

Dubhlain slowly replied, "Life or death is an illusion for those who wish to choose it. What is death if you believe in an afterlife? Is afterlife only an extension of existence? Or is the life you know an abstract illusion or a dream. Are you a dream, and has that dream any semblance of reality? How do you know that I exist, I could be your illusion, and neither you nor I may exist?"

"But! But" retorted Parthalan, "Am I to go to heaven, hell, purgatory or somewhere else like nirvana or karma. And what road must I take to my allotted place?"

Again, following a prolonged silence, Dubhlain uttered, "It is your free choice. You may choose whatever you desire. There are many roads to travel, you will have to decide. You know that you can always come back to where you started, with a semblance of fair winds. Tell me, what is your hell, is it to be concealed under the ground? What is heaven? Are there three heavens; is it a height in this universe? Or is it a human illusion to comfort the obtuse?"

With feelings of bewilderment and confusion Parthalan said, "How am I to know which road to take? Will Saint Peter be there to judge me?"

Dubhlain uttered a harsh laugh, "We don't use titles here: everyone is equal until categorized. You chose your way and your category, everything is written on the road symbols."

"But, Dubhlain" said Parthalan, "I only see a blank screen with strange squiggles on it."

Dubhlain, with a morose look, replied, "It is all digital here now, everything is digital now, we have to keep with the times. Just type in your question and the answer will appear on the screen. Don't think the use of digital is only for the young, not the old like you and I.

Perhaps the old way of doing things was preferable to swipe cards and touch screens. To be honest it is out of my league."

Parthalan looked at a tinted panel, with a strange scrawl that was constantly moving. He turned to speak to Dubhlain to inquire what he should do, however Dubhlain was nowhere to be seen! Was this the reason that he did not have the customary coins on his eyes?

Parthalan was perplexed, wondering what his destiny was, and where he should go. If he stayed then perchance his spirit would wonder the earth as a ghost. Then people would be afraid to meet him, and he would have to remain in places where they would only see him accidentally. Then the people would be talking of seeing Parthian's ghost, and his memory would leave a negative impression on them. All of his unfavourable characteristics would be expanded upon and perchance added to by those fabricators of deceit, to make a good story. All of his good attributes and his charitable actions would be forgotten. Aye it is true, if your spirit does not bother the living, the good you did will be remembered and enhanced. But if your spirit should interfere with the living, they will exaggerate and invent lies to demonize you, and create appalling tales about you when you were on earth. Those thoughts gave Parthalan the impetus to proceed somewhere, either to heaven or to hell. Anywhere away from where his soul would not bother the living by wandering in places it was not wanted on earth.

Parthalan was feeling despondent as he walked the long road that seemed to go to nowhere. There was an extensive stretch of road, then a turn and a further stretch. After a while walking what seemed as an eternity, he came to a crossroads. Now he had to choose which road to travel, the one on his right hand or the one on the left hand. Parthalan chose the road on the right, reasoning that God would be on the right. But was it on God's right hand or his own right hand? As he walked, the road was getting narrower, until it was no wider than his foot. Eventually he could see a shadowy figure in the distance. As he came closer he contemplated who this figure might be, was it St Peter or one of his agents? He hoped that he would get more sympathy or empathy than from the last figure Dubhlain. As he came closer, the figure was turning away as if it did not want to communicate with him.

Parthalan hollered in a loud voice saying, "Excuse me am I on my way to heaven or hell?"

The figure turned slowly and said, "It is you, not I who should know that question, I am not your keeper".

Parthalan retorted hurriedly "Are you St Peter."

The figure replied "No I am not a Saint or Peter."

Parthalan retorted quickly, "I would need to observe a little etiquette and address you by your name. Please what name may I use?"

The figure paused for a while and eventually replied, "If you wish, you can call me Nenio, as I am a nullity and do not exist."

"But," replied Parthalan "Nenio how is it possible for you not to exist, and yet exist?"

Nenio chuckled saying, "Did the so called intelligent scientist say that black holes exist in space and they refer to it as dark matter? Do they not also say that Stella exist with a mass of up to twenty times more than the size of the sun. Yet they cannot see these black holes or Stella, but they propose that gravity is so strong as to bend and hold light and matter."

Parthalan retorted quickly "May I inquire, am I on the road to heaven or hell?"

Nenio replied languidly, "Every person should know their own destiny, and then they can create their own heaven or hell in their own image. All roads lead to heaven or hell."

Parthalan was unnerved as no question was answered to his satisfaction, and he considered a singular query was the best option and said "Where or what is this place?"

Nenio leisurely replied "This could be your limbo or the edge."

"But," riposted Parthalan," I thought that limbo was no longer in use, or that it was annihilated, or it was a delusion of someone's imagination."

Nenio replied, "Aye, you or I could be illusions as neither you nor I exist. If you are on the road to heaven or hell how could you exist if you are dead? Don't you know that the opposite of existence is nothingness? If Limbo does not exist, then how could you be in Limbo? And if you do not exist, then how could you be here? And if you or I do not exist, then how could an illusion exist. Or is reality an illusion that is conceived by delusions?"

"But," retorted Parthalan, "You said that this could be Limbo, however by your own words it exists, and why are you and I here? Why can't you and I leave if this place if it doesn't exist?"

Nenio replied "How can you leave an illusion? If you or I don't exist, choose another illusion and leave this one. Step backwards into another illusion."

Parthalan stepped backwards but now he was falling into what seemed infinity. He was descending down a pit with rapid alternating lights shining with all of the colours of the rainbow, falling down so fast it seemed an eternity. He thought he was falling into hell, until he came to rest on a soft footing as if he had not moved. He looked around slowly, thinking that this place must be hell. Would he be thrown into the fires of hell where he would burn for eternity? Perhaps the devil would prod him with red hot irons for infinity.

Looking down at his feet he saw where he was standing, fearing that he was in the centre of the fires of hell. But there were no fires at his feet, and he could see that he was standing on a broad levelled area. No person or creature was to be seen beside him. Parthalan was now perplexed, wondering if he was heading for heaven, hell or into oblivion? He gave a low call saying "Is there anybody or anything there?" Then he repeated it a little more loudly. "Is anybody there?"

Then a solemn gravelly voice uttered "How can anybody be here, you should know that the body is left to decay in the earth. Nobody is allowed here."

Parthalan replied "Where am I and who am I speaking too; what is this place, is it heaven or hell and who are you?"

The same shadowy Nenio was standing at his side and said, "You are where you are supposed to be, on the same place you left."

"But," retorted Parthalan "I fell down from the place where I was standing. This surely must be impossible, as it is not possible to fall down and be in the same place."

The figure responded with disdain, "Why is it impossible. Didn't I say that this place doesn't exist, so how can you fall from the abyss of nothingness? What you fell from was an illusion, and you should know that illusions are figments of the imagination."

Parthalan quickly uttered, "I do not want to stay here; everything in this place is distorted. Or is it that my mind is in a mirage? Could I return to where this road commences and take another route?"

Nenio riposted slowly, saying, "Are there any fetters holding you to this place, and if not who or what is holding you? If you have a yearning to return, then why don't you? This place is an illusion of an apparition. Everything here is your hallucination which you can accept or reject. Leave it and return to your aspirations."

Parthalan hurriedly replied, "Which way should I travel? Where I am standing is becoming rather too narrow and meagre to allow me turn".

Nenio riposted abruptly saying "Walk on and you will arrive at where you departed. Where you are, is only a distortion of an illusion which can be altered."

Parthalan continued walking the road while he was pondering what he should do. If what he was sensing, was this his punishment? Would this road lead him to obscurity or his eventual damnation? Following it for what seemed an eternity he arrived at the crossroads where he had departed from. He mused, was this his punishment for some unknown transgression? Was this place limbo, or was it a psychotic place where his torments would cleanse his soul of any transgression. Or now perhaps he would have a clear path to hell or to heaven. Following a long trek, he could see a crossroads in the distance with what looked like a figure standing at an entrance.

On arriving at the crossroads there was an entrance, with sweet scented flowers which lay along the pathway. Ah, thought Parthalan, this pathway must surely lead to Heaven with a profusion of every variety of flowers. There were more shimmering roses here and opulent flowers than he had ever seen in his lifetime. As he continued walking, the perfumed air was giving him a feeling of euphoria, as if he was on a good bender of drink, or had a puff of whacky backy. Continuing on, the air was perfumed with a sweet aroma which was giving him a feeling of rapture of sweet music, into a perfect ecstasy. Everything here seemed to be in an ideal state of immense quietness and happiness by being liberated from the cycle of life and death. This place looked as if it was full of people who were smiling at each other. Every person he observed looked as if they were involved in an experience of mystical transcendence that conveys rapture. Anytime he attempted to speak to one of the people, he was ignored or smiled at with the words "purge thyself, purge thyself."

Finally, Parthalan recognised an old neighbour Crochar Beg, he had been at his wake and funeral. Crochar Beg was a kind genteel refined old man, who had experienced many hardships in life. He didn't expect a hurtful answer from Crochar Beg, as he perceived him to be a kind man.

Parthalan said "Crochar Beg, I am glad to see you here, but I did not expect to see you so soon especially in this place. Perhaps I will get a straight answer from you, where am I, and what will I do here?"

Crochar Beg retorted, "In this place we all purge ourselves before we move on to another place. I would advise you also to cleanse yourself."

"But!" retorted Parthalan, "How am I to cleanse myself if I do not know how or where. Is this Heaven, or what and where is it?"

Crochar Beg as jovial as always said, "This process of purifying a tainted soul is a temporary process which restores it to its purified self. It is not intended as punitive, as some postulants maintain."

But Crochar Beg, "Where am I to cleanse myself, and is this heaven or hell?"

Crochar Beg with his usual cheerful smile said "Parthalan, don't you know that you have an eternity to exist, what is your hurry? To cleanse yourself, all you have to do is to have a bath in one of the pools. You can bath in water, or in the flames of purity."

Parthalan replied in haste, "Is this place hell with fires to burn in?"

Crochar Beg, smiling said "No this is not the hell that you were led to believe. You could call this place purgatory. It is on the road to where you are going, but you could always come here for a little bit of purging or cleansing, fires don't burn anything here."

"But, Crochar Beg," retorted Parthalan "Where is this place where I can purge my sins? I was hoping to go to heaven!"

Crochar Beg answered with a chuckle "There are many halls in this place. Walk on and you will find the one that suits your yearning."

"But" retorted Parthalan, "I thought that everyone here is equal so how can there be so many baths?"

"Ah" uttered Crochar Beg, "From my recollection you always had a keen eye for a good looking woman. Why don't you go to the bathhouse where you can be washed and pampered by lustrous-eyed houris?"

Parthalan was in deep thought before he answered, "What is a houri, is it some kind of saint or something like that?"

Crochar Beg laughing replied, "Parthalan my good man, where have you been living, was it under a stone? Or perhaps you are like Diogenes: he was living in a barrel. He at least did not want anyone standing in his sunlight. As I said a houri is a good looking women with glittering eyes that could tantalise your existence."

"But" retorted Parthalan, "Is it not a sin to be with a woman, and aren't all sins disallowed, if one is hopeful of ever reaching heaven?"

"Ah" laughed Crochar Beg, "Follow your instincts! This is a different existence than you were led to believe while you were in your last incarnation. Parthalan, you and all who pass this way have a choice if you wish for another existence".

"What!" retorted Parthalan, "This is not what I was led to believe while I was on earth: it was that following our time on earth we go to heaven, purgatory or hell."

"Ah" said Crochar Beg, "You can stay here if you so wish, or be reincarnated into a new material manifestation, or a force whose original nature is immaterial. Perhaps you could be a new embodiment of a human, superhuman, or an animal form. Here it is as it was on earth: everything can be recycled."

Parthalan was perplexed about this advice, which was contrary to what he perceived what afterlife should be; nothing here was making sense. Saying "Crochar Beg I am baffled, what would be your advice, or how should I proceed?"

Crochar Beg, with his laughing broad smile replied, "Parthalan my old neighbour, perhaps you should go to the bathhouse to be purged. Remember you also have a choice to be reincarnated, to appeal to a younger market. Perhaps after a number of years you could enter into another body for another birth on earth. Some chose to be a wandering spectre of a dead human or animal that can at times appear to the living. They can be the harbinger of good or evil. However, as I have already said, go to the bathhouse and purge yourself after your journey here."

Parthalan walked on until he saw an ornamented door festooned with more beautiful flowers, and a soft sweet perfume filled his brain with an intoxicating aroma. This sweet fragrance filled him with sweet exhilarating contentment and immense gratification. The door was wide ajar as he walked in to see what appeared to be a party in progress. Two scantily attired, good looking young women with smiling faces appeared at his side and said "Welcome Parthalan. We will purge the essence of the land from your soul."

Parthalan was ashamed to stare at the two girls and said "By what name should I address you? I do not wish to offend by referring as simply you!"

The two young women replied "Parthalan you can address us by a name of your choice, what name would you be happy to use, or what names have you in mind?

Parthalan replied slowly, "The last person I was talking to was Crochar Beg and he said it was Houri, but he was always a jester playing pranks on everyone. I do not know if he was joking and was making a fool of me."

Both women replied in unison saying, "Yes the name Houri is acceptable as we said you may choose whatever name your wish."

"But," retorted Parthalan, "I cannot call both of you Houri, can't I have a name for each of you? It is difficult to address you in the plural. Couldn't I address you in the singular?"

Both women replied with their usual smile, "All right you can address us as Houri and Houru. We will cleanse and purge you of the grime of the earth and anoint you with oils of perpetuity and eternity."

Parthalan answering slowly said "I do not understand what you intend by purging, what is it?"

Both Houri and Houru answered again in unison, "Here all must be cleansed of our earth's odour."

Parthalan quickly replied "Is it that I have sinned and that the smell is arising from me?"

Houri and Houru with cheerful smiles replied, "The cleansing procedure a tainted soul undergoes to cleanse it from its spiritual impureness is a temporary one. It is therapeutic in its intent and a balm after your journey, not punitive or unpleasant."

"Aye!" replied Parthalan, "Tell me, is this place purgatory? They told me when I was learning the catechism at school that I could be here for my sins."

Houri and Houru smiling looked at Parthalan, again and replied in unison, "There is no such place as purgatory! Here you purify yourself of the stains of the earth; you are in transition from an earthen entity to a nonentity."

But retorted Parthalan "How can I be a nonentity, which is nonexistence? After all I existed when I was on earth. If I existed, how can I have never existed?"

Houri and Houru with their enchanting smiles replied "Parthalan you seem to be inclined to scepticism. Why can't you accept what is allotted to you? Once you existed in a form, but was it reality or is the present tangible, and was the past a dream or an illusion? Now we will cleanse you by fire of your earthly impurity."

"But," retorted Parthalan, "Will the fire not burn me, perhaps forever and ever?"

Houri and Houru smiling laughed and said, "Parthalan, if creation existed without your approval or consent, then this existence equally may exist with your approval or consent. Now step into the flames with us, for the flames will neither scorch nor burn you, nor I. When you step into the crucible, you are then the cauldron which cannot burn."

"But," riposted Parthalan, "Whoever enters a fire will surely burn. You and I will certainly burn and be devoured like a few bits of dry sticks. Didn't I get burned when we had a bonfire that was at midsummer's night? We were celebrating an old pre-Christian belief of the passing of the longest day into winter Samain, and I remembered the pain."

Houri and Houru again smiling said, "Parthalan you seem very sceptical of our assurances. Don't you know, what applied on earth would not necessary apply in this realm. The laws of nature are not relevant in the afterlife. What was reality on earth doesn't apply here, all earthly pain is analgesia. Pain is here absence of the sense of agony or discomfort. Now take our hands and we will have you prepared for your journey."

Parthalan slowly stepped into the flames with a little trepidation with Houri and Houru on either side of him. Contrary to his perceived fear the flames did not burn him. The flames comforted him as if he was walking through an aurora of psychedelic bands of dancing light of varying colour and complexity. An aura of intoxicating rapture seemed to ascend upon him. Everything seemed as if it was a kaleidoscope with a feeling of blissful euphoria. If this is Heaven, then who would ever want more than this?

Opening his eyes, he was standing alone, his beautiful companions had vanished like straws in the wind. Looking around he considered what his next move would be. Would it be onwards to the damnation of Hell, or into paradise, or was this Heaven? Looking around he anticipated what his next move would be. Everything he had seen seemed to disappear, and before him and behind him was all a road of emptiness, or a void. Parthalan considered that he would continue his journey into the unknown. Perhaps he was on the road to paradise, as no one was there to denounce or advise him. Travelling on he could hear voices in the distance singing and laughing as if a party was in progress.

Parthalan looked inside the room and he saw Aoife, an old flame from his youth, sitting alone combing her golden sunset red hair. He remembered her from his youth, with her hair blowing in a gentle summer breeze like golden shards of gold.

Ah to see Aoife's youthful figure again. It brought memories flooding back of his youth, when both he and Aoife were in their prime of life. It brought memories of joy and sorrow, at the loss of his childhood sweetheart. That hubris smile of haughtiness would dart across her young face. As he gazed at Aoife she looked around in the direction of Parthalan and their eyes met, exchanging looks.

Aoife, with a startled look said, "Is it you Parthalan, or is it that my eyes that are deceiving me?"

Parthalan with a smiling grin on his face replied, "Aoife, is it you, or is it a pleasing illusion of my boyhood days? To hear your voice again utter my name is pure rapture to an old frame that has not enjoyed a friendly voice in my last years on earth."

"Ah Parthalan," said Aoife "You always were a charmer with your sweet words, and big broad smile that was wider than the ocean. I didn't think it was your time to come here."

Parthalan with a look of joy and curiosity replied, "Aoife it is a long time since I looked at your face. When I looked at that old photo of you it was ragged and faded. My mind could always see you as you were, when you and I were young and carefree. I an old man that was more tattered and tarnished than the photo!"

Aoife hastily retorted, "Parthalan it was you who left me and went away to those strange lands beyond the seas."

Parthalan quickly responded, "When I returned you had married that sanguine Dane who was in Scalpimore and went with him to Denmark. When you left you took away my soul and my reason for life. The long lonely years after you left had made my life caustic and grief dimmed my brain. When I learned that you and that bloody Dane had two children, I knew I had lost you."

Aoife with her haunting smile replied, "That bloody Dane and I had one child. Yes, I had two of a family but not as you say with that bloody Dane."

"But" retorted Parthalan, "I never head that you were divorced. But in them foreign countries, I suppose anything goes."

No snapped Aoife, "I was never divorced or I never met another man, if that is what you are thinking."

"But your other child?" responded Parthalan. "Someone has to be the father?"

Yes, smiled Aoife, "Someone is the father; and the father met the daughter and granddaughter."

"Ah" snapped Parthalan, "Is it a riddle Aoife. You were always good with your obscurities and enigmas."

"No" grinned Aoife, "Do you remember one day when you took a young woman and her child out to visit the island of Uaimbeag. Do you recall that day and what transpired? If you can recollect that incident, will you tell me?"

"Well" said Parthalan, "I can remember it as if it was yesterday. Why?"

"Then, Parthalan" said Aoife, "Tell me and I will tell you something you might wish to know."

"Ah" replied Parthalan, "A young woman and child came to my house one fine summer's morning and asked me, or insisted, that I take them out to Uaimbeag, for some reason unknown to me."

And then Parthalan paused for an extended time looking into the cup of his empty hands.

Aoife riposted, "Parthalan are you going to tell me, or have I to beg for your version of that day?"

"No Aoife." whispered Parthalan, "The woman's name was Gitte, and her daughter was Brigitte. As I said, they insisted that I should take them to the little island Uaimbeag. You remember it."

"Aye." uttered Aoife, "Would you please continue with your account."

"As you may know Aoife, that little island was important to you and me, when we were young."

"Aye" smiled Aoife, "You know we have an eternity that we could spend here but will you continue with your version of that day."

"All right Aoife. That day, I don't know why, but I relented and launched the boat and began preparations to take them to the island. Somehow when we were crossing the sea, I felt that little Brigitte may have been getting anxious with the choppy waters. I had her sit beside me and steer the boat to the island. It somehow or other took her mind off the choppy sea. I could see the look of contentment on her face as I praised her for steering the boat. Ah, all children like to be praised, and I suppose so do even the old."

"And then Parthalan continue with your yarn, I am beginning to enjoy it."

"Well," said Parthalan, "On arrival at the island Gitte asked me what the stones in the old graveyard were; you remember? I of course did not wish to go there, and so took them around the island and to the caves. I think that little Brigitte may have been a little scared of the dark cave and she asked me if I would hold her hand. Needless to say I was happy to hold her little hand. Then when we came into the cave where the water was. I asked her if I should carry her for a bit. With her little hands around my neck I was somewhat enthralled by a child holding me. Then she asked me if she could call me farfar. I asked her what the word meant. Gitte replied, farfar was the Danish for grandfather. I of course was a little overjoyed to be called someone's grandfather. Oh how tightly she held me, and I asked if she was scared in the cave. She replied meekly, not as long as you hold me, I will never be scared. How the words of a child could defuse a grumpy old man like me? Ah, you are getting tired of my yapping."

"No" replied Aoife, "Tell me more, all that happened, if you wish to make me happy."

"Well, when we left the cave, wee Brigitte held onto me until we came to the grass on top of the hill. Gitte chided Brigitte for wanting me to carry her like an old donkey. But I was happy carrying her. Anyhow we walked around the island for a while viewing the beautiful scenery, with all the sea birds hovering in the sky and diving into the blusterous sea, with white foam been tossed into a brilliant blue sky. Ah there was beauty as well as anger on the sea that day. Then Gitte asked me what those old rugged stones were for, and could we visit them. I indubitably did not wish to, as in my mind they were my place of joy and sorrow. However Gitte insisted for some reason, and I relented. Then I sat down on the ground and memories of you and I showered me with sheer anguish. Do you remember the promises we made underneath that rugged stone which to me was a large diamond? Do you remember the day that we buried our two secret love stones of betrothal? Aye, promises of young love are more easily made and broken, than upheld."

"Aye" replied Aoife, "Promises of youth are as flimsy as a butterfly's wings: touched by another they are damaged and forgotten. But continue with your story."

"Well" replied Parthalan, "I sat on the same ground that you and I had sat upon years ago. And for some reason, it was the first time in my life, I lowered my head and cried. It was then that Brigitte put her hand on my shoulder and said "Farfar why are you crying? Did I hurt you carrying me?"

"No" I replied, "My little datterdatter Brigitte, you didn't hurt me. Don't you know old men cry with happiness as well as sorrow? I knew that my answer must have puzzled her young mind. However, this was the only half sensible reply I could give her. I thought that Gitte must have thought that I was a fruit and nut head banger. Bur her answer was, that everyone must carry their own love and pain. Then she put her hand on my shoulder and said, "A person without emotions is a despondent soul." Wise words from young shoulders. I was in no hurry to return home, and we spent a little while fishing and we caught a few fish. I don't know why, but I was happy and sad that day when we arrived back ashore. Anyhow I invited them to stay until we cooked the fish we caught. Maybe it was the fishing and cooking the fish we caught that made us all happy. Perhaps it was the only day that I was not grumpy for some silly reason. Anyhow as they were leaving I gave Brigitte the £5 that that I initially asked for the trip to the Island. When Gitte protested about giving the money to Brigitte. I replied, "Can't a farfar not give a little gift to his datterdatter, a little present. That's my silly story."

Aoife smiled and said, "Why shouldn't you be happy? That was your daughter and granddaughter!"

Parthalan was aghast and retorted, "Did they know."

Aoife replied, "Yes they knew."

Parthalan uttered, "And why did they not say something. Did I not deserve to know that they were of my blood? Were they or you ashamed of me?"

Aoife responded, "No, nobody was ashamed of you. It was that I was dying of cancer and this was my request to find out about you. I wanted to know what happened to you, and if you remembered me. Then I could die happy, to know that I was not forgotten like yesterday's newspaper that wrapped chips."

"Ah" said Parthalan, "I never could have forgot you. Didn't I spend my time on earth lamenting your lost love? Perhaps we could be reincarnated and meet again and have a new life on earth?"

Aoife paused for a while and replied, "No Parthalan. I intend to be reincarnated again as a Buddhist somewhere in the Tibetan plateau. If I can grasp the four noble truths, then I may be able to find Nirvana and be one with the universe. Death and rebirth is no longer my liking, with all the greed and deceit."

Parthalan quickly retorted, "Aoife I will go with you and we could be one again."

"No Parthalan, we all must follow our own circle in the Dharma wheel with its eight spokes, wherever it takes us."

"But why Aoife? You and I could have the life we lost."

Aoife smiled and said, "No Parthalan, it is like you or I trying to push the sun back in the sky. It was nice to meet you but I must go. Look behind you again, for my time has come to go, good bye my earthly love."

Parthalan looked behind him, but when he looked back again everything vanished like a puff of smoke in the sky. Parthalan was alone again pondering how to proceed. His only option was to continue.

As Parthalan continued his journey, the scent of exotic flowers was comforting and reassuring him that he was on his way to heaven. The reverberation of laughter and the sound of music was having an euphoric effect. As he got close, Parthalan could see people dancing and certainly enjoying themselves. Parthalan hurriedly hastened his steps as he wanted to see if there was someone he knew. There were many people he knew that had lived a life of chastity, with self-denial of food or other luxury. Surely they would be in heaven? There were other people who had lived a nefarious life of drinking and perversion. The wicked will surely die and be punished, for they would not listen to the warnings and must be accountable for their sins. The wicked who plotted against the virtuous will now weep and gnash their teeth in hell. Parthalan was contemplating that this place must be heaven with all the singing and dancing. One man came forward and bowed to the audience saying, "Once, when I was a young man, I could dance with the best of them. That was before the years extracted a heavy toll of aches and pains on my mortal body. Ah sure in those days, I could make people dance and sing with my songs. Now I am as I was in my youth: I can dance a jig and sing like a lark in the clear air."

Parthalan stepped slowly inside the opened doorway, cautiously searching for familiar faces that he could recognise.

It was Shamus Bán, who he knew could gather the women, with his dancing and carousing of love songs, which he would say was for them only. If this man could get into heaven, then anybody could! Aye he was fond of the girls even if they were another man's. Aye he certainly could be accused of coveting anything in a skirt. However, he had the gift of the gab, and perhaps he would talk his way out of hell and into heaven. If ever there was a man with a silvery tongue, Shamus Bán certainly was that man.

With the dance over, Shamus Bán stepped forward and spoke, saying "Parthalan my good friend what takes you here? I didn't think that you were called, yet."

Parthalan was pleased that someone recognised him. In all his travels no one he met had given him a satisfactory answer. Replying to the retort he said "It is nice to see you Shamus Bán. Tell me am I in Heaven or Hell?"

Shamus Bán replied "Parthalan, you were always in a rush. Why can't you relax and enjoy your time here? This place is one big party. If you are in such a rush, why don't you speak to Taranis? He is sitting over there with a harp."

Parthalan considered his options before confronting the man with the harp, saying "Excuse me, are you Taranis? And where is my allotted place?"

Taranis looked at him with a perplexed expression saying, "Why are you looking for a place? Isn't there enough space here for you? Why come here if you don't know how to enjoy yourself?"

Parthalan slowly replied, "I was in hospital and then I must have died, for I fell through a dark tunnel with a light at the end; I must be dead.

Taranis retorted, "To die is unimportant it, is merely a step to reincarnation. And who are you to change the parameters of reality?"

Parthalan answered "If I am dead I would need to know where I am to go, and where I am?

Taranis retorted "Parthalan, my good man, what is it to you, where you are? We are having a hell of a good time here, enjoying ourselves."

"But," retorted Parthalan, "Taranis, I need to know if I can get into heaven or will I be banished to hell? Where am I to go to, is it somewhere in between?"

Taranis remained quiet for a while and then retorted, "Parthalan you spoke of three places, heaven and hell or somewhere in-between. Where do you imply this place is? Is it that you wish to return to a mortal body?"

Parthalan reflected for a while before replying and slowly said "I don't know what or where I should go to. Is it hell or heaven? If it is heaven, then perhaps I would meet St Peter, and if it is hell then would it be the devil or Satan?"

Taranis looked intently before he spoke and said, "If you don't know where you want to go then how can another know it? Can't you learn to relax and enjoy your new existence? There is irresistible music here, which the small birds would be jealous of. Could you not forget your past existences with all the earthly tiresome drudgery?"

"But" retorted Parthalan "Can't you tell me where hell or heaven is, and what is my future, is it with God or Satan? I hope that I will not burn in Hell, with Satan prodding me with a red hot poker in the fires of hell."

Taranis again paused for a while before replying saying, "Why look for hell and heaven here, when you could make your own hell or paradise, when you were living? My friend Parthalan, everyone can create their own heaven or hell in their own shadows."

"But" retorted Parthalan "I was told that heaven is a place to reward the good, and hell is there to punish the wicked and merciless."

Taranis, shook his head slowly smiled and said, "Parthalan my dear friend you seem to have a preconceived idea of actuality. Perhaps you have listened to a plethora of propaganda about what is the next existence. If you want to speak to Satan, he is over there with the fiddle playing a few old tunes. He will ask you a few questions, but beware for he is a jokester and there is nothing he enjoys more than making an individual squirm in discontent. Beside his little jokes he is not a bad one. He is akin to a picador with his questions, who always like to goad.

"But", retorted Parthalan "Will Satan put me in hell where I will burn for eternity, or couldn't I see St Peter maybe I could be in heaven? In my own opinion I don't think I robbed or wounded anybody either physically or verbally."

"Ah" riposted Taranis, "I am not the prosecutor. Satan is the person that deals with all the regulations. But if you wish I will give you a guided excursion of this entire area. Then you may consider where you wish to abide. There are many mansions in this place; there is room for all. Taking Parthalan by the hand, he led him to many places: some with meadows of green grass, and others with flowing rivers of wine. Here they can enjoy the taste of food and wine as there was no reason for asceticism, as food and drink is hyperphysical and has no influence on what was a body. You can enjoy the taste of the wine and good food and never get drunk or bloated. That was the conundrum on earth: if you did not eat you were miserable and hungry, and if you did eat you became obese. Then the problems were that the body would not be able to function to a person's desire. Too much food was not desirable and too little was also a problem. Was that the hell and heaven on the earth you departed from?

Passing some high walls and closed doors Parthalan became curious about what was behind the closed doors. Eventually he asked Taranis, saying "If you would excuse me, may I inquire why the wall is so high and the door closed, is this place hell as no one can see inside?"

Taranis replied "No, be quiet this is not hell as you perceive, it is a place for the pious hypocritical self-righteous, who believe in their own salvation. It was necessary to have a place where these egotistical self-righteous people can spend a while believing that they were the only ones who achieved salvation. Those inside here refuse to participate in the enjoyment of food or drink and assert that asceticism is paramount. Before we had a place prepared for them, they would raise a row in heaven, maintaining that they were the only righteous ones. Aye, talk very quietly for if they would hear you they could start a commotion with those souls that are unworthy to be with them. You know, I cannot tolerate those who profess to be the chosen people. They are the vainest self-centred egotistical hypocrites. They had poor Peter pulling out his beard in frustration. That man Peter has gone grey twenty times over tying to appease those ignorant Gulpins."

Parthalan was quiet for a while and then said "But Taranis, what is the reason for the wall? Couldn't anyone go into that place with them, or are all forbidden, or is it for the chosen people?"

Taranis smiled, "Parthalan if you wish I will take you inside, if you promise to remain quiet. What you may see could have you wanting to ask questions. But if you remain quiet until we are outside again, I will then answer all your questions! Ok?"

Taranis took Parthalan through a side door which led them down a long corridor that opened onto a large area that was covered in ice.

Those inside were down on their knees prostrating themselves and performing self-flagellation. Parthalan wanted to ask questions as he was amazed at how they could perform self-whipping. Taranis smiled and put his finger to his lips and nodded. They walked on slowly and Parthalan was shaking his head until they were outside again.

Parthalan looked at Taranis and said, "Why, what benefit will they obtain with self-imposed punishment?"

Taranis smirked, "That is their paradise! And who would deny them their choice of self-perception? Some people are as peculiar here as they were on earth. They maintain they are in paradise, and paradise is in the centre of hell. However, if they are happy in what they believe, then why deny them their alternative?"

"But" retorted Parthalan, "I thought that everything here would be orderly, where equality and harmony coincided. Tell me Taranis, is this place heaven or hell?"

Taranis turned and stared Parthalan in the face before speaking. "Parthalan, now you are getting an understanding of this place: it can be heaven or hell depending on how you take it. That is one of the reasons why there is reincarnation, spirits get bored here, after a while. That it is the reason why we have recycling of spirits, it saves congestion and boredom."

Parthalan, who was as baffled as ever, retorted "Taranis, who would have been born the most times?"

Taranis smiling retorted, "Well let me think, did you see that fellow that is playing the fiddle? He was once Aristotle in Greece, Genghis Khan, Emperor Hongwu, Marie Antoinette, Martin Luther and Grigori Rasputin and was both animals and insects. I myself have been through many incarnations. I like nothing better than coming down on the earth with my thunderbolt and wheel, it shakes some fear into the people, and it is great crack."

"But" replies Parthalan, "What about God or gods?"

"Ah" retorted Taranis, "What about Gods: can't we all be Gods or arch villains? Or what is the reverse of god. It can be described in different cultures in different ways."

"Ah Taranis," replied Parthalan, "Was God on earth, and they crucified him because he spoke the truth and men did not like veracity?"

Taranis, smiling replied, "Now I can see that you are understanding something of existence on earth. Some had a good experience in that cycle of existence, while others were shown contempt and ridicule. Anyone who confronted the status quo and spoke caustic words about their masters, they sometimes left everlasting memories of their time on earth. All are deities: Gautama Buddha, or Laozi or Daoism or Zou Lu Zhou, better known as Confucius or the countless divinities that persist. You may be more concerned with Jewish Nazareth carpenter Vasus, but incarnation endures. Also you have the many people who declared themselves God. Those have and would burn you on a slow fire to inflict pain and terrorise others from speaking. Now do you understand, proclaimed gods can be either man or woman?"

Parthalan, trying to comprehend all that was said, replied "Excuse me, did I misunderstand you, did you say that Emperor Hongwu, later became Marie Antoinette? Was she not a woman? Surely that can't be right, a man and then a woman, did I not understand you correctly?"

Taranis laughed and said, "No you understood me quite perfectly. As I have already stated you can be reincarnated into whatever you wish. However, if you keep changing gender, your body may not know if it is supposed to be masculine, feminine or neuter. Then confusion may occur at times! They may be intersexual, transsexual, nonsexual, bisexual or parthenogenetic. The latter would be the least desirable as far as I am concerned. Now do you understand the variations and the confusions that can and do occur?"

Parthalan was perplexed by the answers. Some of the explanations were confusing to his mind; he thought that he understood all the fetishes and obsessions. There were people he knew who were as odd as two left shoes. However, he knew how to avoid those peculiar weirdos. There always seemed to be one or two weirdos in every parish. The elucidation he was given seemed to create more obstacles to his basic understanding. When he was alive, if he told some of it in confession, he would have to pray for twenty-two out of the twenty-four-hour day.

Parthalan, turning to Taranis, said, "I thought in all my years that I knew all when I roamed the earth. But now my understanding of existence is dishevelled, in this place where everything is as peculiar here as it was where I left."

Taranis smiled and replied, "Aye Parthalan, old age is a tremendous price to pay for maturity. As you know vanity and old bones crumble with old age. Nevertheless, there are more mysteries in heaven and earth than any mortal mind can comprehend. However, come with me and I will introduce you to Satan, I suppose that you will have to experience that formality."

"But" retorted Parthalan "I would prefer never to meet Satan, I am afraid of what he might do to me, like burning and tormenting me with red hot pokers in the fires of hell."

"Ah" laughed Taranis, "Where did you get the idea that there are fires in hell? Hell is a mistranslation from a Saxon word helan, to cover; as in setting potatoes. Hell or Gehenna was the municipal dump outside Jerusalem where the city's garbage was discarded. All kinds of offal and the bodies of animals and criminals were disposed in it. A continuing fire was kept burning to consume the waste in the dump. You and all were indoctrinated with absurdity to collect money and keep overfed racketeers sitting on their fat pompous seats. Now Parthalan, have you any more indication of reality?"

Parthalan eventually replied, "I hear you, but it is difficult to comprehend all this, which was never spoken to me or others. It is as if what was once truth is now a distorted myth of false ingenuity. I am hesitant of what is ahead of me, and perhaps more than a little apprehensive."

Taranis quickly retorted "Ah you needn't be too anxious, we are going to meet Satan and your paths have to cross sometime." He called out in a loud voice "Satan! We have someone here, perhaps you should have a little talk with him."

Satan, speaking in a rasping voice, said "I see we have a new recruit. Well how are you settling in here?"

Parthalan being hesitant and fearing what might transpire replied, "Well I suppose not too bad yet, but I fear for what might happen. I was told that you defied god and was thrown down to hell".

Satan roared a hearty laugh saying "Where in your book of the Bible is it written that I defied God? Defied is written six times and defy is five times. If you care to look at the book of Job you will see that no spiritual force opposes God. When the Divine Court decides that someone deserves to die, then I am dispatched to claim their life. I investigate their past to see if they had opposed God, so therefore I would be the diabolos or prosecutor. I am a spiritual entity that faithfully carries out my celestial task that is assigned to me. How have you lived your life on earth, did you kill anyone either by deed or by denying them substance of life?"

Parthalan replied, "Are you, or who is Lucifer, prince of darkness?"

Satan again roared with laughter replying, "Don't you know Lucifer was a title given to a king of Babylon? Or Lucifer could be the name of a morning star like Venus. Or a fiery ball in the sky that fell to the ground and caused damage. Tell me Parthalan did you ever hear of a meteorite or comet hitting the earth, with its burning tail lighting the sky. Did one of those meteorites not fall on Russia, within your lifetime? Could this burning light not be referred to as Lucifer?"

Parthalan was getting more befuddled by his retorts and said, "Perhaps Satin, are you are here to tantalise and tempt me with false promises that will torture my reality? I implore you, do not torment me."

Satan uttered, "You do not need anyone to torment you as you are a master of affliction and self-flagellation. Who do you want to pacify your unsettled ailments?"

Parthalan retorted "I thought that Saint Peter would be here to examine me of my life deeds, which I consider not too grievous. I strove for a fair deal with any dealings, but I never left a debt unpaid. I certainly endeavoured to have as much money as could make life comfortable."

"Ah" laughed Satan "Man's worldly riches soon thaw away and deceive the hungry miser. However as for Peter, santus was a Latin prefix for a righteous or just person; in around 1300 the prefix was added to a dead person. You can call any honest person santus or saint, either living or dead without conformation."

Parthalan retorted "Where is Saint Peter, am I not entitled to speak to him to see if I have any sins written in his book. Then I would surely know that I would not be deceived by thy lips or actions."

Satan hollered, "Peter come here. This is one of those doubters, who would need to put his finger into your side before he believes. He is well indoctrinated into the philosophy of the financial bureaucrat."

Saint Peter walked over to where Parthalan was standing saying, "What is all the commotion about, can't a person get any rest from turmoil and grief. I thought that you Satan would take some of this drudgery from me."

Satan answered quietly, "It is this newcomer Parthalan; he is insistent that he would see you in person. I have tried to persuade him to blend in with others that are here, but to no avail."

Saint Peter, after a little while spoke "Tell me who are you, and who called you here. Satan did you call this person Parthalan to come here? Why did you not inform me of this obstinate newcomer?"

"No" retorted Satin, "I was of the opinion that you may have called him as it is one of your many privileges."

"Well Parthalan," snapped Saint Peter "who or what brought you here?"

Parthalan was a little hesitant in replying. "I was in hospital, and I must have died because the next thing I knew I was here. In my opinion I lived a frugal but thrifty life. I owe no person money nether did I allow them to be indebted to me."

Saint Peter said, "State what is your name and number, where did you come from, and again who called you here. Satan said you are Parthalan but I have no record of you on my books. If there is no record of you, it seems you are a refugee or an interloper."

Parthalan was in dread that no one knew about him; "Surely everyone is called here by God." he replied hastily. Speaking quietly, he said, "Saint Peter I do not know where I am to go, is it heaven or hell?"

Saint Peter was becoming a little perturbed as he rubbed his bedraggled white grey beard. After a long pause he responded saying, "I have looked for your entry on my computer but there is no record of you. Have you your entry number so I can check your bar code on the computer?"

Parthalan somewhat mystified replied, "I didn't think there were computers in heaven."

Saint Peter snapped! "Parthalan how do you think that we could run this place, don't you know we had computers here before you could spell the word."

"But" said Parthalan, "I am here, surely someone called me because I must be dead."

Saint Peter replied irritably, "When the divine court decides that someone deserves to die then Satan is dispatched to call them, and to adjudicate. All that Satan does, he does for the sake of Heaven. Without Satan the defence wouldn't bother to unearth all the virtues of a person's past life. As neither Satan nor I have any record of you here! You are an intruder and will have to be deported."

"But" responded Parthalan "I must be dead if I am speaking to you, and if I am dead then inexorably my place is in heaven or hell."

Saint Peter snapped "Nevertheless regretfully there is no place for you here, and we will have to deport you until your records are in order."

"What?" quipped Parthalan "Is there no place for me in heaven or hell? Don't tell me that I will have to walk the land as a ghost!"

Satan quipped, "Peter, is there another way around this quandary? Surely we could send Parthalan back without having him walk the land as a ghost? This predicament doesn't seem to be of his making. Perhaps you or I may have overlooked something. It would be no problem for you or I to change time, for time is transitional."

Saint Peter answered quickly. "As Parthalan was here he would tell people where he had been, which we could not tolerate."

"Ah" said Satan "Who would believe him if he told all he now knows? They would make him the founder of a new religion, and you know how dangerous that could be for his happiness. He would never attempt to walk on water with punctures in his feet. Anyone who ever started a new religion had to be a murdering psychopathic pervert to survive, or the men in white coats would take him away wrapped in a coat with bonded sleeves, and he couldn't put his hands in the pockets."

Saint Peter snapped, "He will have to return and walk the land as a ghost until this mess is cleared up. We can't have souls coming and going here. It is bad enough with those who are reincarnated."

Satan replied quietly, "As we have the authority to reject him from here, why can't we return him to where he was before his soul departed? The people will call it a miracle and all will be satisfied. You know how a miracle answers all their irrational superstitious questions."

"Aye" said Saint Peter and he laid his rod on Parthalan's back.

Parthalan was instantly transported back through the roads he arrived on, through the dark passage, and into the blinding lights of the hospital. The nurse who was at his side said in a loud voice, "It is a miracle! It is a miracle. This man, whose heart seemed to have stopped, is now breathing again, he is alive."

The doctor who was standing by said "Don't be stupid, I have resuscitated him with the defibrillator. Enough of that rubbish to me, it is the work of modern medicine."

Some days later, the doctor began to write a paper eulogizing the wonders of modern medicine, extolling his skill as a modern doctor who had saved a life against all the odds.

The following week Nessa Mór came into the hospital saying, "The miracle was granted to me, as I was praying to Blessed Coné Anism. I have prayed night and day for your recovery. You know there is power in prayers. I am going to petition the Pope to have blessed Coné Anism beatified into a saint. Yes, Parthalan, we will go to the birth place of blessed Coné Anism in Italy to pray that he will be declared a saint."

Parthalan retorted, "Nessa Mór, have sense woman, it is nothing to do with any blessed person, and Nessa Mór, you could not afford the money to travel to Italy. It is a long distance away and the expense to travel there would be exorbitant."

Nessa quickly replied, "I will try to organise a dance to collect money, to take you and I to Italy. Then perhaps we will petition the Pope to have blessed Coné Anism declared a saint, Parthalan. I have already begun collecting some money for the trip, and you will come with me to tell all the people about your miracle. Maybe we could start a house of prayer to let the people know about the miracle."

"What!" barked Parthalan, "Nessa Mór, no way would I be interested in that rubbish. If you were to be frugal with your spelling, then you would have your heart's desire, and I will have peace of mind. Now would you leave me in peace, and give my head a rest? You are raving like a lunatic. There are saner people than you locked up and they say that they were psychotic."

Nessa Mór with her religious enthusiasm hollered, "I am saying a novena of the nine Fridays to the good Saint Peter to have blessed Coné Anism declared a saint."

Parthalan jumped up agitated, spluttering and said, "Saint Peter! I don't want to hear that name mentioned to me as long as I live. That man would create a dilemma in heaven! It's Satan, not him, that should be called a saint. It is a pity that your St Peter was not kept incarcerated in the Mamertine prison when he was there. And for good measure perhaps they should leave Coné Anism in jail with Peter, the insurgent.

Pete

When we were young, we would all enjoy some devilment on Halloween night, the 31st October. It was an expected part of life that the young would play some pranks on their neighbours.

Pete, who lived alone, was the most acerbic, difficult, and temperamental old man that had ever existed. He was annoyed at what had happened to him every year. Not wishing to have his door hit by cabbages or turnips, he decided not to stay in the house that night. Before he left he put spadder (white turf) on the fire. This way he would have heat in the house then he returned home later. Then he went to his local pub to spend the evening, cursing and damning as he walked the road, kicking stones before him.

After he was gone, some of the local boys came to his house and were disappointed not to find him there. He was always the person to give them a good chase every year. Not wishing to accept that Pete had outmanoeuvred them this year, they had a long talk of how or what they might do to rectify the matter. They boys went to the field where Pete had a donkey grazing. They took the donkey and tied a white sheet around it, opened the door of Pete's house, and put animal inside. This they thought would put the fear of god into this mean crabitt old bitch. Perhaps he would think it was a ghoulish ghost ---or maybe even that the devil was in his house. They had visualised Pete running from the house in a state of terror: Ah, this will be the best night's crack. We will have this old clouster!

After a good night drinking in the pub Pete staggered home. As he went to open the door to his house he thought of how he had fooled the boys this night. Pete was so pleased that he was talking loudly to himself now, "I have suffered at the hands of these young blackguards for too long. That young John is a bad looking prig, his eyes are too close together to be any good. As for them Mickie Joes, they were never any good and will never be. If they are not got for stealing they will surely kill someone and spend their days in jail. They would steal the milk out of your tea and come back for the sugar. Them Frank

Mickie's boys, how could they be? They would not take anything from their own fields. It would have to be rotten before would throw it at my door. It would have to be some other person's that they would throw. I have never seen them give anything away. They are so miserable they would take their shite home in a paper bag." With this he gave the door a couple of good kicks and shouted "You did not get me tonight to annoy me, you b****ds!"

The poor donkey was by now getting very nervous by the kicking on the door, and the roaring of Pete was further adding to its distress. It recognized that voice and remembered all the beatings it had received from him. It thought that it would be better to avoid him when he was in this excited manner. With this Pete opened the door to his house, and to his horror he saw a white object that had the feet and the head of the devil, two big red eyes, and what looked like two black horns on its head. The afterglow of the fire gave an eerie look and feeling to the house. The shock of this apparition had the hair standing up on the back of Pete's neck. There was wild commotion in his kitchen, with tables and chairs being thrown about and with the stench, he thought that the smell could not be of this earth. Pete was sure that Satan himself was waiting for him this night. Not wishing to spend the rest of his time in hell Pete roared at the top of his voice. His screams could be heard in ten townlands. "O mother of Jesus save me this night from this black ba****d! I will never f*****g curse again."

The poor donkey was now so upset that it was trying to get away to safety. The donkey saw a cleft of night sky through the opened door. It knew that this was its only means of escaping from this madman and that the only way out was through the door beside where Pete was standing. The donkey tried to escape from this place of danger and fear by the opened door.

Pete thought that it was the devil coming for him this night, to drag his living body and soul into the depths of hell for all eternity. If it was devil then he reckoned that it was better to confront it rather than to run away. He turned, thinking that if this was his end he would not give up so easily. Shouting "You fu****g black ba****d devil out of hell, you will not get me so easily: I will fight you every inch of the way.

I will not give up so easily! You have met your match tonight! I do not want your fires of hell to roast the arse off me for the rest of time." Pete reached to try and find anything that he could use to protect himself, and finding a crowbar he swung it with all the energy that his body could muster at what he thought was the devil. Saying "You will not take me tonight, you god dammed f*****g devil out of hell. You were chased out of heaven and you will be chased out of my house if it is the last thing that I do on this earth!"

The utter trepidation that filled him had flooded his body with desperation. The induced delirium of dread gave Pete the strength of a crazed man. He was now roaring at the top of his voice calling for god's help and cursing this devil. "You f*****g b*****d, goddamn and f**k you to hell and damnation." Swinging the crowbar he rained blow after blow onto his worst fear, who now was lying at his feet screeching and moaning in agony. The more it screeched these terrifying sounds that clawed at his body and soul, the more Pete swung at it, blow after blow, with the cold sweat of fear oozing from every pore of his body, until it groaned no more.

The neighbours were alerted by the unmerciful noise coming from Pete's house and rushed to his aide. They met Pete outside his house in a state of dread, crying "I have killed the devil this night. I have killed him the b*****d devil."

When the commotion was over and the neighbours gathered, lamps were lit. Pete saw his own donkey lying dead on the street in a pool of blood.

A Refined Courteous Gentleman

Murish Rua had returned from America to build himself and his wife Meabh a gorgeous new house near his old home at Doras-feasta. Following many years of toil in America, he had an American Army pension, Old Age pension, work pension, life insurance and to top it off they had a financial return on stock market shares. His wife Meabh had an American Old Age pension, an insurance pension and a nursing pension. To say they were financial comfortable was to under state their wealth.

Murish Rua decided to build his new house at Doras-feasta where the old family home once stood. He was proud of the name Doras-feasta, and said, "It stands for the door of knowledge." Where in older times monks lived ascetically in huts or cells, they lived separately but in a coenobium". He would continually boast; "The name indicates that it means the door of knowledge."

Murish Rua hired diggers to remove half a hill, to level a site for their new home. His intentions seemed to be that he would move heaven or hell to level an area for his intended new house. No expense was spared as he continued to retort. "This is the way we did it in America, and that was this was the way we did it in America!" sometimes ad nauseam. What little soil there was on the site was cleared or swept into a pile, to be returned when the job was completed.

The design of the house was contradictory to the type of houses in the surrounding area, or perhaps anywhere in Ireland. Some of the hotels in the area did not have as many rooms as this grand residence had. There seemed to a room for everything, including two master bedrooms. There was a little sarcasm from the neighbours about the two masters who were to live there. However, the house was built by a squad of men to Murish Rua's fanciful wishes, or capricious whim. He would often say, "Aye, whoever pays the fiddler calls the tune."

The house was something of a wonder even if it was seen in another country, with its east and west patios and its granite flagstone paving.

Hugh Bán would often say, "It was a sight for sore eyes with all its dudas."

When the house was built, the next project was the garden, which required that any protruding stones in or around the house had to be removed, and the ground was pulverized to gravel.

The garden was filled with four inches of gravel, then the topsoil was spread over it with a light layer of sand which was raked into the soil, and of course a good sprinkling of lime to enrich the ground. The next year there was a good covering of grass. Around the boundaries Murish Rua set a range of flowers, and hedges that would gladden any eye.

The neighbours admired the beautiful manicured lawn, which could feed a cow for a week or more. The well-ordered hedging and the neat flower beds adorned his garden. Some said it was a welcome sight that would gladden the eye and lift the heart. Others would say that maybe God made the world, but Murish Rua had built a house and made a garden out of a barren mountain. It was sarcastically referred to as "Murish Rua's garden of Eden, with or without the snakes."

Murish Rua and Meabh travelled to Cork to visit old friends they knew in America, and to renew their onetime friendship. While they were away, Cahal Sean's cows entered their garden and ate the flowers and hedging, and ploughed holes into the lawn. None of the neighbours were going to intervene as they knew that both parties could be obstinate. If Murish Rua and his wife came home, they could blame the person removing the animals for the damage. Murish Rua's temper could be as inflammable as his red hair once was, then the person being neighbourly would get a tongue thrashing. They considered prudence and caution was the best part of valour, and if Cahal Sean saw you chasing his cows, he may blame you for causing them some hurt. The neighbours considered that it is better to avoid a fight than to try and settle one. They considered it unwise to get involved in other people's wars.

When Murish Rua and Meabh returned home, they were enraged at the damaged that was caused to the garden. The beautiful flowers were gone as was the hedging, and the lawn was full of holes from the cow's hoofs. There was also cow's manure covering their new granite stone flagged patios. None of the neighbours were prepared to confirm whose cows caused the damage to their property. The usual retort was, "It was not mine, my cows were in this field or that field". Murish Rua made his typical inquires, especially in the pubs where a few drinks could make men talk. The generosity of a few drinks loosened tongues, and the truth eventually emerged to see sunlight. He found out it was Cahal Sean's cows that had caused the damage to his garden.

Murish Rua was enraged that the garden, his pride and joy, was destroyed, and no one came forward to apologise. He had a sturdy wall built around his property to impede further intrusion of any other animal. He repaired and restored the hedges and flower beds around his house; it now resembled Fort Knocks, overbearing or over ostentatious.

When all the work was completed he went to his solicitor and directed him to send a letter to Cahal Sean, asking for compensation for the repair and replacement of the plants in his garden. The solicitor's letter threatened Cahal Sean that if he did not pay for the damages Meabh and Murish would take him to court.

However, it would be easier to get the Pope to play the fife at an Orange march, than to try to get money from Cahal Sean. Cahal was a person who could be blind, deaf, illiterate or play plain stupid, whenever it was to his advantage. Cahal was the shrewd idiot whenever there was money involved. There was no response from Cahal, as he customarily ignored any letters seeking money.

Murish Rua was aware that Cahal would probably not pay, but he was hoping that at least the letter would prevent him from allowing further trespass by his animals. Each avoided the other, preferring distance and peace rather than confrontation.

One Saturday night, Murish Rua, Meabh and some of their old friends from Cork who were visiting them, went to the local pub for a few drinks, and to reminisce of their time in America. Cahal entered the pub and went to speak to some of the people in the bar. Murish Rua thought that his presence in the bar would be upsetting to Cahal, and he would leave the bar fearing ridicule from his friends, or to avoid him.

However, the crack and the laughter that was emitting from Cahal's social gathering was ecstatic and this was annoying to Murish Rua. Cahal could drive a mill with all his talk and hearty laughter. Murish Rua refrained from speaking to Cahal, although he was exasperated that someone could be so brazen as to stand up in his company, as if nothing had happened. Had he any shame in him?

When Murish Rua was leaving the pub, he tapped Cahal softly on the shoulder and said, "Did you get my letter Cahal?"

Cahal turned and smiled at Murish Rua, and said "Aye I certainly did, I certainly did Murish. It was kind of you and your wife Meabh to think of me. Meabh is a lady. You were lucky to find such a good looking woman; I hope that you appreciate and look after her."

Murish Rua was determined that he would not let Cahal distract him with his talk about his wife. Replied, "Never mind your palaver, about Meabh! What are you going to do about the letter that you received from my solicitor?"

Cahal with one of his smiles replied, "Oh that letter, aye."

"And well," retorted Murish Rua "What are you going to do about it."

"Well said Cahal with his usual smile, "I showed it to the cow."

"And what then Cahal!"

"Well Murish, the cow looked at it and just shook her head. I don't think that the cow could read."

"Well" replied Murish "Did you read my letter Cahal?"

"Aye Murish you could say I did. I was sitting shitting as I read your letter. The more I read I shit the better, the ground was bare and scarce of grass so with your letter I wiped my ass."

The retort made Murish livid with anger, as everyone in the pub overheard the spat between Cahal and Murish, and all in the pub were trying to smoother their giggling. Even Murish's friends from Cork were bending over trying to smother their laughter. But all the people in the pub were ecstatic with laughter. They could see the humour in a tiff between Murish Rua and Cahal and were waiting for the response from Cahal. They were aware that it would be easier to get blood out of a stone than to get money out of Cahal Sean. Cahal was a man that would talk his way out of hell and into heaven. He had a sweet tongue that would charm the snakes out of the grass. So the little wrangle between Murish Rua and Cahal faded into an unpleasant memory.

And now Cahal was prepared to move on to his next victim.

Murish Rua's mind was smarting from being outwitted by Cahal's drollness. The hurt remained in the back of his mind. However, he endeavoured to have the last laugh, as he did not like anyone to get the better of him. He spent days planning how he was to achieve his retributions on Cahal. Finally, an idea was hatched. A young couple from Europe were looking for somewhere to stay. They could be described as "over schooled and under educated." Like all that are over educated, they lacked country wit, or a good dose of cop on.

Their parents had spent their hard earned money on the best schools for their family. Greta had burned her bra, and her partner Johan had burned his socks, and was content to wear sandals. In their thinking they were endeavouring to return to living off the land like it was in 'Grimm's Fairy Tales.'

Murish Rua hired a field bordering Cahal's land with an old house on it that was close to ruin. It had in the past been used as a cow byre, although the corrugated iron roof was adequate with just a few leaks. Murish Rua thought if they were living there they could hinder Cahal, as they had the education, and could understand law, so he offered the place to them to stay. Then he offered them a goat and said that he would try to get a few more nanny goats for them. Of course this pleased Johan and Greta as they could see themselves living with nature.

Cahal knew that Murish Rua was extracting retribution, and Greta and Johan were to be his catalyst for reprisal. Cahal was prepared to let time and a congenial tongue be his weapon. He went to visit Greta and

Johan to welcome them as neighbours. They of course were pleased to be made welcome.

Cahal said, "If there is anything that I can do, don't hesitate to ask me. I know that you have been to the best colleges and university and are very smart people. Unlike me, who is uneducated and ignorant and knows nothing."

Greta and Johan were unused to such praise and laudation from a stranger. Their shield was down, and they dismissed Cahal's compliments saying that he must know a lot about the land and nature.

"Well" said Cahal, "If you don't laugh at me for my stupidity! But don't touch the fairy tree, whatever you do!"

This remark has them interested and they said, "Where is this fairy tree you spoke about? Is it nearby?"

Cahal knew that he had them hooked, and was going play them like a salmon on a light string. He was going to let them run their halter's length, then reel them in.

"Ah" said Cahal, "I have said too much. You can laugh at my nonsensical chatter, an ignorance country fool. Forget everything I said. That is my ignorance; I know that you educated people will have a good laugh at me."

Greta and Johan tried in vain to get Cahal to talk about the fairy tree, however, he refused to comment. Cahal knew it would be too soon to spring the trap. Time, and wonder of a hidden country belief was a better bait. Whenever Greta or Johan spoke about the fairy tree he would reply, "Ah, we should not be talking about old superstition, especially to you that are educated. Ah forget all about it. Perhaps that is best."

Cahal was building a wall for a cattle crush, but the goat crossed the boundary fence and tossed the wall in the middle of the night. Not wishing to have a dispute with Greta or Johan, he felt he could use this to his advantage. The next night he put some animal fodder in an old barn of his. Cahal closed the door on the goat which had gone in after the fodder, and left it there until the morning. He always had a few bottles of poitín in the house for emergencies. He took his bottle of poitín and pored it down the goat's throat and let the animal free. The goat walked or staggered to Greta and Johan's house and fell asleep at their door. Cahal visited them and commented how the goat seemed to be sleeping for a long time. "Ah", said Cahal, "Maybe the goat is tired."

The next day the goat was still sleeping and Greta went to ask Cahal to ask if something was wrong.

Cahal immediately went down the field and returned with a few branches off a tree that he had broken that morning. He said, "Who was at the fairy tree? Didn't I tell you not to harm that tree? It is bad luck!"

Greta and Johan replied, "We didn't go near any tree; I promise you we did not."

After a long pause Cahal said, "Someone or something has damaged the tree. There is your evidence: the broken branches."

Johan uttered, "The only thing that was outside at night was the goat."

After a lengthy pause Cahal replied "Aye that makes some sense. Has anything else happened to you or the house?"

Greta retorted quickly "Well there must have been something around the house last night. There was some strange noise outside. And a fan belt had broken on the car yesterday; that's all."

Cahal kept quiet for a while and then cried out loud, "God save us! Why have you upset them? They wouldn't have bothered you if you don't bother them. You should never get involved with the unknown."

Greta exclaimed, "Cahal who are you referring to? Who is them? Please explain."

Cahal answered with haste, "Those that I told you not to upset. The fairies of course, didn't I tell you not to damage their tree?"

But cried Johan, "It must have been the goat not us! What are we to do now? Is there anything worse coming?"

"Hold on a minute!" said Cahal who left the house and returned with a few old iron rods. Then he placed them at the four corners of the house and said, "Don't for the love of God leave the house tonight. I will leave a bottle of whiskey for them, maybe it will pacify them; but I don't know! And I will say a prayer that they will not trouble you."

Cahal could see the nervous look on Greta and Johan's faces as they asked, "What will we do?"

Cahal sat down and put his head into his hands and groaned lowly, "I don't want to tell you to leave here. But if I was you I would leave for at least seven years. You may never have a day's luck here!"

Greta and Johan uttered almost in unison, "Perhaps it is better that we leave now." Greta said, "The noise last night must have been them. But what about the goat, what will we do with it? Do you want the goat Cahal?"

"Well no" retorted Cahal, "Leave the goat back where you found it. If you leave all as you found it, then maybe you will be free of the fairy's curse. I would advise you to put the goat out of this field, and don't tell anyone what has happened."

"But Cahal," said Greta, "Will the goat die? That would be terrible."

Cahal lifted up the goat's head and he could see that the goat was suffering with a hangover. Cahal knew how people used to make a horse or a donkey dance to sell them at the marts or fairs, by rubbing ginger on the animal's backside. Then he played with the few iron rods while chanting a mantra of gibberish. Then he rubbed a paste of ginger to the goat's backside. The goat jumped up and ran out of the place in the direction of Murish Rua's. Greta and Johan were mystified of how the goat that was lying for two days had suddenly jumped up.

They said "Cahal, what did you do to cure the goat?"

Cahal replied slowly, "I didn't cure no goat. I lifted the curse for a while and the goat may have seen something, and wants to disappear. I would advise you to escape while you can. And never tell anyone what happened here."

Greta and Johan threw their few belongings into their car. Then they gave Cahal some money to cover his expense for the whiskey. While saying, "Thank you Cahal for all your help. Only for you we would not know what we should do. When we get home we will send you some more money for your kindness."

And now Cahal was free to plan how he could get more land, for grazing his animals.

A woman by the name of Mary Rosha lived in that large old house named Ardmuckvill. In its glory days it had been the optimum house in the area, while others lived in houses that could be described as shantys. Ardmuckvill House was more splendid than any other house for miles around. It sat on a high mound surrounded by various trees. When the house was in its prime, the owners employed many men to carry out work on its farmstead, as they owned at one time over 200 acres of prime land. It had orchards and flower gardens. When the Roshas spoke or demanded the people to follow their dictates, they were compelled to listen.

As years progressed the families in the area renovated, or built new houses.

The older people remembered the influence the Roshas had on the neighbourhood. If Ardmuckvill coughed, the people dreaded the consequence of what might follow. However, through time and changes to farming practises, coupled with the boys of the family joining the army, who either died or had mental or physical disability, the house and land fell into disrepair. Whatever money the sons could obtain by borrowing they spent unwisely, or on the cursed drink, and then the solicitors swallowed whatever money they had left, through family infighting. Now only the house and about ten acres of land was left with Mary Rosha, which made her bitter. The days of grand parties in the house were now only a fading memory of past grandeur.

Some people remembered how the Roshas treated them when they were young, and were unkind to Mary Rosha whenever she spoke. Murish Rua could be particular rude with his American mannerism. He would openly refer to Mary Rosha as, "Lady Muck from Clabber Hill."

This remark was upsetting to Mary Rosha and at times she would cry out, "Excuse me, my name is Mary Rosha. You are an unmannerly discourteous man lacking any manners. You have no breeding. A bad weed will grow anywhere. You don't know how to speak to your betters. Just because you got a few American dollars!"

Murish Rua would reply, "Your betters! What a laugh. You are no better than the tinkers. You hobo, the Rocha's were the parasites that lived on the people; but no more. Once you could order people around, but now no more. Now we are richer than your lot. You were a have been, but no more. Lady Muck from Clabber Hill. Ha, ha! Now you are the tramp of the country. As for breeding! You are like an old hen that is past her time for laying. You wouldn't get a stupid blind man into bed with you. To lie with you would be like going to bed with a bunch of nettles."

Mary Rosha was obviously very upset by Murish Rua's remarks, and would if possible stay out of his way. His rude mannerism was reprehensible to her. She was aware that Murish Rua's family were as poor as church mice, but now he was lording it over the country. The other people of the area were respectful towards her, and if they held any animosity they did not openly show it. Her monetary fall from her perceived refinement was annoying, but she was determined to put on a brave face. She had a little garden where she grew some vegetables and the fruit bushes that would supply her with some sustenance. Mary Rosha was determined that no one would see her in penury. As always, the family name was to be protected it all costs.

Mary Rosha's house had only the memory of its splendour to live on. She was perhaps now a little envious of those who lived in more comfort than herself. Envy and pride makes an uncomfortable combination that breeds resentment, which took the form of extreme enmity. Mary Rosha was more than a little bit eccentric. She kept a few unusual cats who sat on the table while she ate her food. She had a bizarre attitude to life and could be as pleasant as the summer's sun, or as bitter as a winter's frost. If you were to have any prospect of obtaining any comradery with her, you had to pretend to agree with her sentiments. A person had to treat her with utter respect, for her tongue would shave gooseberries. There were few people in the area who would speak to her, or tolerate her saline attitude. Mary Rosha was friends to few, if they could even be found, and an enemy to many.

One morning Cahal went to Mary Rosha's house with the intention of asking her to rent her lands to him for grazing his animals. Saying, "Excuse me Miss Rosha for bothering you who has better things to do than to be speaking to me, as you are a lady. I know that it is unmannerly of me to ask you, but I must ask you, then you can chase me away."

Mary Rosha was pleased that someone should address her with such refined decorum. The unpleasantness with Murish Rua was fresh in her mind. The courtesy of Cahal's address brought back memories of when she was young and all the people had respected her family. Any bitterness that she harboured towards the people faded away like snow on the mountain with a summer's sun.

Mary Rosha smiled as she looked at Cahal and said, "What do you want to ask me Cahal Sean? Ask; I won't bite your head off. You seem to be a gracious gentleman with good manners, which some people we know lack."

"Well Miss Rosha, I suppose that you heard that Murish Rua was blaming me for destroying his garden. He is saying that it was my cows that was in his garden, when they were grazing on the hill. And now he says that I can't put my cows into my own field. He is threatening me that he will take me to every court in the country. You know that I can't afford solicitors to defend myself. He said that he will take me to every court in the land until I am penniless. I don't know what to do, that is why I came here. I am sorry for bothering you."

Mary Rosha said, "Tell me, what do you want of me Cahal Sean? I can't finance you in your legal fight with Murish Rua. I know all about that rude person. Now that Murish Rua has some money he is bullying people; he has no manners."

Cahal Sean replied slowly with a demurred smile, "I don't know what I am to do. Maybe he would attack me, after all he was in the army and he know how to kill."

Mary Rosha now had an affinity with Cahal. And as she had had a verbal skirmish with Murish Rua, she was willing to give succour to anyone who opposed him. She smiled and replied "Cahal, don't you know that the fly that rises from the midden always flies the highest. Never mind that midden fly Murish Rua. Now settle down and tell me what you want."

"Well" answered Cahal, "It is like this: would you please consider renting me your field. I know that Murish Rua said that he was going to buy it."

Mary Rosha face lit up and retorted, "Buy my land! That person will never put his two dirty feet on my property. Cahal! You have good manners and courtesy. I can't tolerate people that don't know their place in life. Of course you can rent my land, and that bully will never stand on my ground. I can promise you that if Murish Rua ever stands on my ground I will be the person that takes him to court for trespass. I should know the law as I studied it in my younger days at college. I still have those law books in the house and I will study them in preparation for any attack by that bully. Mr Murish Rua may have bit off more than he can chew. If he thinks that he can bully you or me, he is in for a big surprise. That insolent tyrant."

"But Miss Rosha" said Cahal, "What if he sends me a solicitor's letter telling me to remove my animals from your land, what will I do?"

Mary Rosha face lit up like a light bulb, she was in fighting mood as an adrenaline rush of confronting her enemy surfaced. She felt young again, and could oppose any adversary like she felt when she was young. The dispute with Murish Rua was a challenge that she was unwilling to refuse. Her supressed anger was rising within her body at the opportunity to mortally wound her perceived tormentor. It was an answer to her prayers to hinder the person who mocked her.

Mary Rosha said, "Cahal come in please. Would you like a cup of tea as I was going to have a sup myself?"

Cahal was aware that he had won a victory with his cunning words, and he would refrain from careless words that could lose him an advantage. He was aware that a person's words could also be the noose that would hang them. Now he would play the saint and keep praising Mary Rosha and her family.

"Thanks Miss Rosha, but your house is too grand for me. A lady like yourself has better things to do than to be speaking to me, an uneducated labourer. I often heard my father say that the Roshas had fed the people during the famine. The Roshas were always good to the people, whenever they had trouble. I suppose that you know that your grandfather bought the boat ticket for Murish Rua's uncle Anthon to go to America? I often heard my father say that only for the kindness of your grandfather, Anthon would be locked up in jail. Did Murish Rua ever thank you for your families help? I suppose not! And Anthon was the person that Murish Rua went to stay with when he went to America."

Cahal was feeding her ego and Mary Rosha was savouring the accolades. She was of the opinion that the Roshas were descended from chiefs or kings.

By now Mary Rosha was purring like a cat after a saucer of milk. She was unaware of what the family was supposed to have done. She, or no one in the district had ever heard of these stories, as Cahal was composing them to suit an agenda of appeasement.

Mary Rosha was highly delighted with Cahal's eloquent eulogy. Now she could wallow about in her preconceived ideas of past grandeur. She had the strange idea that the Rocha's were of nobility, and now Cahal has stoked her fire of superiority.

Cahal was a master at laudation and he knew that 'A spoon full of honey would catch more flies than a bottle of vinegar.' And he continued to heap commendations on Mary and the Rosha family. Cahal had what he wanted: the use of her land. If he played his hand right, there were always the prospects that he may in time have the rest of the land for himself.

Mary Rosha was insistent that Cahal should come into her house to see it for himself.

Cahal was pleased to get into the house. It was another step in his endeavour to somehow acquire more of her land.

The inside of the house, in its days of glory, was glamourous with large pelmets that extended around the four walls of the room. There were numerous paintings hanging from nails in the pelmets, of deceased family members. Cahal would look at the pictures as in wonder, for an extended time at each picture, inquiring as to who the image was. Mary Rosha was pleased to explain who each family member was. Whatever little knowledge Cahal knew of the family he was sure to include it in the conversation. Sometimes he repeated the stories that Mary told him, saying that he had heard it from his father.

That day was extremely pleasing for Cahal and Mary Rosha. Now there was a perceived symbiotic bonding between them. She was living on past glories and of course Cahal would use it to his advantage.

One evening when Cahal was in the pub, he met Andy Corab who worked on various jobs, and at present for Murish Rua and his wife Meabh. Cahal knew that Andy Corab was a gossiper and would carry any stories to Murish Rua. If Cahal could come up with a plan, he would spin a yarn that would be to his interest.

"Good day" Cahal said to Andy Corab, "Will you have a drink with me."

"Ah thanks Andy" replied Cahal, "However I am afraid that I am in no mood for conversation: I have too much on my mind."

Andy Corab retorted, "You know a worry shared is a worry divided. Are you sick or something? Good luck to you; I heard that you have rented Mary Rocha's land, fair play to you. You are the only man in the place to get the use of that land."

Cahal replied, "Andy, I am sick, but not in the sense of illness. Thank you for your kind words. I know that you don't begrudge me or any man in the area anything, not like a lot of people you and I know. We will mention no names! But my luck may be short-lived. I don't want to talk about it".

Cahal's remark made Andy Corab curious about what was happening. Now his curiosity fed on speculation, which he would have to satisfy. Cahal knew that Andy Corab's mind would conjure up a multiple of answers to his refusal to talk. This would make it easier for him to bait his trap. He knew that to set a good snare he would need to be patient, and wait until the trap closed. Cahal bid good night to Andy Corab and went home.

Two days later Andy Corab came to visited Cahal saying "Cahal, how are you feeling to day? I thought that you may have been getting the flu when we spoke in the pub. Is there anything that I can do? You know that you and I are friends and neighbours for many years."

"Aye you are right" answered Cahal. "We have known each other for many years. However this is a burden that I must carry alone. Isn't that right my old friend? Let's change the conversation; how are you keeping yourself?"

Andy Corab replied, "I am all right, working away at a few little jobs here and there. I suppose that you know that I have a few jobs to do at 'Doras-feasta' for Murish Rua and his wife Meabh."

Cahal was slow in replying and said, "Are you! Well good luck to you Andy, you are a great tradesman who can turn your hands to anything. Maybe I would be better off if I was like you, working for a day's wages."

"But Cahal, you have a nice herd of cattle and, and you have Mary Rocha's land, which is the best land in the neighbourhood."

Cahal slowly replied, "Aye Andy, but for how long? You know how money talks any language. You or I would never be in league with those with pockets full of money, would we?"

"And tell me Cahal, who is buying the place? Is it the land, or the house and land, what auctioneer has the sale of it?"

Cahal, looking at Andy said, "Auctioneer! It won't be any of the local auctioneers. I heard her on the phone to someone, it may be London or Dublin; it will be a very hush-hush job. The first we will know will be when the new person takes over the place. I think Mary Rosha does not want anyone to know she is selling. It will be a quiet private sale. I wish I had the money to buy the place. I am sure that she would grab any money offered, and vanish from this place. I think I have said too much. Don't under God tell anyone what I was saying! Maybe it is because I am upset. Please don't breathe a word of what we were talking about."

"No" said Andy, "You have my word Cahal, this is between you and me: my lips are sealed."

Then they parted company. Cahal knew that Andy could not "hold his water". If he got any story he would put legs on it by telling it in his own version.

Andy was busting to take the news to Murish Rua. If Murish Rua bought Mary Rocha's place there would be abundance of work for him. The house was old and would need plenty of work to make it comfortable for Murish Rua and Meabh. They always aspired to be the lord and lady of the area. Andy Corab could then picture himself with a handy job for life. The old stables and byres could do with plenty of revamps. The more he thought of the many options of how he may have paid work for himself.

Andy Corab went to Murish Rua with a big smile on his face singing. He had a habit of singing when he was in a good mood or if he had some juicy scandal.

"Well" said Murish Rua "You are looking happy today Andy. Did you by any chance find a pot of gold somewhere?"

Andy Corab replied, "I found out some information about Ardmuckvill. Mary Rocha is selling the place to someone from London, it may be through an auctioneer from Dublin or London. She is mad to get her hands on money and she could not care who they are, she is broke."

Murish quickly snapped, "And who is the auctioneer in Dublin, Andy?"

Andy replied, "I am not sure, they are keeping things quiet. The first thing we will know is that someone with money will snap it up for a song."

"And Andy" snapped Murish Rua, "Can't you ask someone? Perhaps Cahal Sean knows. I wouldn't be surprised if that man knows what is going on."

Andy replied, "Cahal is as much in the dark as far as I know. Why do you think that he is in such a cantankerous mood these last days? It is not like him who always had a laugh and a smile even when he was robbing someone. Don't you know that Mary Rosha has been visiting the town a lot in this last while? It is my opinion that something is afoot. The Rosha's were always a secretive lot; they never told anyone their business. The first thing we will know is that Ardmuckvill is sold. And she will vanish into some town with her own kind."

Murish Rua was quiet for a while, pondering on what had been said. Then he replied, "I know someone in the council that should know what is going on."

Andy quickly retorted, "Everyone will know when everything is sold, and the papers signed and sealed. Is that any good to us now? Well, is it? I suppose that there is nothing we can do but wait for the new owners to land on our doorsteps. Whatever they are like; maybe some strangers that will torment us, in our own country."

Murish Rua jumped to his feet bellowing, "I did not spend my time in a foreign country to have some jumped up alien guttersnipe upset us in our country."

"But" said Andy, "Maybe he is from America and you and he may have met over there. You could know him."

"Know him!" yelled Murish Rua, "Do you know how many people there are in America? It is millions. If the person who has their eye on the place was from America don't you think he would have contacted me? It could be some bloody Russian communist who wants to take over the country. Then where would we be, but in some bloody Russian gulag in Siberia."

Andy with a look of mystification on his face said, "Where is Siberia? Is it in America?"

Murish Rua looked into Andy's face with a look of utter disgust and replied, "Don't you know anything? You always have half a story. If you want to find any information it is, who, what, when, why, and how. The first question is who is interested to buy Mary Rosha's place. Do you have any idea Andy, or can you find out?"

Andy replied meekly, as he feared his job could be at risk, "I can only tell you what I have heard. Maybe there is nothing in it and it will blow over. Sure, who would have that kind of money?"

Murish Rua was agitated and upset, fearing that someone would usurp his standing in the district. Suspicion sets its own seeds of distrust and thrives in a vacuum. Now Murish was determined to find out who was interested in the land. He could buy Ardmuckvill, if it was only to keep others out. If he had to, he would speak to Cahal Sean, to find out what he knew. Yes, perhaps this was his best option, to find what Cahal was devising. If it was a new owner, then Cahal's situation would be precarious.

Early in the morning Cahal saw Murish Rua heading for his house, and he hid. Murish rapped on the door but there was no one to answer, and when he tried the door he found it was locked. This was annoying Murish as he thought that everyone should jump to his beck and call. Cahal was purposely avoiding Murish as he knew that his absence would give birth to all kinds of nuances and connotations. This cat and mouse game was played by Cahill. When he went home in the evening he did not light any lamp, so Murish did not know when he was at home. Most days Cahal would go to Mary Rocha place and sit with his head in his hands without moving.

Mary Rosha would look out the window of her house, wondering what was wrong. It was unusual for Cahal to sit still as he was always on the move. Her curiosity was getting the better of her and she confronted Cahal and said, "Cahal is there something wrong with you? You are sitting there like a scarecrow. Tell me what is bothering you; it can't be that bad."

Cahal retorted, "Miss Rosha, I don't want to be bothering you with my troubles."

"Come-on" snapped Mary Rosha, "we are all grown up. A troubled shared is a trouble halved. I know that you are a decent person with good manners. You always have a cheery voice and your songs are always cheerful. The happy laugh and songs have left you lately; tell me what is bothering you. I look on you as a friend; please tell me what your problem is."

Cahal with a demure look on his face replied, "Well I don't want to be prying into your business, and the place is yours to sell to whoever you like. It is none of my business."

"What do you mean? Who told you I was going to sell the place? This is Rocha's land and will be until the day that I die. Where under heaven did you get that unfounded notion?"

"Well" responded Cahal, "It is that I was talking with Andy Corab and he said that Murish Rua was going to buy all of Ardmuckvill and chase me off the place. Andy Corab said that he had the money to buy the whole county."

"Buy!" Said Mary Rosha in disgust, "I wouldn't sell him as much land that is under my finger nails. Let him come here with his big mouth. That man Murish Rua has no manners. Where did he get the money? Perhaps he was one of those gangsters in America. Now Cahal go home and rest yourself and don't tell him that you have being speaking to me. I will give him a piece of my mind, if ever he calls here!"

Cahal went home contented: he had his seed of doubt firmly planted. Now he would wait for it to flourish. Tonight he would light the light to see what moths flew into the flames. He did not have to wait long until Murish Rua was knocking at his door.

Cahal shouted, "Who is there at this time of night? I am intending to go to bed as I have been working all day."

Murish replied, "It is me, Murish, come on, open the door until I can speak to you."

Cahal responded, "Could we speak to morrow; it is late and I am tired."

Murish retorted "Open the door and we will speak man to man. After all we are friends and neighbours. Maybe we could go and have a drink. I have plenty of drink in my house. What do you say to that? I am not going to shoot you, am I Cahal?"

Cahal answering slowly, "So you have a gun, have you. Perhaps you came here to shoot me, like they do in America."

"No Cahal! Where did you get that crazy idea? It is only for a friendly chat, perhaps there is money in it for you, if you are interested."

"Aye" responded Cahal, "How could I get money. If it is to kill someone, I am not interested."

Murish gave a dry laugh and said, "No it is not to kill anybody; it is for a little information that may benefit you. How do you feel about having a little chat?"

Cahal replied, "I don't know what you are talking about. What information are you talking about? Are you drunk?"

Murish was getting irritated by Cahal's stalling tactics. It confirmed his suspicion that there was some truth in the rumour that Ardmuckvill was on the market. Finally, he said, "I hear that Mary Rocha's land is for sale. I suppose that you know all about it. What will you do then for grazing? Who is interested in that place, is it you?"

Cahal paused for a while before replying, "I don't know. Maybe it is you that has all the American money. You are the only person that could afford to buy that place."

Murish gave a dull snigger saying, "Cahal you must have heard something. After all you are well in with that old bitch, Mary Rosha."

"I heard nothing" uttered Cahal. "I don't know where you are getting your information from, but if I was you I would forget all about it." With that Cahal closed the window.

Murish Rua went home cursing Cahal, and talking to himself. Cahal's refusal to open the door to him was confirming all kinds of implications in his imagination. When he opened the door, his wife Meabh asked, "What information did you get from Cahal?"

Murish roared, "That man would make the gangsters in Chicago look like altar boys! He knows something but is telling nothing. I will go and talk to Mary Rocha in the morning. I will get it from the horse's mouth."

Meabh said, "Murish Rua, calm yourself, maybe there is nothing to be gained by getting worried about what may never happen. What if that place is sold? We have a good house; you have nothing to worry about. Now calm your nerves and don't think about it. Aren't we happy here; say no more tonight."

Cahal was up early as he assumed that Murish Rua would visit Mary Rocha, and wanted to be there before him. He saw Murish Rua heading for the house and he hid behind the back of the house, where he knocked into some pots, creating a racket.

Mary Rosha opened the back door and she saw Cahal crouching. "What is the matter with you Cahal? You seemed scared of something."

Cahal replied "It is him! He is coming maybe to kill me; it is Murish Rua!"

Mary Rosha said, "Come in Cahal. I will deal with that rascal: how dare he put his two dirty feet on my property. That man will never but a foot inside my door. You sit in the front room until I chase him away. It is fortuitous that we have seen him coming. I will deal with him in my own way."

Cahal and Mary Rosha were sitting in the large room with the pelmets and the pictures hanging, waiting for the knock on the door and her cats sitting on the table.

Murish Rua went to Mary Rosha's house and knocked loudly on her door. She and Cahal waited until it was knocked again. When she left Cahal he was playing with a bottle of poitín that was in his pocket, and the bottle fell from his pocket and spilled on the floor. Cahal was wondering how to dry it when one of the cats began to lick it off the floor. That was the end to Cahal's worry and he sat in another part of the room.

Mary Rosha was upset that anyone should hammer on her door when she had a bell.

Mary Rosha opened the door and snapped, "What is it that takes you to my house without an invitation?"

Murish Rua retorted, "Are you selling the place. Who are you selling it to?"

Mary Rocha was unused to people demanding her to answer any questions. She slaked her thirst for vengeance on her perceived tormentor, bellowing, "Mr Murish Rua, how dare you speak to me in that brusque manner? This is my property, please leave, and do not return. You are like a needle that has no head or point. You have progressed from adolescence to senility without ever reaching maturity!" and with that she slammed the door shut onto Murish's face.

But Murish Rua had his foot in the door and he threw a tantrum, and began to lambaste the Rocha's family saying, that there was never was any good in them; they were liars and thieves and that was the truth.

Mary Rosha had an old fashioned walking stick beside the door, and she jabbed with venom into Murish Rua foot shrieking "There is as much good in the Roshas that we know how to get rid of vermin! Now clear away. You are a sewer rat, and never stand on Rosha's property ever again, or I will shoot rats or parasites."

Murish Rua was taken by surprise and backed away from the door as it was firmly slammed in his face.

Mary Rosha came back into the room smiling as she was happy to have chased Murish Rua away. She had been waiting for her chance to lambaste Murish Rua who had insulted her in the past. Revenge is a bitter sweet fruit which she was now relishing, while basked in the past grandeur of Ardmuckvill.

Mary Rosha was normally a serene reserved woman, but now her face was red with anger and she said. "Did you hear the rubbish that person uttered before I slammed the door shut on him?"

"Yes" replied Cahal, "I certainly did. If that man ever found the truth, he would squeeze it so tight in his hands that he would suffocate it. Perhaps that man lives on lies, which is the refuge of cowards and fools. And truth to him is only a false illusion."

The retort from Cahal pleased her as she walked across the room smiling, she was happy to have chased Murish Rua away. She had for a long time been waiting for her chance to castigate Murish Rua, who had insulted her in the past. Revenge is a fruit that is sweet; which she was now savouring.

Mary Rosha smiling said, "Cahal, we put a fly in that person's ear! I don't think that he will bother you or me again. We will have a cup of tea: it will settle us down. I know that you were a little agitated when you came in this morning. As a matter of fact, I will enjoy a cup of tea myself."

As they sat there drinking the tea, the cat that licked the poitín off the floor began to run around the room. It jumped up on the furniture and up onto the pelmet and began running around the walls, knocking pictures onto the floor. Cahal was busy gathering the pictures from the floor and putting them on the table. Mary Rosha was saying, "Toby, Toby what is the matter with you? My Toby come here to me." However, the cat kept running around the pelmet with pictures dropping to the floor. Then it jumped to a large chandelier and was swinging from it, and began trying to climb up the chandelier. All of a sudden the cat fell to the floor without moving.

Mary Rosha lifted the cat up unto her lap crying, "Toby what has happened to you my Toby?" But the cat was dead and Mary Rocha said, "What has happened to my lovely cat, it is dead?"

"I don't know." replied Cahal "Maybe Murish Rua has poisoned the cat."

"Yes" replied Mary Rosha, "How did he get his money in America? It must have been by killing. I will get a court order to prevent him from coming near me or my property. When you are on my land you will be covered by the court order. That man will never come next or near this place again. I will make sure that person never darkens my door again. That man is lacking knowledge or sophistication and doesn't deserve to be spoken to. He, the ignorant buffoon, doesn't deserve to be acknowledged, let alone be tolerated in any company. Cahal, you can have the remaining part of my land for grazing your animals as spite on that eejit, Murish Rua!"

Cahal was pleased with the outcome and he knew that if he could keep Mary Rosha isolated, he might in time get the place to himself.

Mary Rocha said "Oh Cahal, by the way, you are a refined courteous gentleman."

The Vet and the Hypnotist

Canice McGregor was a young man who came to the area of Loughcorr as the new vet. Like all young men he was full of devilment, playing tricks on everyone he met as well as his own family, who sometimes would be amused and a little annoyed by his devilment.

Cundy, who lived in the neighbourhood, was a strong man and lived close by and was glad of any opportunity of a job, to earn a few shillings. Cundy was a strong naive man of early middle age who trusted everything that was told to him. He had experienced many years of handling difficult or contrary animals. Canice would give Cundy a casual job at times, assisting him while visiting the various farms that he had to attend in the neighbourhood. Cundy helped Canice with the various onerous day-to-day jobs a vet has to perform in the locality.

Often Canice had to visit the farm of Turlagh to remove the horns of his cows, as no animals would be allowed into a mart with horns. Turlagh at times would not be the most congenial of men and he was easily annoyed by frivolous matters, or people's attitude. At times he behaved more like a child who had lost his rattle.

Cundy's erratic attitude was what Canice relied on to annoy or please him, and he showered him with praise Whenever Canice called on Cundy he was glad to accompany him to the various places where his service was required. Canace's payment to Cundy was a small payment of money plus embellished words of eulogy.

The vets at times had to work in places that were precarious or unpleasant. There were many locations where the vets had obligations to serve, sometimes with distasteful individuals. Vets, akin to doctors, have to endure acerbic censure over what is not under their remit or control. Neither are praised for curing, but are scandalised if those in their care die. If the vets or doctors get the patient well, it is supposed that the patient was cured by some saint.

The cattle marts insisted that no animal with horns would be allowed to enter the mart's property. They are afraid that they could damage each other, or some person on the mart's property. To circumvent any future litigation, they insisted that any animals with horns would not be allowed to enter the mart. This annoys some farmers as they insist that their animals are quiet, and would not harm even a mouse.

One evening Canice and Cundy arrived at the farmyard of Turlagh, who was waiting for them, somewhat a little annoyed by their late arrival. Canice reached into his car and produce a small box of strawberries, which he at times he used to pacify unsettled clients.

Saying, "Turlagh, do you have anything as good as this growing on your farm? Cundy is a dab hand when it comes to growing things. He had the best potatoes last year."

"Aye" retorted Turlagh "I always have the best crop of spuds in this parish or the next ten, for that matter. My spuds are real balls of flour, with an onion and a bowl of milk they would feed any man or woman."

Canice smiling, "Said grab a handful of these strawberries and, tell me what you think of them Turlagh."

Turlagh took a full handful and pushing them into his mouth and began chewing with the red juices dripping down his face. After a while chewing he began to spit the remainder out of his mouth with a string of profanity which was unimaginative. Saying, "These goddam things, are full of gravel!" as he spat the remainder out of his mouth." Those things are under my false teeth. They would wear the mouth of me with all the gravel that is stuck in them."

Then Turlagh walked to an old stone trough, and took out his false teeth and washed them in the trough. Then he bent down and took a handful of water and he washed out his mouth and spat it in front of him, some into the trough.

Canice said, "That is not gravel Turlagh, it is little seeds of strawberries, if you kept them you could have a nice garden of them next year."

Turlagh with a look of distaste hastily replied, "Them straw things are good to neither man nor beast: they are full of sand or gravel. That thing would wear the gob of any man or beast and would have a person supping porridge every day of his life. Dammit! They are only some old weeds that you boys have, maybe they could poison a man. Now are you going to get my animal ready for the market? You buckos may have plenty of time to talk, but I have a day's work to do. We are wasting time here talking about nothing. You buckos could talk all day and say nothing."

Canice looked at the cow that was tied in the byre. He said to Turlagh that perhaps it would be wise to have a basin of lukewarm water with a bar of good red carbolic soap, as it is the best antiseptic. He said that he would cover the horn stumps with coal tar as he found it the best to seal the wound and prevent any infection.

Cundy readily agreed with Canace's decision saying, "The carbolic soap which was used in older times is far better at preventing infections than what they have today, with their new-fangled-gangled rubbish."

Aye, said Turlagh "I always had great faith in people that relies on the old ways rather than them new-fangled gangled ways. Them new boys of today, with their armful of papers and computers! They would know nothing if their computer broke down, or if they lost a page of their books. They have everything in books and nothing in their head. Aye their heads are like a big drum, empty in the middle, but it makes a loud racket. They slap powder around like a woman baking bread, which is only fit to cover a baby's backside."

"You are right!" said Cundy, "I always wash myself with the good old red carbolic soap like my father did, and his father before him. This new soap is only for the lazy people that are afraid to get their hands dirty with a good day's work. The people nowadays smell like a rat that was covered with butter on a hot day. Aye, next day they would stink half the people of the parish."

"Aye you know," said Canice "Some of the men in my own job are peculiar, I would not trust them. The say they know everything, but you can't beat a country man for wisdom who can read their mind.

Those that say they are smart deviates from or perverts their truth and are telling lies."

"Aye snapped" Turlagh, "Half the lies them bullshitters tell are not true!"

"Well" retorted Cundy, "What about the other half of their lies they tell? Should you let a bullshitter think you believe them?"

Turlagh quickly responded, "It takes one to know one, and you should know your friends. Now we are wasting our time standing here talking, do you want the water and soap?" When Cundy and Turlagh went to the house to get some warm water and carbolic soap, Canice gave the cow an injection that would cause drowsiness and have the cow sleeping in 10-15 minutes. Then he could remove the horns from the cow with ease, as he considered that the cow might be difficult to hold. He was well aware that a contrary man spreads conflict, and a gossip could separate close friends and have them arguing and fighting over frivolous topics.

Canice walked to the farmer's house saying "You know maybe I should have a cup of water. You know my throat is parched dry."

Turlagh retorted, "Aren't there plenty of good water in the stone trough outside. If it is good enough for the cows, it is good enough for you. Did you not see where I had a drink, dammit man! Are you blind or stupid?"

Canice was a little taken aback by Turlagh and the caustic remark, but was not surprised as he was well used to obstinate and rude men in his work, thinking that there is nothing more dangerous than original stupidly or false vanity.

Canice quickly replied, "Aye I know, but I was told that you had the best spring well in the parish and I would like to taste it to confirm if what they were saying is right. I had a drink from Owen Charlie's well last week, and it would be the greatest spring water I ever tasted."

The remark about Owen Charlies well unsettled Turlagh as both were in constant hostility with each other. This was one remark that he could not tolerate about Owen Charlie having anything better than him.

Turlagh roared, "Quick Mary, get this man a mug of our best spring well water. He is only used to drinking that rubbish out of Owen Charlie's well. Owen Charlie's water would give the cows the skitter. This man doesn't know what good water is."

Mary, a little timidly, handed a mug of water to Canice, out of a rusty bucket, saying "Mr Canice, here is the water. What you don't want you can always throw away."

Canice raised the mug of water to his mouth and drank it hurriedly, he was aware that his actions and comment could pacify or inflame emotions. After a long pause he let out a rift of sound and uttered a loud exclamation: "That must be the best water I ever drank. You know if you were in France you would be getting a fortune for that water. Isn't that right Cundy?"

The grin abated from Turlagh face and was replaced by a quasi-half smile. When his water had been adjudicated to be the best it pleased Turlagh, and he insisted that Cundy should also have a drink of his water.

Cundy at first refused, saying that he was not dry as he had a bottle of water with him.

However, Canice was insistent that Cundy would also sip from the unwashed chalice of a rusty bucket, proclaiming that this water that came from the earth would cure even a dying man. "Isn't that right Turlagh?"

"Aye" answered Turlagh, "Drink it up man it will keep the drought away."

Cundy slowly held the mug to his lips and replied, "That is good water! I wish I had a spare bottle to take away with me to drink later. I might even keep it for a cup of tea it is so good."

Turlagh again yelled "Mary! Have we any spare bottles in the house so these men can have a decent sup of water to take away with them? They have been used to drinking rubbish."

Mary took some uncorked bottles that lay in an untidy cupboard and filled them without even rinsing. Then she handed them to Canice and Cundy with a demure smile.

"Ah" said Canice, "I will put them into the car in a place where they will be safe. If word gets out that I have your water someone will raid us, isn't that right Cundy?"

"Aye" replied Cundy with a grin, "Isn't it a wonder that somebody didn't steal the bucket: it could be a treasure. Maybe I should put the bottles in the car where they will be safe and won't get broken."

"Aye" responded Canice, "Maybe it is because I had too much beer last night. You know I can't take drink like I used to. How about you Turlagh can you hold your drink?"

"Aye" retorted Turlagh, "I can drink any man under the table, and still walk home as sober as if I never had a drink. Here in the country we can always have a good drink of poitín. It is real whiskey, not that rubbish you have. That is government whiskey".

Canice replied, "You know Turlagh you are right, I believe in it myself. They say that there is nothing better than poitín for an animal that had a foundering".

"Well" said Turlagh, "if you have a foundering, you needn't be looking to me for poitín. That scamp Mackie Joe was here last week, and what he did not drink he took away. You know that man would drink it out of a cow's foot track. I would need to get a few bottles again in case the cow was ever to get sick. A good drink of poitín would in no time have a dead man dancing a jig on the table".

"Aye" replied Canice, "You know that I have a few bottles that I use on any wound on animals or myself, but I have to hide it on Cundy. However, I must attend to the job we came to do."

Returning to the byre, Canice started a conversation with Cundy on new ways in medicine, and said he saw of a film on hypnosis, where a man who was crippled walked. "Wouldn't it be marvellous if we knew how to perform it?"

"Aye" said Cundy "wouldn't it be great if we could hypnotise the cow? But it would never work on an animal."

"Ah! I don't know." retorted Canice, "Do you think we should give it a try anyhow, Cundy? There always new things being discovered. Perhaps you and I would become famous for discovering a new treatment. Our pictures could be splattered all over the papers for discovering something new. Perhaps we should give it a try to see if it works. Will we start counting?"

"Aye" said Cundy to Canice, "You are a smart man, with all the time you spent at school you must be as smart as any fox, with your education".

"All right." said Canice and he began counting from one to twenty. But the cow stayed standing. "Hum! Hum" said Canice, "Maybe I do not have what it takes to be a hypnotist. Maybe Cundy you should try, they say it is not everyone has the power to hypnotize. You have a way with animals, which is why I like to have you with me; you know there is something miraculous about you."

Cundy with his innocent grin started counting from one to twenty, but the cow was still standing.

"Hum!" said Canice "Maybe you should count from twenty to one. Maybe that will work, what do you think? But, Cundy you did not tell the cow to go to sleep, that could be the way to hypnosis. We are only learning."

Again Cundy began counting from twenty down to one saying "Nice cow, go to sleep. Nice cow, close your eyes you are getting tired. Go to sleep nice cow your eyes are getting tired." and commenced counting, "twenty, nineteen" and on down to one. But the cow was standing shaking her head. This process was repeated a few times but the cow only shook her head.

Canice smiling said "I still believe you have the power in you Cundy, keep trying I can see her shaking her head. To me it looks like as if she is getting tired."

Cundy with a despondent look on his face said, "It is no use, the cow is still standing, maybe I will never a hypnotist."

Try again said Canice "We counted a few times, God willing the cow could lie down this time. But this time say it in Irish, maybe she knows it better, wasn't the cow reared in the Gaeltacht?"

"Aye perhaps it is worth a try." said Cundy and he began his countdown from twenty to one in Irish."

By now the anaesthetic from the injection was beginning to work and the cow was dropping to its knees.

"Ah! Good man Cundy, I knew you had the power in you. I knew it was in you!"

In a few minutes the cow was sleeping and Canice and Cundy removed its horns. Canice continued praising Cundy, telling him what a great man he was. Obviously Cundy was smiling and purring like a cat after it had drunk a saucer of milk. Cundy believed he had hypnotised the cow, and his pride was rising like the moon on a spring tide.

Following a bout of congratulations subsequent to the removal of the horns from the cow, the next predicament was getting the cow standing again.

Canice, smiling, said to Cundy, "Now tell the cow to stand up. You are the hypnotist."

Cundy began his incantation, "Nice cow, nice cow; when I count from one to twenty you will rise up a happy cow." and the rendition of counting continued, but the cow did not rise up; it was lying snoring on the floor like a drunken man after a bellyful of Guinness.

The sweat was falling from Cundy as he was getting frustrated. His period of success had been shattered and his recent euphoria was turning to calamity and disappointment. He kept thinking, what if the cow never wakens up, and to make matters worse Canice kept saying, "You must undo your hypnosis."

Turlagh entered the byre, and hearing Cundy at his mantra, was beginning to think that they would need a period in some mental hospital for the bewilderment, with his ramblings "nice cow, nice cow, stands up nice cow."

Canice exchanged a few pleasantries with Turlagh and asked if he spoke to the cow in English or Irish.

Turlagh retorted in disgust, "In Irish! In Irish of course, my own language, the only way and the right way to speak to man or beast is in Irish".

Canice smiling said "I suppose your wife also speaks to the cow in Irish?"

"No!" retorted Turlagh "She came from that skittery wee town of Polmor where they couldn't bless themselves right in Irish, of for that matter in English."

"Aye" replied Canice, "I know! Haven't I one myself that was breed in a town. It isn't that I wasn't told often enough, that any women from a town were hard to keep with all their fancy rings powder and lipstick.

"You are right!" snapped Turlagh, "The money they spend on all these God damn powders! Wouldn't a dollop of corn flour do the same job, and it would be cheaper? They waste good money on lipstick and that other rubbish. If they boiled a few beetroot and chewed them in their gob, that would give them red lips and feeding. Musha! My mother, God rests her soul, she never once put lipstick on her lips, and she lived to a ripe old age of 95 years".

Canice quipped, "Don't be telling me about extravagant women, don't I know all about it! I have a woman that would spend a fortune on her hair. They have more clothes than would cover a townland. Then they cover themselves with more powder than would plaster a house."

Cundy smiling interjected "But Turlagh they need the lipstick for kissing the men and making love."

"Ah" retorted Turlagh, "You! The superstitious idiot that knows everything. Yet you don't know much about cows. The cows are the same as woman: if they get plenty of grub and their nuts they are happy. And as for kissing, it is for those who do not know how to do the job or haven't the equipment".

"Aye" said Canice "It takes a man to do a man's job; you can't beat a country man to do a good job. A country woman who speaks Irish is always happy with what they have."

Turlagh with a look of revulsion on his face replied, "Aye there are lots of country people that you could put in the same category of being thick. That includes some that I can see standing before me. "What about my cow! Have you finished the job yet"?

"Aye" said Canice, "Cundy won't be long tidying things up here, isn't that right?

Cundy retorted, "I am not sure that I am of much use to the cow, maybe you should try Canice".

Canice smiling said to Cundy "You should try speaking to the cow in Irish, maybe she will understand it better. Cundy do you think you could speak in Irish again. After all it worked once with the cow, why not again?"

Cundy riposted sharply "Yes I certainly can speak Irish as good as any man." and he began in his best of Irish. "Bó deas seasamh sua, bó deas seasamh sua, seasamh sua, bó deas seasamh sua, ardú suas bó sona." (Nice cow, stand up, nice cow, stand up, nice cow, stand up, nice cow, stand up.)

However, the cow was still lying on the floor, and beads of perspiration were dripped from Cundy's brow. And Canice was urging Cundy to undue his hypnosis. Saying "Come on man, you can do it! Say it, you did before."

Turlagh was looking discontent at the two idiots he had let near his good cow. The thought crossed his mind that they had no idea what they were doing. He considered that Canice was not a real vet, and who was the idiot that was talking to the cow? Maybe they killed or are killing his good cow. In a fit of utter revulsion, he roared, "Clear to hell with you two wasters. You two have killed or are killing my good cow. Who in under hell ever said that you are a vet? You two could not bury a dead cat!"

Canice, intending to pacify Turlagh, smiled and with a little wink said "It is all right, the cow will rise in a wee while, the thing will wear off in a wee while, and she will rise of her own accord in a wee while."

Tulbagh's face was getting redder with anger as he grabbed a long hay grape shouting "Clear to hell with you two F****n chancers. Get to hell out of here before I stick this grape through you two preposterous imbecilic backsides! You two eejits. And for you! You, moron! You Mr Moron, you, numbskull dim-wit, standing there with those long-winded gobbledygook ramblings. It is not here you should be, but locked up in some mental hospital and the keys thrown away".

Turlagh made a dive with the grape for Cundy uttering a mouthful of profanities in rage saying "I will stick this f*****n grape up your big fat ass, you, you!"

Canice and Cundy made a race for the byre door, each fearing that Turlagh would in his rage stick the grape into one of them. He was in no mood for explanations.

As they ran for the car Turlagh was shouting to his wife, "Mary, Mary, quick, get me my gun and I will fill these two idiots f*****n asses with hot lead."

Mary, being an obedient or browbeaten woman, duly took the gun to Turlagh, muttering, "Don't kill them or we will never go to heaven. Put a few shots in the air. That will be enough to scare them away. What will I do, if you are sent to jail? I will never manage the farm on my own. Have sense Turlagh, we can sue them, if they harm the cow."

Mary did not have time to finish her sentence when Turlagh grabbed the gun from her hand, saying, "I will send them two wasters to hell where they belong. The killers of my good cow."

Rising the gun to take aim at the car, with Mary pleading with him to call the guards, saying "They will do whatever they do to criminals, maybe lock them up in jail."

However, Turlagh was in no mood to listen to reason as he loaded the gun and lowered it to shoot.

Mary, fearing that someone would be killed, shoved the gun away from where he was aiming. The discharge from the gun hit the corrugated roof of the byre where the cow was lying. It left the corrugated byre roof looking like a strainer with all the small holes in it.

Was it the effect of the injection beginning to deplete, or was it the shot from the gun that rattled on the roof of the byre? The cow came running out the door and into a new netting wire hen's yard that Turlagh built a week ago. The poor cow was so frightened that in its haste it completely wrecked the yard. And Turlagh shouting a loud string of profanities as long as your arm, did not help to pacify the cow. The cow now in its haste jumped into a field of newly planted potatoes, wrecking the drill that Turlagh prided himself on its neatness, and now his wife Mary was on the receiving end for pushing the gun that hit his good galvanised roof.

There was commotion as Canice and Cundy jumped into the car fearing for their lives. They heard the shots being fired and were afraid that the next shot would hit them. Then Cundy started reciting a partial mantra of prayers that he had half-forgotten from his youth. When he prayed as far as he knew he said, "Jesus Mary and Joseph how the f***, what is the rest of the f****** thing? I can't remember it now. We were nearly killed.

Cundy was amazed by the furious kerfuffle that Turlagh had caused and said to Canice, "I thought that you had quieted him by drinking from his rusty bucket! Maybe you did not drink enough?

"Ah" roared Canice, "You did not drink from her bucket! Maybe that was what upset him."

As Canice and Cundy was speeding down the winding road, the cow was following behind them with froth exuding from her mouth, along with Turlagh, followed by Mary, and he shouting. "Come back you blackguards and I will put you two scoundrels to hell where you belong."

Irish Poems

Request for an Irish Grave.

Give me but six foot three (one inch to spare),
Of Irish earth, and dig it anywhere.
And for my poor soul say an Irish prayer.
Above the spot.

Let it be where cloud and mountain meet,
Or vale where grows the tufted meadow-sweet,
Or boreen trod by peasants' shoeless feet,
It matter not.

I loved them all - the vale, the hill,
The moaning sea, the flagger-lilied rill,
The yellow furze, the lake shore lone and still,
The wild bird's song.

But more than hill or valley, bird or moor,
More than the green fields of my native Suir,
I loved those hapless ones, the Irish poor,
All my life long.

Little I did for them in outward deed,
And yet be unto them of praise the need,
For the stiff flight I waged against lust and greed,
I learnt it there.

So give me an Irish grave,
Mid Irish air, with Irish grass above it anywhere;
And let some passing peasant give prayer
For my soul there.

Settle the Question Right

However the battle is ended,
Though proudly the victor comes,
With flaunting flags and neighing nags
And echoing roll of drums;
Still truth proclaims this motto
In letters of living light,
No question is ever settled
Until it is settled right.

Though the heel of the strong oppressor
May grind the weak in the dust,
And the voices of fame with one acclaim
May call him great and just;
Let those who applaud take warning
And keep this motto in sight,
No question is ever settled
Until it is settled right.

Let those who have failed take courage,
Though the enemy seem to have won;
If he be in the wrong, though his ranks are strong,
The battle is not yet done.
For sure as the morning follows
The darkest hour of night,
No question is ever settled
Until it is settled right.

O men, bowed down with labour,
O women, young yet old,
O heart, oppressed in the toiler's breast
And crushed by the power of gold,
Keep on with your weary battle
Against triumphant might;

No question is ever settled
Until it is settled right.

Ella Wheeler Wilcox

The Dream

I dreamt that I woke up last night
And found myself alone
The room was bare but for a chair,
A tooth brush and a comb,
The doors were locked the window barred,
The walls were solid stone,
I wondered what had brought me here,
And I pined for my humble home

Rory P Cunningham

Ban na Tra

On the road to Damascus I was overtaken on Porter's brae.
By Bannatra who had filled her tanks in Joe's that day,
Where she drank good beer whiskey and wine,
And began yelling "I will live until I am ninety-nine!"
She had a bellyful of distilled water to carry her on,
Her chariot was full of fag and rubbish of all kinds,
On Porter's brae she discarded her old burden,
Of fag ends, drink, empty beer cans, bottles of whiskey, and wine.
But now she walks the Tra lamenting and squeaking.

Caoineadn Anthoin Uí Ghallchobhair

A Nóra Ní Dhomhnaill ní mhaith loim do sgéal
Fa do bhuchail breág, dhoigheamhail nach rabh a leithid sa tú
A Anthoin ba chalma do dhream in ngac slíge
As a Chlainn Daibhid mo gháir mhallaght chighaibh le gaoith.

Idir a fiche a's a dó sin aois an graiscí a bhí a sáimh
Gan mhairg, gan bhrón mo lean mar loitheadh do lár
Clan Daibhid ar an ród caithruigh thusa le grán
Tá díoghalas mhór a dtóir fa do leagaint gan fáth.

Nárbh iontach nár imigh tú ag amach ó'n ród
Nuair a chonnaic tú ag teacht iad a's n a gunnaí leo
Ba bheag a shíl to go scaoilfí na hurcháir romhat
A Mhuire a chroidhe! Fríd do thaobh a chuidh an piléar a bhí mór.

Mo mhallach don ceathar sin buchall óg
Bó na bólan na béarac na'r eírigh leo
Sgéal cráidhthe 'ach eile chugath A Dhoimnic Óigh
A Éoin bháin! Do leas ná'r theánaidh tú.
Na dtug cead a anama do.

Níl a fhois cé a anama chum. 1798

Lament for Antoin Ó Galchoir

Nora Ó Donnell I am sorry about your sad story.
About your fine handsome boy, the finest in the land.
Anthon your clan were courageous in every way,
And to the McDevitt clan my curse on you with vengeance,

At twenty and two years old, your hero met his fate,
Without regret or sorrow he was fatally wounded,

The McDevitt clan on that road, killed you with a shot,
This is a revenge with cause for murder without reason,

It is a wonder you didn't leave the road,
When you saw them approach with guns,
Little did you think that they would shoot you down,
Dear Muire of my heart, it was through his side that large bullet went.

My curse on those four young men.
That a cow or a bullock they will never own,
A tranquil story, young Dominic and Eoin Bán
That you will not thrive, that you didn't allow him to save his soul.

Writer unknown (1798)
Translated by Martin Whelan. Invite further translation

Yesterday

Yesterday that shy young girl with the enchanting smile and dancing
eye captured my heart,
Today that enchanted smile is frozen like the granite hills and smiles in
my memory,
Yesterday a mother and father smile, and comfort and protect their
children
Today her children and grandchildren gently walk comforting only in
spirit,
Yesterday, those eyes danced like flowers in a gentle summer's breeze
Today they stare silently like water frozen in a winter frost,
Yesterday your laugh warmed my spirits like a new summer's morning
Today it is silent like the calmness before a terrible storm,
Yesterday we danced and twirled and danced with the light of moon
Today that light footstep is locked like the mountains unmoving

Yesterday your laugh danced on echoes booming happiness and joy
Today its silence is deafening and the memory of the laugh fetches
sadness
Yesterday you carried your children on the warmth of your breast
Today they carry your memory with the coldness of their anguish.
Yesterday through the nights you fretted over your children's every
cough and moan
Today your children fret over you and damp your face with their tears
of despair
Yesterday we looked forward to a new life of what might and could be
garnered
Today I look back on what was, and scatter dreams like dust on the
wind
Yesterday how sweet the morning sun of life glowed never seeing the
chill of winter
If today was only yesterday were today, who would wish for tomorrow
when winter is today?

Which one

One of us dear, but which one, will sit by a bed with a nameless fear
and clasp a hand,
Growing cold as it feels for the spirit hand, darling, but which one
One of us dear, but which one, will stand by the others coffin bier, and
look and weep,
While those marble lips strange silence keeps darling, which one,
One of us but which one, by an open grave will drop a tear, and
homeward bound will go,
The anguish of unshared grief to know, darling, which one.
One of us dear, but which one, shall speak glad words the other cannot
not hear,
Nor fully know,
All we have dimly groped for her below, darling, which one,
One of us, darling, it must be, it might be you it must be me,
It may be you will slip from me, my little life be first be done,

I'm glad we do not know, which one.

Mo gisa beag, mo grá mo chroí
Mo gisa beag, mo grá mo chroí
With my hand on my heart it is true to say
You were never spoiled if you got your way
Ah daddies little pet is she going away
You fly away from daddy this bright new day
What new nest will you rest in from today?
I watched that small kernel grown into a flower bright.
Bathed by the soft dew of morning's light.
Will that small flower soon be gone from my view?
That little child has grown in to a flower bright
But you were never spoiled if you got your way
Those little tantrums were merely a growing vogue
How could you be noticed between arduous boyos?
I think of those nights I carried you while you cried.
But now the tears of bliss slides upon that face of joy
I look at the exhilaration that shines upon your face
The vale of tears will it lie upon your face or mine
I know you were never spoiled if you got your way
And now you ask me to give you away

The Glenties Harvest Fair

Come all ye loyal countrymen and listen if you please.
I'll sing for a verse or two to put your mind at ease,
Tis all about the bygone days when friendship we did share,
On the twelfth day of September at the Glenties harvest fair,

All the boys did turn out in suits of navy blue,
Their sisters were along with them, their dads and mummies too,
The hay and corn was all saved, they didn't have a care.
When they all did meet upon the street at Glenties harvest fair,

The ballad singers they were there, the rich, the poor, the small,
The sheep were tied along the street lined up against the wall,
With mediator at each deal the difference to share,
Saying "Sell them, they'll be lucky" at the Glenties harvest fair,

The people came from far and near with trade of every art,
Some were selling duilse, more with apple carts,
The fiddlers and pipers played, their music filled the air,
You would think you were in heaven at the Glenties harvest fair,

Bullig

I steer my boat beside your mighty billowing white foam
Exhilarating beauty of desire with white a hypnotic smile
You tempt men to dance beside you to feel your alluring grace
On calm days you smile shuddering your body with a placid dance
But when the wind upsets you you're mighty thundering roar
To dance my boat along that narrow edge as if to balance life or death
I love your dance in and out along the seas of sorrow and joy

Again on these dark days we awe, in reverence at the obsequy to a
dying sun
But why not have a mighty wake with all its feasting drinking and
pulsating heads
Let none say that we have not given the sun a decent funeral with all its
protocol and ceremonial rituals.
But why despair with the solstitial death will come its resurrection
when it will crawl again across a new sky
And embrace the birth of a new morning
So to hell with expenses let's put more salt on the dinner

The Banshee

Long, long ago when I was young the banshee sat in cold damp stones

Weeping and lamenting for some poor soul that was soon to depart
this life
In that lonely place she sat wrenching her hair for the impending death.
And the strongest man shuddered with terror to walk those narrow
roads at night.
Who not I wanted to see banshee on these moonlight night sitting
waiting to pass on her summons of death.
But then I was young, long, long ago the country of ours was a
different place,
But now the banshee so longer sits and wails along a lonely road with
untidy hair
Nor will she sit on cold damp stones that would founder a mortal's
bone.
Here she sits in skimpy jeans and shortened belly tops,
There are rings on her finger and her nose, and ones where the wind
should not blow
And her hair is a psychedelic shade or hue of green or pink but others
say it is something in-between
That was invented in some psychotic or neurotic chemist's sink.
Now she has her own luxurious condominium
Where she is suavely combing and pampering her latest hair-do
Sending her warnings of impending death by text, or electronic mail,
with little logos of treats and threats.
Saying: your time is up, it is time, for you are going to do a belly flop.
You are for the recycling body shop where your spare parts will enrich
a destitute

The time passes slowly on as I sit in my chair waiting for the favours
that I thought were owed to me
Who are those that you have given freely to when hinted at?
What fool gives all that he has and is left with nothing?
Have you not a fleeting gratitude that disperses quicker that what is
given?
Aye I have given freely, but now I have the audacity to look for a
reciprocation
Aye, a fool, one that has emptied his larder to one that has a fat belly

What is left is a vacuum

Babies are looking outwards in amazement
The young are looking forward in anticipation
The old are forever looking backwards in demise
The dying are looking inwards to bareness in doubt

A perverted head

O to dance all night and march all day
And chase those clowns and amadans away
Heavy sticks are there to beat you down
If you refuse to part with that half a crown
The hungry monkeys must be fed
Why lament if you have no feather bed?
Don't you know that man must live
By the salt that falls from his tired brow
Baboons and buffoons are protected species
Truth, is it an illusion to a final conclusion?
Fill empty space